FLIRTATIONS WITH FAME

Memoirs of a Celebrity Manqué

NEIL D. ISAACS

ISBN 978-1-957582-22-1 (paperback)
ISBN 978-1-957582-23-8 (digital)

Copyright © 2022 by Neil D. Isaacs

All rights reserved. No part of this publication may be reproduced, distributed, or transmitted in any form or by any means, including photocopying, recording, or other electronic or mechanical methods without the prior written permission of the publisher.

Printed in the United States of America

Also by Neil D. Isaacs

Bay Area Trio

The Doaker's Story: A Novel

You Bet Your Life: The Burdens of Gambling

The Miller Masks: A Novel in Stories

Vintage NBA Basketball: The Pioneer Era

Batboys and the World of Baseball

Innocence and Wonder: Baseball through the Eyes of Batboys

The Great Molinas: A Novel

Grace Paley: A Study of the Short Fiction

All the Moves: A History of College Basketball

Sports Illustrated Basketball (with Dick Motta)

Jock Culture, U.S.A.

Covering the Spread (with Gerald Strine)

Checking Back: A History of NHL Hockey

Fiction into Film: A Walk in the Spring Rain (with Rachel Maddux and Stirling Silliphant)

Eudora Welty

Structural Principles in Old English Poetry

CONTENTS

I: The Call of Fame 1

II: Look-Alikes 5

III: Early Promise 10

IV: Spring Break among the Stars 18

V: Liz No Show 28

VI: Transition and Spencer Haywood 33

VII: Hollywood Comes to the Smokies 38

      Keep Thinking Sinking 45

      The Cassavetes Connection 49

VIII: MusicMusicMusic 52

IX: Collaborationist 57

X: Lefty Gets Counted Out 67

XI: The Wisdom of Solomon 75

XII: Jock Culture, U.S.A. 83

      The Course 85

      The Book(s) 90

      Cosell, Gifford, and Exley; Molinas and Me 94

      The Column 100

XIII: In the Tank 103

XIV: Crossing the Bar 107

XV: Man of Letters 113

      Obiter Obits and Provoked Connections 117

      The Critics' Critic 119

XVI: Burt and Brooks; the Tosh and Dollar Bill 127

XVII: Brief Encounters (a.k.a. Zelig Photo-ops) 138
    Heisman 139
    Dominic Frontieri 140
    The Champ's Corner 141
    Lena Horne 141
    Globetrotters 142
    Ted Straeter 143
    Harvey Swados 146
    Camelot 149
    You Can't Beat City Hall 150
    Mallon Faircloth 151
    Robert Penn Warren 152
    Red Smith 153
    Sam Jones 155
    Len Elmore 157
    Tony Kornheiser 158
    Roy Jefferson 159
    Bob Fachet 161
    Dick Darcey 162
    K.P. and the Gang 166
    Chet Forte 168
    E. L. Doctorow 170
    John Barth 171
    Grace Paley 174
    David Ignatius 176
    Valerie Plame 177
    Barack Obama 178

XVIII: Envoy 181
Acknowledgments 185
Family Album 187
Praise for The Great Molinas 229
Praise for The Doaker's Story 231

I

THE CALL OF FAME

For a long time I used to think that it was in my DNA, this hunger for fame that I felt gnawing in my gut and recognized in a whole family's focus of conversation. And then I realized that it all could have been learned behavior, a deep-seated element of a clan's subculture. Maybe it's a false dichotomy, nature/nurture. Maybe what I have always experienced--whether in anticipation or disillusion, in surprise or disappointment, in avidity or dismissal, in self-pity or self-deprecation--is a product of both and therefore all the stronger because it comes at me from both sides. Whatever. It is a fact of my life.

On the wall above my writing station in the part of the house I call "studio" or "study" or "workplace" is an arrangement of five framed 7 x 11 photographs. One, vintage 1948 (as seen here), shows Charlie Parker and me at a table in the Royal Roost smiling over our drinks between his sets; I am 17.

Another, circa 1973, catches Robert Penn Warren and me, seated in uncomfortable straight-back chairs on a stage platform in Boone NC, sharing a laugh. Then, sometime around 1977, we see Sam Jones and me with our game faces on, waiting to go on the court for our doubles match in a "celebrity" tennis tournament: Sam towers over me by almost a foot, but we both look like players. The last, shot in 1997 in the assembly hall at Montgomery College in Rockville MD, shows me sharing a platform with John Barth.

This array (with accompanying narrative at appropriate places in the pages below) raises two questions: Is this a capsule of my life? Is this a great country or what?

On an adjacent wall, in a place of honor above the shelf where my compact OED, my Webster's New International (2nd. ed.), my Columbia Encyclopedia, and my Baseball Encyclopedia (1984) stand ready for use in a throwback to pre-Google days, in a somewhat larger frame, is a signed original copy of a segment from the "Tank McNamara" comic strip. Three panels feature a character, featured in the next day's strip as well, who to all intents and purposes is based in appearance and attitude on yours truly. The full story of this marginal immortalization will be told below in Chapter XIII.

A good many of my earliest memories are set in Grandma and Grandpa Isaacs's sixth floor apartment on East 175th St., two blocks from the Grand Concourse and the subway station in the Bronx. It was there that the family regularly congregated on Sunday afternoons, for pinochle, gossip, and dinner (Grandma's roast beef or lamb). And it was there that I internalized the importance of fame, celebrity, or at least a close association with big-name players in a larger world. This central part of a value system was hard-wired in my developing awareness--along with such other qualities as integrity, loyalty, and a respect for authority--of the kind that earned rather than imposed it.

It seemed that the individuals who were most highly regarded in that family were those who had formed relationships with folks whose name appeared with some frequency in the newspapers. For example, my grandfather's position as patriarch (if not benevolent dictator) was enforced by his first- name acquaintance with Herbert Lehman, governor of the state 1938-42, U.S. Senator 1950-57. Hanging on a wall in the apartment was a framed commemoration of that friendship, a proclamation honoring Grandpa for his contributions to the war effort and signed by the Governor.

His son, Uncle Bert, achieved whatever admiration he was given by the fact of his friendship with Jake Pitler, for more than a decade a coach for the Brooklyn Dodgers after a brief playing career for the Pirates and a minor league manager in the Dodgers system throughout the war. In fact, Bert met Pitler through Jake's daughter, with whom he had struck up a friendship in the garment industry where they both earned their living. But in Bert's absence from family get-togethers, he was always referred to as Jake Pitler's friend.

As an indication of how far this tradition extended, I offer the case of a cousin or second cousin whom I never met, Cousin Sylvan. His name was mentioned with uncommon frequency in those Bronx chitchats for the simple reason that he was the long-time accompanist for Beatrice Kaye, star of vaudeville, night clubs (headliner at Billy Rose's Diamond Horseshoe), theater (Mercury Theater with Orson Welles), radio (hosting her own show), movies, and even early television. Cousin Sylvan may or may not have been the star's lover as well, but he was not one of her five husbands and is mentioned in none of her published obituaries. On 175th Street, however, he was big-time.

My mother's characteristic modesty precluded frequent mention of her most distinguished connection. But on the rare occasion when I was present in her absence it was whispered in hushed tones of awe that she had worked as private secretary to Gregory Zilboorg, a protégé of Sugmund Freud, who was best known in the family not for his influential writing but because he had the Gershwin brothers among many prominent patients.

What we have here is a kind of composite of the Boswell complex, the obsessive attraction to illustrious figures as a way to create one's own fame, and the compulsion of Woody Allen's Zelig, for whom just to appear in the same frame with the famous is recognition enough. If the former is a precursor of the kind of impulse that can lead to a morbid fascination with a John Lennon, Jody Foster, Dick Waitkus, or David Letterman, the latter can produce the kind of toxic behavior that characterizes gate-crashers, barrier- jumpers, paparazzi, groupies, stalkers, avid autograph hounds, and intrusive collectors of personalized memorabilia. None of that would seem appropriate or be acceptable to an Isaacs, but if a connection comes one's way, one will be highly regarded for it.

In the middle of the eighteenth century, when George Frideric Handel came to England to capitalize on his status as the master of the classical music world, he encountered a young writer named Tobias George Smollett. Smollett had walked down to London from Scotland, hoping to make his way as a Grub Street writer, and indeed had been fashioning a reputation for energetic pursuit of whatever opportunity might be afforded his pen. But before Smollett had earned more than passing recognition with *Roderick Random* and *Humphry Clinker,* Handel directly offered him the chance to write a libretto for an opera.

For reasons that have never been revealed, Smollett declined the invitation, though he believed he could turn his hand to any kind of writing that might turn a pound or shillings. The maestro is reputed to have said, "Dot damned Scot, I could haff made him famous."

I find that whole exchange incomprehensible. In Smollett's well-worn shoes, I would have jumped at such an opportunity. Imagine writing lyrics for a Sondheim or a Lloyd Webber! But even if the connection hadn't been productive, I'd have dined out for months on the invitation itself. And such a brief encounter would surely have found its way into the chronicle that follows. I was bred--or perhaps even born--to reach for fame and to seize the main chance for achieving celebrity that draws me on like a brass ring on the merry-go-round (an appropriate metaphor for the way my world has turned). The possibility of associating with stars, rubbing shoulders with household names (a metaphor as mixed perhaps as the habit of mind it depicts), has always shown me a way to go.

No wonder, then, that this tale of ambition falling short will often read like the story of a name-dropper on steroids. Name-dropping, after all, is an occupational hazard of one whose career is that of a fame-seeker. But the narrative will not focus on whatever irony, bitterness, or envy it may betray. I see it instead as a comedy of near misses, missed chances, and the pleasures of the road to anonymity.

II

LOOK-ALIKES

A curious byproduct of the hunger for fame that seemed to be endemic in the family, whether embedded in some intricate combination of genes or the result of behavior learned from the cradle onward, is the notion that if one looks like someone famous it would be tantamount to being famous oneself. A few examples that I remember, although I may have missed many more, should make the point.

One day, my Uncle Bert took his three children to Ebbets Field to see a Giants-Dodgers game, but as I've heard the tale it seems that Aunt Alice had chosen to absent herself from this sporting felicity. Because Grandpa Isaacs was a dyed-in-the-wool Yankees fan, and because there were few avenues available for expressing rebellion against Grandpa's tyrannical ways, the whole family grew up as Giants fans. This was especially true of Bert's family because they grew up living close enough to Grandpa to bear the brunt of his imperious impositions. My father and brother carried on the tradition, at least until the Giants decamped for California and my brother had to wait four years before adopting the newly-formed Mets (my father, by this time, no longer caring about baseball at all). I had stubbornly if unconsciously carried the rebellion a step further and taken the Detroit Tigers to my heart, adding the St. Louis Cardinals when they might possibly take on the Yankees in the World Series.

When the game was over, and no telling of the tale ever makes note of who won, the Isaacs spectators lingered in the emptying ballpark because Uncle Bert wanted to visit for a few moments with his friend Jake Pitler, a Dodgers coach. The visit was brief enough so that, when they left through the gate that the players would use, a crowd of rabid Dodgers fans was still waiting outside for the possibility of getting autographs.

The twins, Richard and June, were fourteen or fifteen at the time and their brother Stanley was eighteen or nineteen. Just as they approached the crowd, one eager fan pointed at Stanley and yelled, "Hey, there's Peewee Reese."

Suddenly a madding crush attacked the family group. There was no time to explain or claim innocence or identify themselves, so Uncle Bert grabbed June by the hand and they ran after Stanley and Richard as fast as they could dodge and plunge, out toward the parking lot. The eager believers gave hot pursuit, and the Isaacs four barely made it to their car before being swamped, blocked, or tackled by their pursuers. June says she was never so scared in her life, while Stanley bragged for long afterwards about how he was a ringer for the Dodgers shortstop.

Dad never bragged about it, but Phil and I did when we recognized another striking resemblance to a major league baseball figure. A photo of Birdie Tebbetts, who as a big-league manager had taken on some weight since his playing days as the Detroit Tigers catcher, could easily have passed for a picture of our father, himself grown pudgier in middle age.

More flattering resemblances came from Mother's side of the family. My cousin Marilyn, who in her early teens was an eye-catching figure skater, matured into a lovely young woman, who on occasion was mistaken, in her West L.A. and environs habitat, for Angie Dickenson. This pleased her, as her attractiveness was always a source of some quiet pride. But it was nothing like the enormous satisfaction her mother experienced when mistaken for Jane Wyman. And this was something that had happened with unsurprising frequency because the resemblance was uncanny. The dark-haired, dark-eyed beauty of her youth had given way to a more mature handsomeness, but she had always carried herself like a star. And she never liked to be teased, my Aunt Ruthie, except that when someone in the family called her Jane she would always grin.

Aunt Ruthie at 16, and in Jane Wyman mode

Her daughter (my cousin Marilyn), as teen figure-skater *As Angie Dickenson look-alike*

My own experience as a look-alike was minimal and I thought ridiculous. I can remember once in the summer of '53, when Mal, George and I had reached the *Cote d'Azur* on our summer tour. We had insinuated ourselves one day onto the private beach where the rich and famous basked, and from the boardwalk high above someone pointed at me and yelled, "Jerry Lewis."

It must have been the haircut, because that was the only matching part. But in the years just before and after that summer, when I might be found drinking in Minetta's or some other bar in Greenwich Village near where my brother was staying, I might be mistaken for Dustin Hoffman--although again it would take a purblind witness to have said so. I thought those mistaken look-alike sightings were ridiculous; I looked too little like either Lewis or Hoffman to suggest a connection; and I guessed that it was the location, location, location that had prompted the errors. And yet I confess to experiencing them with a touch of excitement, a kind of frisson at fame-by-proxy.

George Graboys, however, my roommate and traveling companion that summer, and I were often mistaken for each other. He had arrived in Hanover the year after I did, and until he met me couldn't understand why he'd be greeted as "Diz" on campus by guys who acted as if they knew him. We were built alike, we dressed alike, and our features were similar. One morning, when I was visiting him in Fall River, his mother came down the stairs for breakfast and addressed me as George. That's how close it was. But by the time he had achieved a degree of fame far beyond my own aspirations, we had reached a parting of the ways in terms of appearance--still built alike and still good friends, but no one calls me George or him Neil (or Diz).

That was all when I was twenty or so. Skip forward thirty-five years or thereabouts, and some people started calling me "Willie." With my full head of long hair and my beard grown out to its longest, both with some reddish highlights in the dark brown, I may well have looked a lot like Willie Nelson. So much so that in a kind of narcissistic way, in the laundry room of the house on Pewter Lane, I hung a window-size poster picture of the great song-man's face. No wonder, then, that just a short time ago, my son Daniel, on a business trip to Austin, bought a great t-shirt for me ("Have a Willie nice day" with a cartoon Nelson face).

More than self-indulgence, it was also a commemoration of the first evening spent with my wife Ellen, on March 14, 1983. Four of us had gone to a Willie Nelson concert at the Capitol Centre, Ellen with my shy friend Charlie, me with doll-face Eileen. She and Ellen were good friends, divorced single mothers, and when Ellen met the "older Jewish professor" Eileen was dating, on Christmas Day of '82, that old dog knew right away he was seeing the wrong friend. It took some time for us to get together, and fixing her up with Charlie for that concert was just a way of getting closer. Three months later, we were first a twosome at Memorial Park, sitting right behind the Orioles dugout and on our way to wedded bliss. No wonder that a few years later Willie would be looking benignly down on us, our own country-western Cupid, giving us his (appropriately stoned) blessing to what a shared appreciation of him had helped accomplish.

My brother Phil might be called a look-alike Manqué. He has always maintained an appearance of being vaguely familiar to people who don't know him well, a little Gary Moore here, a little Sonny Tufts there, and provoking some to insist that he had been a minor character actor in an indie movie. Twice he appeared on the game show, "Who Do You Trust?"--among three men who pretended to be the real guest. On neither occasion did he ever get so much as a single vote from the panel. He just didn't look enough like the person he was supposed to look like to convince anyone. "I know your fooling face," I would often say to him, whether at the poker table or when he was trying for some practical joke.

And the beat goes on: this is my granddaughter Sara,
who continues to look like a young Nicole Kidman

III

EARLY PROMISE

You might say that as a child I was of two minds: one was the child who wanted to be alone and be left alone, who wanted to amuse himself as he wished, mostly by reading, and who did not like being told by anyone what to do or how; the other was the child who wanted attention, enjoyed performing, and basked in the admiration and applause of others. But the truth is that there were many other parts working in my head: the shy non-social dreamer and the gregarious anything-for-a-laugh socializer, the solitary sports fan who memorized a world of statistical data and the eager competitor, the mean mocker of others and the open-minded seeker of broadening experience and variety of acquaintance, the opera lover and the jazz fan, the self-made individualist tennis player and the dedicated team-player of team sports, the idealistic dreamer and the cynical naysayer. In other words, looking back, I find it hard to put a finger on what I was at any given period, though I can often come up with anecdotal evidence of what I seemed to be at a particular moment in time.

The earliest moment of this kind is beyond actual memory, though I've heard the story often enough to think I may actually remember it. It happened during the year we lived in Providence before we settled in New Haven, and that means that I was no more than fourteen months old, and in the telling perhaps not quite a year old. Mother and Dad were the first in either the Isaacs or Braun family to move outside New York, and they were only "permitted" to do so on the understanding that they would make regular visits back to the City, as often as every weekend if at all possible. On this occasion, my mother and I were making the trip by bus, and I have no idea why my brother wasn't with us or why my father wasn't, as usual, driving us all in the car.

My mother, with her characteristic modesty, never bragged about any of my accomplishments, though she would often betray her pride whenever I would show the family what I could do. Fully toilet-trained at seven or eight months, for example, I brought admiration to both of us. And that I walked at ten months and was already speaking in full sentences were duly noted with the oohs and ahs that mark any sign of a prodigy in the making. So it was without apology or bravado that she first told a family gathering that weekend of what had happened on the bus. As it comes down to me, this is what she reported.

"We hadn't even reached New London when Neil told me that he had to go to the bathroom, so I went up to the bus-driver and told him that we needed to stop. He asked me how I knew that, and I said that my son had said so. Looking back at where we were sitting, the driver said that a kid that little couldn't have said that, so I told Neil to go tell him himself. He just marched up to the driver and said, 'Would you please stop so that I can go to the bathroom.' That man was impressed that a child who looked like he was maybe seven months old could walk and talk as well as Neil did, so he just pulled off the road and opened the door. He must have thought that it was a good story he could tell and he was laughing to himself about it when Neil got back on the bus and said 'Thank you' to him."

One other time my mother told a story that may seem like bragging about her child prodigy, but in her way she made it sound like a confession of her not knowing quite how to deal with me. And this time I remember the incident quite clearly.

We had moved to the two-family house on Edgewood Avenue, with a fringe benefit of being just over two blocks from the school that I was due to start. On the first day of kindergarten, enforcing my demands of independence, I was allowed to walk by myself to school. Mother was a lot more anxious about it than I was and hadn't slept much the night before. So when she saw me off after a light breakfast that was all I would tolerate, she went back to bed. About two hours later, she was shocked to discover that I was sitting in the room I shared with my brother, quietly reading a book.

She was shocked, cried out almost frantically, "What happened? What happened? Why are you home so early?"

"Nothing. I decided that I could play with toys just as well at home, if I wanted to, but I'd rather be reading anyway."

I had my way and never did another day's time in kindergarten. That's the last they saw of me at Edgewood School till the first grade, when I had the great good fortune of having Mrs. Wood as my teacher. She knew what she had on her hands and allowed me to spend much of the school day reading by myself off in a corner of the classroom while she led the class through material that I had long since mastered. She and my brother took turns suggesting what I might want to read, and they kept gently pushing me well past the curve.

In any case, apparently what most impressed the family about these little tales was that I paid no attention to them, treating them as if for me they were hardly worth listening to and surely undeserving of the noisy responses they elicited. At age six and a half, however, when I stole the show at my brother's bar mitzvah, I understood immediately what I had done, though I've always said to Phil by way of apology that I hadn't planned it at all. When he had approached the bema for his haftorah reading I jumped to my feet in the forefront of the B'nai Jacob sanctuary and called out, "That's my brother." There was much laughter in the congregation, and if I blushed deeply at the time I believe that it was from instant pleasure in the moment and not at all in embarrassment.

The urge to perform came on me unexpectedly. At Camp Everett where I began almost a decade as a summer camper in 1939, there was a major interest in "dramatics" that took second place only to sports as a staple of camp life. I have a cast photo of my first role, one of a chorus of younger campers who played the "forty thieves" in an original musical called "Ali Baba," written and directed by the music/drama counselor, Arthur Block. I was content to be one of the crowd at the time, just fitting in and going with the flow. Or so I remembered it as my debut, until I came across two bound volumes of the 1939 and 1941 "Everett Echoes," the camp's daily mimeographed bulletin, where I discovered that two weeks earlier I had played the role of one of Noah's sons (which one is unrecorded) in a piece called "Revolt in the Ark" and that I had followed the "Ali Baba" role by playing the part of Shawn Early in Lady Gregory's "Reading the News" a month later. The busy summer on the boards ended with another "chorus" role in a camp spoof called "It's the Bunk."

I'm the towel-head in the plaid shirt

Master Slouch, far right

What I've never forgotten, though, is that several years later a juicy role lured me back to the boards in the form of Sergeant Major Morris in a dramatic adaptation of the classic W.W. Jacobs ghost story, "The Monkey's Paw," giving me the opportunity as a senior camper to scare the bejesus out of the youngest kids from the first four bunks of the camp. I could feel the shudder of anticipation and the sharp intake of breath when I came forward and spoke to them, rather than the other players, the immortal words: "...but I warn you, I warn you."

The only other time the dormant thespian emerged in my teenage brain was in junior high school, when I was recruited to play the part of the court jester in a production of "The Forest Prince," a cheesy operetta with music by Tchaikovsky. I couldn't resist, having been identified as small enough, witty enough (I was something of a class clown in those days), and bold enough to tread the boards. I couldn't sing worth a damn, but I got to give a little comic solo dance and the script gave me all the best lines--if you can call "Waste no time on the windbag, captain, I'll tell the czar" a good line. It was a star turn and I loved it, but never wanted to do it again.

If the stage didn't beckon, then (remembering that all the world's a stage, after all), there were other opportunities to perform for an audience. There was a place downtown in the City, the Central Plaza, featuring Dixieland jazz, where I'd get up on one of the big round tables after a few beers and dance the Charleston to applause, applause. There were occasions during college when I'd sit in on drums at fraternity house parties or in Northampton at Rahar's. There was a place in Berkeley where, on rare nights out during graduate school, I'd take advantage of the live amateur entertainment encouraged by the establishment to deliver a stand-up comic routine.

And perhaps most memorably, there was the Sunday afternoon of Carnival weekend in my senior year, when I stood in the intersection in front of the Hanover Inn and directed traffic for a couple of hours, doing my best imitation of an Italian orchestra conductor, doing nothing to relieve the legendary congestion of Carnival visitors leaving town but giving them something to be amused by. At least that performance was memorable to many who witnessed it and thanked, praised, and toasted me for it years after the event.

But the fact is that I have no memory of it whatsoever. I had drunk so much of Marsh Smith's legendary "milk punch" concoction at the Pi Lam house that I was not conscious of my immediate surroundings. It was only after I had crashed and woken up mid-evening that I heard the first rave reviews of my performance.

Clearly, the brief flashes of notoriety for one or another live performance gave neither hint nor prediction of future fame. And nor were they consciously undertaken with that in mind. Spontaneous bursts of an ordinarily hidden aspect of the personality would be a more accurate category of those events, while juvenile accomplishments of intellect or scholastic distinction were seen in the family as predictors of what would make me famous one day. For example, I was given kudos for a trivial event like an appearance on the "Dr. IQ" radio quiz program when it visited New Haven; I was the "boy in the balcony, Doctor," who answered the set-up question with a confident if squeaky little voice. Likewise, when I was awarded a certificate for being a "Quiz Kids" finalist in open auditions, it proved an anticlimactic prize when the show folded shortly thereafter and before I had a chance to be chosen to appear among the gifted young wonders.

My grades throughout elementary and secondary education were uniformly superb, but when it came to prizes won, like the Janet M. Purdue Prize my junior year and the Susan S. Sheridan Prize senior year, they came in statewide competitions judged on the basis of an exam for which no preparation was called for. I was happy to accept those awards, in part because the competitive instinct drove me in the process, in part because they gave in my view testimony to an innate brightness, and in part because all I had to do was sit for the tests themselves; in other words, I valued winning when no studying was involved, a sign of a strain of laziness I would often struggle against. Unless the payoff came easily I didn't want to be bothered.

There were, I think, only two occasions throughout those years when I made an effort to gain recognition. One came during junior high school, when for reasons I can't recall I decided to enter a city-wide contest for an essay commemorating Fire Prevention Week (yes, there was such a thing). I think my dad had something to do with my participation; in fact, it was he who suggested that instead of a piece of didactic writing I put what I had to say in the form of a story. Appropriately, then, and cleverly, I thought, I began my story/essay with a dialogue between a father and son. "Something must be done," the boy says at the dinner table. "To or for what or whom?" says the somewhat pompous but kindly needling dad. And in the event I believe it was that introductory setting and innovative format that led to my winning the contest. I still have a framed certificate to show for it and a clipping from the New Haven *Register* to prove the public recognition of that very minor triumph.

The other one I worked for was another writing contest, when, a seventeen- year-old showoff, I strained to put together a very short story called "Biography á la Gertrude Stein." I still have a copy of "The Gleam," the magazine in which it appeared, my first published work of fiction.

There was one other occasion I can think of when I got some ink in the local papers. It was 1948, a presidential election year, and until 2008 the last one in which I became actively involved. Starry-eyed and full of hope, not with the audacity of it but with the kind of unrealistic, unworldly, utopian, daring-to- be-different, and cruising-for-disillusionment innocence of it. I had read Henry Wallace's recent book, *Toward World Peace*, and became enthralled with its vision, charmed by its rhetoric, and thrilled that a candidate for office could espouse a plan to achieve exactly the era of global peace that I thought any rational person would recognize as the only appropriate response to a half century of world wars.

I volunteered to work in the local headquarters of Wallace's party, called The Progressive Party in most places, but The People's Party in Connecticut. What a great platform, clear, logical, and absolutely right in my view! Its planks were to me like pillars of a new world: international peace based on cooperation with the USSR, thus nipping the nascent Cold War in the bud; a total end to racial segregation; and universal health care. So I not only did the office scut-work of stuffing envelopes and helping to distribute flyers, but I did in this case what otherwise was something I avoided at school, namely, volunteering for an active extracurricular role.

Civic-minded Connecticut, with an eye toward evenhandedness, had organized through its public high schools a series of debates among student representatives of the three (!) parties, and when a blind draw assigned the People's Party to Hillhouse I was first in line. The debates were organized by broad topics with a format of statement and response by a two-student team. The New Haven *Register* was impressed with this notion of real-life civics education and gave our debates some good coverage. I have a yellowed copy of the page that featured this program, complete with a picture of us kids all dressed up and ready to tell it as we saw it. I'm the littlest one in the group but feeling like a big person leading the way to a bright future. No score was kept; these debates weren't really contests, and it was clear to me that nothing my teammate Bernie Oxnam and I said would influence any of the other kids--or a single voter, for that matter.

As the campaign wound down there was a general feeling of discouragement (though Wallace himself remained upbeat), but there was also the sense that we were being utterly dismissed from serious consideration, the Connecticut school system notwithstanding. This genuinely surprised me because I thought that a strong slate of candidates, including John Marsalka for a Congressional seat, and the presence in the campaign of the brilliant Yale Law School advocate Thomas Emerson, unlike most third-party ventures, would demand reasonable open-mindedness. And then one evening late in the campaign, still doing whatever was needed in an office that had steadily lost volunteers, I made a damning discovery. Partly hidden behind the campaign literature was a stack of other material. Inquisitive as always, I took several pamphlets home to read.

Young as I was and wet behind my political ears, I recognized Stalinist propaganda when I saw it. Marsalka and others in the state party, it seemed, were card-carrying members of the Communist Party. (Years later I learned that Emerson was commonly known around the Yale Law campus as "Tommy the Commie.") My dreams were obliterated. I felt deceived, duped, and suddenly dead to political activity. I had been used, and so, I believed, had Henry Wallace been. To this day I believe that he did not know of his Connecticut campaign's true red colors. As a voter it took me a long time to recover from this shock, and my ballots were cast over the years all over the political spectrum, ricocheting right and left before coming to rest with Barack Obama--from a generally patriotic and pacifistic Socialist Labor side.

In the spring of my senior year, I earned a brief athletic triumph. I was voted onto the fraternity league basketball all-star squad, which meant I got to travel to Bridgeport for the annual game against their all-stars. A scouting report of my game would surely have been called "mixed reviews" at best. I was always the smallest boy on the floor, and at the peak of my vertical leap I was still the shortest. Not only was I small but I was also relatively slow-footed, and besides my shooting was erratic. My assets were my quick hands, which made me a pesky defender; relatively good ball-handling skills; a quick first step, which along with my ability at faking and feinting, got me open often on offense; and especially my court vision and perception, which made me a good passer and accounted for my steals in passing lanes.

Bridgeport was beating us pretty badly, with me sitting on the bench, mostly because we were just missing our shots. With five minutes left in the first half, our coach Chucker Alpert sent me in with just one instruction: "Shoot." I brought the ball up court, dribbled past midcourt about ten feet and quickly released a two-hand set shot. Swish!

Bridgeport came down and missed a shot, our rebounder gave me the ball to lead the play again, and I did the same thing. Ten feet over the line, quick release, two-hand set shot. Nothing but net!

Well, I said it was a brief triumph. In fact it lasted about thirty seconds, and not because I started to miss. For the rest of the half, I never touched the ball again. My teammates didn't want the instant gunner to take all the shots and they shut me out. Chucker just shook his head, and I sat out the whole second half.

Looking back on those so-called formative years, a.k.a. developmental stages, it is easy to see, with the unremarkably perceptive vision of hindsight, the predictors of my future. The theater, politics, sports, and diplomacy, not to mention science, medicine, or anything that required acquiescence to authority, were out; the appeal of performing in front of an audience would translate readily to the classroom. And if I could summon the energy to work at it, my most likely avenue to any kind of popular acclaim would come through my writing.

At the time, of course, no such thinking had reached the level of consciousness. In my largely wasted undergraduate years, loafing through what could have been a challenging curriculum, I avoided anything that would take time away from poker, drinking, and the pursuit of the opposite sex. Self-indulgence, indolence, intellectual arrogance, the joys of athletic competition and non-physical games, and lustfulness dominated what I see now as defenses against depression. Though I took one writing course, short stories with Arthur Dewing, I otherwise avoided the practice of what I should have been working at. And when I started graduate school in the English Department at Berkeley, my thoughts about pursuing creative writing under Mark Schorer were prematurely undercut when the austere eminence of the program in the person of Bertrand Bronson said to me in his famously stentorian tones, "Creative writing is the Cytherea Bog of the graduate program." I didn't know what that meant, except that it was a warning that if I wanted to succeed at Berkeley, I'd have to bury that yearning.

The writing itself became narrowly focused in an arena of devotion to academic minutia. And the allure of contact with avatars of fame and celebrity was suspended, except to the extent that the sheltered groves and ivy-covered dwellings could nurture a simulacrum of such desires. But let me go back and pick up the narrative thread of those urges that could never be completely repressed.

IV

SPRING BREAK AMONG THE STARS

One of the great advantages of being a teenager in New Haven in the late '40s was that there was no deterrence to hitchhiking, except for the largely unenforced laws on the Merritt Parkway. Few of us had cars that we could borrow, but we went virtually everywhere we wanted by walking to the start of a route and sticking out our thumbs.

Mostly, when I use "we" for the last three years of high school, I am talking about Marty Danzig and me. The Danzigs lived a block and a half up the Boulevard from our apartment building, and Marty and I were a regular twosome. That extra half block had put him in a different junior high zone from me, so that I really didn't know who he was until we went to Hillhouse. He knew me, though, largely through the Garfinkle twins who lived across the street from him and knew everyone in the neighborhood including that smart little kid down near the corner of Whalley Avenue.

Marty made it his business to become my friend, and as I remember it, he introduced himself to me as Gordon Finman's cousin. Gordy had gone to Sheridan for junior high, like Marty (and my brother before them), and not Troup, like me, but he and I were classmates in sabbath school at Temple Mishkan Israel. Whereas Gordy was known for his quick wit, his cousin Marty was known as a smart aleck who knew everyone in town. I quickly learned that he knew more than names and faces, that he could rattle off addresses and five-digit phone numbers and license plate numbers by the score. He knew the familial connections of every Jew in the community, and he could identify the owners of most cars we'd see in the neighborhood. It was Marty who famously said, "If you walked the block up Chapel Street between Temple and College in New Haven and didn't see anyone you knew then you just didn't know New Haven."

It amused Marty to be my friend because he thought I knew everything he didn't, and besides, as one of the tallest boys, he could appear as the protector of the "brain." It amused me to have a kind of Little John as a sidekick to my Robin Hood-like merry-making. He and I used to talk in a language of our invention that only a few could figure out and none could follow. It was to say everything backwards, as if reading words from right to left. We'd talk about going to the Lwob Aps (Bowl Spa) for lobster rolls (retsbol sllor) or down to Retsoow Teerts (Wooster Street) for zzipa (apizz'--the Neapolitan slang for pizza long before "pizza" became a national staple) at Sepep or Syllas (Pepe's or Sally's--still the best anywhere). Taken to another level, this became in time a parlor trick of mine, singing songs with all the lyrics backwards (a gimmick that to this day some folks regard as my greatest claim to fame).

Marty and I would hitch to Hartford for a jazz concert or anywhere within a four-hour drive for a sporting event. One memorable Saturday we hitched to New York to see the Army-Illinois football game where a pint-sized Illini running back named Patterson (naturally the player I rooted for) ran rings around the Army defense. But clearly the highlight of our tandem hitch- hiking career came during spring break of our senior year.

This was no Cancun or even Fort Lauderdale week, not in 1949, and there weren't even any school-sponsored tours. But neither Marty nor I had ever been to see our nation's capital, so we decided to hitch down to Washington. Did our parents approve? Well, they weren't enthusiastic about it, but we were accustomed to having our own freedom-loving way. Besides, there seemed nothing to worry about; we could take care of ourselves.

Less than a year earlier I had had an experience that should have scared me out of the thumbing habit. It was during the summer that I had gone back to Camp Everett as a camper-waiter, along with my friend Mitch Strickler. When I say friend I mean someone who went through grades one to three with me, a year of high school before he transferred to Hopkins Grammar, several years at the Temple in our confirmation class, several summers as bunk-mates at camp, three semesters as roommates at Dartmouth, and now after more than seventy-five years we still meet every other week for lunch at Ruan Thai in Silver Spring.

Mitch and I flanking Jay Karp, our all-around-athlete star

So he is my oldest living friend, at whose retirement dinner from the general counsel's office of the Pension Benefit Fund, I was the secret guest speaker who had more memories of Mitch than anyone alive and who had the rest of the attendees rolling on the floor. Among his many characteristics he has always been a lover of classical music and an encyclopedic automotive maven (even now, he drives an RX8 with the license tag "LSTFLNG").

Well, on our one day off that summer at camp we decided to hitchhike from camp, located in Taconic, Connecticut on the Twin Lakes, to Tanglewood in Lennox, Massachusetts, for some good music. The day is memorable for a number of things, including a huge bunch of grapes that we bought along the way on one of our many walking stops between rides and then wolfed down with some bloated results, the glee with which Mitch spotted a brand new 1948 Packard V-8 sedan in the parking lot, an afternoon of watching the great Serge Koussevitzky direct a rehearsal of the Boston Symphony and hearing his meticulous demands for precision called out with measured authority, and later in a chance encounter when the maestro asked Mitch to take a picture of him with his young granddaughter on the day of her visit.

All this we both recalled in a series of vivid mental snapshots we shared just recently at lunch, along with the most vivid memory of all--the return hitchhike that night. On those winding country roads through the foothills of the Berkshires, we were picked up by a local hayseed who happened to be driving back to Canaan, just the other side of Taconic. His rattletrap Model A was barely roadworthy, and we soon learned that maybe he was the same. He entertained us with his gems of driving wisdom, especially about the difficulties of seeing at night on the dark roads.

"The later it gets the harder it is to see the road," he said. Mitch looked at me and pointed to the holes in the floorboards where we could see the road very well as we passed over it.

"In fact," our driver went on, "it's safer to turn off your lights. Otherwise all you can see is what your lights show you on the road up ahead so that you can't hardly make out the lights of anyone coming the other way."

With that, he turned off his headlights and drove on through the dark. We may not have been in that car more than twenty-five minutes, but it seemed more like many hours after midnight until he dropped us off a short walk from camp. We said our trembling thanks, and he had one more hint for us: "By the way, if you're out thumbing some time and see me heading away from town, don't get in my car because I'll probably be drunk."

We had survived--and the hitching habit never wavered. So on a fine late April day Marty and I walked over to Derby Avenue, the road out to the parkway, to begin our adventure. For some reason it took us longer than usual to catch a ride, even though Marty identified the owners of several cars that passed us by.

"We know who you are and where you live," he'd say, "and you should recognize us."

Our luck was running so bad that when we got out to the ramp up to the Merritt, we agreed to take any ride we could get rather than hold out for a straight shot to New York for our first leg. So after a half hour wait we got to Bridgeport and then after another frustrating forty minutes were taken only as far as Greenwich.

We were beginning to think it just wasn't our day and that maybe we should go back home and try again tomorrow, when a Ford station wagon, the classy kind with the wooden paneling, stopped for us. The driver was a middle-aged woman with a plump smiling face, who asked if we'd like to get to New York, though she might have to let us off on the West Side Drive.

We said that would be fine if we could get from there to a tunnel to New Jersey, and slid into the back seat. The man sitting shotgun didn't acknowledge our presence, but when we were seated Marty nudged me with his elbow and nodded excitedly towards the guy. I took a quick look, then a double take, when I saw that it was Henry Fonda.

Marty indicated that I should talk to him. "Say something." he mouthed to me, as if I was the one who would know what to say. But I was struck dumb in awe and couldn't think of an appropriate gambit. I knew he was currently on Broadway in *Mr. Roberts* but hadn't seen it and didn't want to appear stupid. I could have quoted his classic Tom Joad speech of omnipresent inspiration from *Grapes of Wrath*, but his manner was totally aloof and I didn't want to intrude on his leave-me-alone attitude. I thought it would be better to enjoy the company in silence, and I wondered what had possessed his wife to stop for us in the presence of that forbiddingly concentrating face.

Then it came to me that I could address our driver. Off and on during the preceding couple of years I had done some part-time work at my dad's place. Mory Sales Corporation was a wholesale appliance dealer, the mainstay of which was Bendix Home Appliances. We had the franchise for the counties of southern Connecticut, and part of the way the business worked in those days was that the wholesaler was responsible for installing and servicing all the machines sold by the retail dealers. I had done some scut work in the warehouse, some simple washing machine installations on the road, and a bunch of file-clerk duties in the office. The latter had made me privy to the knowledge of which prominent people in Fairfield County were the proud owners of our top-of-the-line home laundries, the Fonda family of Greenwich among them.

"How do you like your new Bendix?" I said--and I thought Marty would fall off his seat.

"Well, it's working fine," she said, evenly, never questioning how I had known about it.

As for her husband, he gave no indication that he had even heard the random remark.

That was the end of all conversation, and we rode silently all the way to the West Side Drive, where they dropped us off before turning into midtown. Looking back, I've often wondered what that trifling incident was for them. For us, of course, it was a kind of thrill, an amazing piece of good luck. There was no hint that Mrs. Fonda, nee Frances Ford Seymour, was depressed or anxious in any way, though I doubt I could have recognized psychiatric symptoms at that time anyway. Henry was the one who seemed withdrawn, but I thought he was concentrating on the play, saving all his attention and energy for the performance to come. Nor was there any vestige of the woman often described as a "society beauty" in the jargon of media bios. The fact that six months after this ride the Fondas had separated never registered on my consciousness, nor, I confess, did I have any knowledge of her suicide the following April. I only learned of it, with its gruesome method, several decades later.

Clearly, our luck had turned, and Marty and I were recharged in expectations for the rest of our trip. We had to wait only a few minutes before a sleek black Lincoln stopped and offered to take us through the tunnel to New Jersey, though the driver said he was only going into Newark. "Driver" was what registered, our racial profiling suggesting that he was probably a chauffeur on an off-duty jaunt. But then he said he had a job to do that night, and, tongue loosened after the Fonda diffidence, I asked, "What kind of job?"

He hadn't said "gig," so we hadn't a clue that he was a musician. And not just any old musician. It was Louis Jordan, Louie of Tympany Five fame. As jazz enthusiasts, we had plenty of questions to ask, and he responded graciously to every one. I wish I had a tape of that half hour; I'd probably be embarrassed at my naivete, but his answers would be a treasure for jazz historians. Standing on the shoulder of the New Jersey Turnpike, waiting for a ride that was another hour to come, Marty and I were exulting in our incredible parlay, Henry Fonda and Louis Jordan back to back. "Just one bad thing," Marty said, "no one will believe us." But in some ways the best was yet to come.

We were way behind schedule and decided to stay over in Philadelphia and get an early start in the morning. The Broadwood Hotel, to my amazement at the corner of Broad and Wood Streets, was our nondescript way-station, but we got to D.C. in time for lunch next day. We checked into the G Street Y, and then the first thing Marty did was make a phone call.

We had a friend and fraternity brother, Jerry Weiner, who had often mentioned Uncle Ben and Aunt Mae who lived in D.C. In fact, when Marty had asked him if it would be okay to call his aunt and uncle, Jerry said sure, even though the families had not been in close contact for years--for reasons unknown to us or to Jerry himself for that matter. So it came as a surprise to me that Marty would actually make that call, and I had had no clue that he had concocted a plan until he introduced himself to Aunt Mae as "your nephew, Jerry, Al and Lois's son. My friend Neil and I are in Washington for a couple of days," he told her, "and thought I'd say hello."

She insisted we come for dinner that very night, and when he said we would and asked for directions, she told him that Uncle Ben would pick us up at six sharp. I thought the joke had gone far enough and said so, that we needed to come clean before bumming a meal at some strangers' home.

"Strangers, hell," Marty said. "I know as much about Jerry's family as he does. They haven't seen me, I mean him, since he was little, and they won't know the difference. We'll all enjoy it, and we'll have a good laugh with Jerry when we get home."

"Don't you think it'll piss him off? It's *your* joke on *his* family." I didn't mention it, but I had a private misgiving that had no place in a discussion of friendship and the ethics of practical jokes. I had a bit of a crush on Jerry's kid sister, the fun-loving Sandy, had yet to make any move, and believed this prank would kill any chances I might have with her.

"Well, he might get a little embarrassed, but we'll laugh it out of him and promise never to tell his folks. You know he wouldn't dream of telling them. Come on, it's a chance of a lifetime, one in a million. We can pull it off, but if you don't want to enjoy it on the spot and play your part, which would help back me up, I'll go there myself."

I had no doubt that he could pull it off, and I gave in to my curiosity to go along with the gag, as I was used to hearing Jack Benny say on Sunday nights. And it was a memorable dinner in one of those ample ivy-covered apartment buildings on Connecticut Avenue in Northwest that reminded me of the places out Whitney Avenue where "old Jewish" money was tastefully lavished in New Haven. Marty regaled "his" aunt and uncle with stories about cousins and other relatives they'd been isolated or perhaps estranged from since before the war. "That would be just like her," Aunt Mae would exclaim about an absent-minded gaffe that Marty had made up on the spot. It was an improv worthy of Second City. I laughed so much I thought for months afterward about whether our hosts wondered what the hell was so funny to me, the "outsider" at the table. But they enjoyed the evening so much, they insisted on being our tour guides to see the city's sights next day. I tried to tell Marty that was a bad idea--I had my own agenda of what I wanted to see--but he ignored me and said he couldn't deny these good folks their pleasure at a grand family reunion.

So we did the obligatory tour of the monuments, museums, and historic landmarks, and I never got to the Library of Congress, where I was to spend so many productive hours two decades later. On our last night in town, I had my heart set on a plan of my own, an evening of live music at the Capitol Theater. There was a hidden agenda in that, too, but when I told Marty about it he heartily agreed, although he was not quite the jazz aficionado that I was. How could a Jewish kid with an ear for music and good native rhythm grow up in New Haven and not dig the big band sound? After all, the Elm City was where Artie Shaw grew up (though his later protestations about the difficulties of anti-Semitism resonated with me not in the slightest). It was also the home town of Buddy Morrow, ne Moe Zudekoff, whose family's home was right across the street from us on the Boulevard. Buddy played a mean jazz trombone, but it was and remains little known that his kid brother, Milt, who never made it outside of town, was even better on the trumpet.

That wasn't my favorite sound, however. I had jumped onto the bebop bandwagon around 1946 when I heard my first Slim Gaillard records and went to my first concert at the Arena to see Dizzy Gillespie and hear the great vocals of Al Hibbard. So devoted to that "modern jazz" was I that my nickname right up through college was "Dizzy" and when I had a short-lived radio deejay stint in Hanover, my theme song was "Manteca." Many a night in the late '40s I could be found in New York, passing for eighteen and getting a hearty dose of Gillespie and Parker at the Royal Roost and Birdland and elsewhere on and around 52nd Street.

So I was delighted to discover that Woody Herman was in Washington, the big band leader who had most prominently incorporated bop into his arrangements. He had been headlining the show at the Capitol all week, and this was getaway night. This was the so-called "Second Herd," maybe the second greatest big-band jazz ensemble after Duke Ellington's all-time all-star band. He had Terry Gibbs on vibes and Shelly Manne on drums, two of my favorites, and his special guest co-headliner was Mel Torme, a masterful jazz drummer in his own right, a fine songwriter, and with a vocal delivery characterized as "the jet-propelled whisper of the velvet fog." This herd would soon be disbanded, sending such outstanding jazz musicians as Al Cohn, Stan Getz, Shorty Rogers, Ollie Wilson, Jimmy Raney, Gene Ammons, Oscar Pettiford, and Zoot Sims scattered to many gigs elsewhere.

For me the highlight of their final set was a long version of "Caldonia." I was on my feet and practically sent big Marty to the floor with an excited elbow. "What's that for?" he yelped, and I said, "Don't you get it? We got a ride with Louie Jordan this week and here's Woody doing Louie's greatest hit."

Our big move, though, came after the show. My idea was that we'd bum a ride back to New York on the bus. We had no trouble finding our way backstage, this being a time before security measures needed to be enforced to keep determined groupies out. The first star I met was Mel Torme, and unlike my tongue-tied embarrassment with Henry Fonda, I knew I had something to say to him--after praise for the performance.

"We have something in common--an early love named Susan Perry."

I knew he was recently married but his earlier romance with a model of that name had been tabloid material not that long before. My Sue Perry had been since junior high the primary object of my adolescent affections. For every occasion that required a date, she'd get my first invitation--and first refusal. I'd never gotten close to a date with her, and it became a standing joke.

Ironically, we would start dating that summer, after both of us had our senior prom plans cancelled, and by the time she was my date at Winter Carnival in my freshman year at Dartmouth, I had had the great good fortune of having my first genuine love affair with my longtime first if foolish love. Another story for another time, perhaps, but mentioned here because of what I thought was a clever remark to connect with a celebrity--which he of course ignored.

When I told him what out mission was that night, he said, "Sure, why not? Just ask Woody."

And so we did, but not before I had a moment with Shelly Manne, who I thought was the greatest drummer ever. I had spent several hours about two yards away from his kit in a club in the City, trying to match his hand movements in my dream of getting a chance to beat the skins myself. There was no way I could match his speed--for him a triple paradiddle was standard exercise. He had seen what I was doing, though, and spoke to me briefly between sets, and I never forgot his advice. "If your feet can keep the beat," he had said, "your hands can riff any way they want." I reminded him of that night, and he kindly said he remembered. I told him he'd just given me another lesson when he picked up the brushes to accompany Torme. He liked that and said, "Maybe we can talk on the bus," after I told him what we had in mind. Those two encounters with Shelly Manne were the sum total of my hands-on instruction on drums, but enough so that sometimes I could sit in during house parties in Hanover and in odd sets at Rahar's in Northampton, the rare occasions that mark the totality of my career as musical performer--until the outburst of song-writing almost two decades later.

Anyway, it was with some confidence that it might actually happen that I approached the bandleader. Woody was friendly and brisk, but not dismissive. "Fine with me," he said, "but you'll have to clear it with the bus driver," and pointed the guy out to us.

And that's where it fell through. "Can't do it," he said, as if he was really sorry, "the insurance doesn't allow anyone but the band on the bus."

Later, Marty said he thought they all knew it all along, were just being professionally cordial, and I had to accept that canny observation as accurate.

Back in New Haven, I found Marty to have been wise about other things. No one believed our encounters with the celebrities were anything but pipe dreams, and we had to quit trying to tell the story. And Jerry Weiner didn't believe our tale of the welcome that "he" had received from Aunt Mae and Uncle Ben. When he finally caught on that we had actually pulled it off, he was, as I had feared, not at all happy, whined at us and sulked for months.

We followed his example, though, by not sharing the tale with our respective parents. And as for his sister Sandy, I never got to second base with her, so the joke was on me after all.

V

LIZ NO SHOW

Some detail about my dad, deliberately postponed from earlier chapters, has been saved as background for this incident. Mory Isaacs settled with his family in New Haven in 1932. As a wholesale appliance distributor he established his business on Brewery Street, near the Wooster Street corridor where the famous kitchens of Sally and Pepe developed their widespread "apizz" fame. The closest business to Mory Sales was a moving company named Smedley's. It is a measure of my father's egalitarian nature that the moving men at Smedley's became his friends as readily as his accountant Jack Zemsky, his lawyer Ben Levine, and his doctor Meyer Etkind.

And there was the butcher, Sam Metler, and Al Rivers, apparent proprietor of the garage where Dad's car was serviced. I say "apparent" because it was suspected that Al fronted for a well-known "family" organization, and that the correct designation of his profession was "driver." This suspicion got a bit of support for me when, after Mory Sales moved to a location near the railroad station, Al Rivers introduced me to Broadway Jonesy, the local bookie who ran a so-called social club across from Dad's place and was willing to take my occasional action on a horse race. Al may have been connected, but Jonesy was more likely a soldier.

In any case, all these men considered my father a friend. At the restaurants we frequented, Casey's for fine food, the Tivoli or the Oneco for Italian, the Far East or Chunking for Chinese, the owners and the wait-staff all greeted him as a friend, just as readily as long-time mayor and undertaker Celantano did. Two other loyal, long-term friends were his barbers, Frank Fiascanaro and Charlie Esposito, whose shop had a prime location up a half flight of stairs from the entrance to the Chamber of Commerce building on Temple Street. Frank and Charlie were the eyes and ears of the Elm City; they knew everybody in town and knew who was doing what to whom. And all they knew they reported to Dad on his regular visits, as gleefully as any fair and balanced reporters of our time.

FLIRTATIONS WITH FAME

The point I am making is that my father had achieved a local fame that may have been good for business and was certainly good for his ego, while my mother was the quiet beneficiary of the warm regard in which she was held wherever she went in New Haven. When Connecticut began to issue vanity license plates, Dad saw fit to advertise his small-town celebrity by getting a tag with his name on it. MORY identified every car he drove from then on, and the only possible confusion was that some folks who were not in the know thought the car belonged to the proprietor of the restaurant featured in "The Whiffenpoof Song" dear to the hearts of Yalies.

When I got my driver's license, it was always the current "Mory-mobile" that I was allowed to drive. Decent cars, all, but with a built-in or added-on disadvantage to me. No matter where I went, whatever girl's house I was visiting (with whatever intent), whatever party I was privy to, whatever poker game I got into, whatever public showplace or eatery I frequented, the next morning my father would know about it and that evening at dinner I would hear about it. I entered my senior year of high school bound and determined not to go or even apply to Yale. I knew I had to get out of town, to be somewhere where every step I took, every move I made, everything I might try to jump into would not be common knowledge at home.

Yale offered at least partial scholarships to any Hillhouse graduate who was worthy of admission, and I could easily have fulfilled that long-cherished dream of my father's. I would not do it, I told him why, and he understood. Now here's why I ended up at Dartmouth. I applied to five schools, UConn as the perfunctory "safety school" I knew I wouldn't attend, Cal as a lark because the distance to Berkeley was more than my parents would tolerate at that time (a dream deferred till much later when I went there for my Master's and where my first son was born), Princeton, Columbia, and Dartmouth.

Imagine my shock when two of those three Ivies rejected me. With my scholastic record and my lofty SAT scores, I believed it was my choice to make. Not so in the spring of 1949. I had never really experienced anti-Semitism until then, never thought about the fact that I was applying to the two colleges that had the most niggardly quotas to keep Jews to a minimum. My letters of rejection tell the tale. Columbia said that although my academic record was excellent, my test scores did not measure up to their incoming class's standards. (I had scored 800 and 750 on my only sitting for the SATs.) Princeton said that though my test scores were competitive, my high school record did not measure up to their incoming class's standards. (I would be one of a dozen graduates out of a class of almost a thousand with perfect records.) I later learned that only one Jewish boy from the state of Connecticut was admitted to Princeton that year. I knew him, one of the dullest members of my confirmation class at Temple Mishkan Israel. He had gone to Choate. So that was why I matriculated at Dartmouth in September.

The background of this incident, then, prominently includes a father who is a well-known figure in his adopted hometown and a son who often wished he could be anonymous. Now I had decided to turn the tables. I was going to throw a party that would make me famous in New Haven--and not just as Mory's younger son. If it went off as I had hoped and planned, the news would be broadcast as widely and quickly as if a town crier had spread the word from Westville to East Rock, from the Yale Bowl to Woodmont. And the headline would be that Elizabeth Taylor had been at a party in the Isaacs apartment on Winthrop Avenue.

She was not Liz yet but no longer the enchanting child of *National Velvet*, just Elizabeth Taylor, the most beautiful girl in the world. She had just appeared in *A Place in the Sun*, George Stevens's brilliant adaptation of Dreiser's dour and melodramatic *An American Tragedy*. I think it's safe to say that for every Dartmouth undergraduate in the audience the most memorable part in the movie was not Lee J. Cobb smashing his crutch down on the rowboat he has had placed in the courtroom, not Montgomery Clift's ambivalent attempt to save the pathetically clingy Shelly Winters; it was Elizabeth Taylor's face in which even on a black and white screen the extraordinary violet eyes gleamed. What we took away was the look on her face and the sound of her voice as she says to Clift, "Every time we say goodbye I think it's the last time."

Stevens had directed her into a timeless maturity and captured that moment that stirred every adolescent boy's guts and loins. She was the iconic target of every wet dream in Hanover. She was nineteen. I was nineteen, too. And she was coming to my party.

Looking back, I think the whole idea of the party was just that she would come. I was not one to host parties in my parent's apartment in New Haven, though partying at the fraternity house in Hanover was one of my favorite ways of killing time. But that Christmas break of 1951 was going to be special, because my friendship with Jim Goldstone, my very own pledge-mate, was about to pay off big time.

The Dartmouth fraternity system had fixed rules about maximum membership numbers (sixty-five at the time), so that no house could pledge more new members than graduation had left openings for. Pledging took place early in fall semester sophomore year, but that year Jim and I failed to make the cut for Pi Lam, the only house that we considered or that considered us. But in the spring, thanks to the early graduation of two brothers, we were tapped in. I was playing in a basketball game for my dorm team in the intramural league when Mal Brochin appeared courtside and said to me, "You're playing your last game for the dorm; you'll be in uniform for Pi Lam next game."

Jim, I discovered much later that year, was the son of Jules Goldstone, Miss Taylor's Hollywood agent, and they had gotten to be good friends. (Jules was also the agent for Budd Schulberg, among others, including the classic director Clarence Brown.) The Taylors and the Goldstones would be in

New York during the week before New Year's, and Jim was expected to be Elizabeth's escort when needed or appropriate.

"Come into town if you want to meet her," he said to me.

"Why don't you bring her to New Haven and I'll throw a party," I said. "Great idea, perfect to get away from the parents."

"And mine will be away."

"Just let me know what night and we'll be there."

I was not shy about advertising the coming attraction, and I invited a lot of people. There were the other New Haven Jewish kids at Dartmouth of course, Mal Brochin, Wayne Weil, and Ed Winnick, all Pi Lams There were the high school classmates I had kept in touch with, mostly from the fraternity trio of Delta Rho, Mu Sig, and ULP. And I had called up a few friends from the two high school sororities that mattered to me, the classy (Waspy) Alpha girls and the (Jewish) princesses of Phi Sig.

None of the latter came; none believed the Elizabeth Taylor fantasy. The girls who did show up were mostly Hillhouse seniors with designs on the Dartmouth guys, hoping, I suppose, for invitations to Winter Carnival.

By nine o'clock it was over. I knew Jim had not come through, that his date would remain a figment of dreams. And I knew I'd be stuck with all the booze I had managed to buy. So I did what I suppose anyone remotely like me would do. I organized a poker game with the five or six guys still around that I knew were players. Why not? We had the apartment to ourselves and had all night to use it.

Back at school, Jim never told me exactly why the plan fell through, saying that it just didn't work out. When years later he had become a successful screen writer and director (*Winning,* with Paul Newman and Joanne Woodward, his best credit, I think), I was proud of the connection. His father Jules, meanwhile had made it possible for me to connect with the philanthropic director Clarence Brown (more of this below). But I never got to meet Miss Taylor or Liz.

I did encounter her once, at Orly Airport outside Paris. It was the spring of 2002. Ellen and I were on our way home from a wonderful week in Italy and there was Liz, being wheeled through the international waiting room, with a little white dog on her lap. She looked old, bloated, and ill, barely recognizable. It was all I could do not to cry.

Truth be told, any tears I shed would have reflected an adolescent pipe-dream: I had fantasized not just a meeting with Elizabeth Taylor at my very own party, but inviting her to be my date at Winter Carnival that year.

Winter Carnival pipe-dream

VI

TRANSITION AND SPENCER HAYWOOD

In the neon glare of hindsight I can see two decades or so blocked out in almost biblical terms: five lean years of waste in Hanover and Boston; five fat years of learning in Berkeley and Providence; four anxious years of scrambling in New York, Mount Vernon, and New Canaan; and eight years of branching and growth in Knoxville. The move to Tennessee, to paraphrase George Saintsbury (that most impressionistic of English literary critics), was like emerging from a cloying sickroom into a bright springtime garden. I had anticipated some culture shock but found it cushioned by gracious folks, a graceful passage of the seasons, and gradual realization that I could find and assert myself in the role of an outsider.

To those who questioned the wisdom of such a move I offered assurances that I knew what I was doing. On Martha's Vineyard that summer of '63, for example, my tennis buddies and other friends in the Black and inter-racial community of Oak Bluffs were astounded to hear where I was moving.

"Are there any Blacks at U-T?" they would ask. "Not enough--yet," I'd say.

"And that Southeastern Conference isn't even integrated," they'd sneer. "It will be, and soon," I promised.

I had, in fact, conceived a plan to carry out that little boast of mine. At the Oak Bluffs tennis courts I had eventually joined the ATA, the African- American counterpart of the USTA. I played regularly in their Labor Day Weekend tournaments, and got to know some of the folks who had been junior champions in that league. One, Doris Mitchell (nee Downing) was married to a lawyer (later judge) friend from Boston, Joey Mitchell, and she was a dean at Harvard. Here's how well I knew them. Playing on a court adjacent to hers one day, I looked over and saw that she was wearing a small bandage just above her knee. I waited for an opportunity when she was retrieving a ball nearby, and I said, "Is that one of those flesh-colored band- aids?"

She wheeled around in an instant rage, Doris Mitchell never brooking in silence a racist remark, and for a long second I thought her racket might be slung in my direction. Then she recognized the source of the "slur" and we both burst into laughter.

My plan was slyly simple. I thought that the way to break the race barrier in the SEC was through a minor sport instead of football or basketball. So I would make contact with the godfather of the ATA, Dr. Johnson, in Lynchburg, Virginia, where he ran a facility at which Althea Gibson and Arthur Ashe (and Doris Downing and her brother Lewis, a doctor in New Haven and one of my doubles partners) had learned important tennis lessons. We'd then groom and recruit a promising youngster to be the Jackie Robinson of SEC sports.

Not long after adjusting to a new life in Knoxville, I knocked on the door of tennis coach Tommy Bartlett. He was a former Vols basketball player and was now an assistant coach, earning part of his salary by serving as tennis coach. Practically all he did in that role was open the cans of balls for matches, with inter-squad play determining the line-up. Tennis was small potatoes there at that time, before players like Lenny Schloss, Jack Jackson, Lenny Scheuerman, and Paul Annacone came along, with some coaching assistance from Louis Royal and Dell Sylvia. So I told Tommy what I had in mind and he burst into raucous good-ol'-boy laughter, took me by the hand, and said, "Let's go next door. I want Coach Mears to hear this."

Ray Mears was sitting at his desk, drawing up charts of patterns. It was my first meeting with him, but I already revered him as one of the true geniuses among collegiate coaches. "What's so funny, Tom," he said. And his towhead assistant said, "Dr. Isaacs here has a plan. I'll let him tell you himself."

So I did, and Tommy kept snickering while Coach Mears heard me out and immediately waved his assistant out the door. "Sit down," he said. And he told me that he was hard at work on the integration problem. He said that minor sports wouldn't do, that he wanted to start big in basketball and tear the rotten fences down. "And it won't be an ordinary player," he said. "He's got to be a star. I've got a lead on one, and I expect him to visit soon, name of Spencer Haywood. I'll let you know how it goes."

A few weeks later he told me he had some bad news. Spencer had failed to pass U-T's entrance exam. "I have plan B," he said, "and I'd like you to come in and talk about it with me and Spencer." When I got there I met an impressive, large young man, cordial and surprisingly articulate for someone who hadn't been able to pass a routine test. But when I heard the back story I was no longer surprised.

Haywood had grown up in Mississippi, and ten years of "separate but equal" education had rendered him functionally illiterate. He'd made progress after moving to Detroit, but his focus had remained on basketball, successfully. He had led Pershing High School to Michigan's Class A championship and was being recruited by big-time schools. He was intelligent enough to have as first choice a school with a great coach. He didn't really care about breaking any racial barrier in any league but thought he could handle that. Right away I was as confident about that as Coach Mears was.

The coach had been in contact with Knoxville College, the small Black school across town, and was trying to set up an intensive remedial reading program for Spencer to pursue during the summer. And would I take part, in part to make sure that the re-take of the entrance exam was handled under academic scrutiny?

I jumped at the opportunity. I thought of it as a chance to "make a difference," just as I had two years earlier back in New York when I was asked to be a proper-English-language tutor for Sugar Ray Robinson, the greatest pound-for-pound boxer in history. Sugar Ray was planning a theatrical career and needed help with the way he spoke. It never happened, I didn't even get to meet the champ, and that career plan flickered and died. Now here was a more likely opportunity to contribute something to progress.

My contact at Knoxville College was a dean who had the misfortune of bearing the family name of Martin, with the inevitable jokes about Jerry Lewis as a price to pay for his rank. The dean became an acquaintance of lasting value, but the proposed arrangement was never consummated.

Spencer rejected the plan. A summer in Knoxville was not what he was looking for, with little chance to play ball at his level. Ray Mears had a Plan C as back-up. He'd get Spencer into a complaisant junior college and transfer him over to the Vols after one season. The only reason that didn't work was that Spencer got a better offer from another school's junior college "farm system." After that first season, all he did was star for the American Olympic team in Mexico City and then make the University of Detroit the winner in a recruiting competition with a deal that included an assistant coach's job for his high school mentor.

In his one-and-done year at Detroit he led the nation in scoring, then jumped to immediate stardom in the ABA, where he led the league in scoring and was MVP and Rookie of the Year. And then he made basketball history after all, the first "hardship" case in an innovation called the Haywood Rule. The NBA had been off limits for him because of its rule requiring four years after high school for eligibility. Challenging that rule in court and drafted by Seattle, he won battles in court and on court, the first player under twenty-one in the league, and a steady rebounder, scorer, and all-star selection--all this while being booed by fans for his fight against the establishment, which might have seemed to him an ironic reminder of what he might have faced as a Tennessee player in places like Starkville, Mississippi and Baton Rouge, Louisiana.

His career took him from Seattle to New York and then Los Angeles where he was a role player on a champion team, then dumped for using recreational narcotics. He finished his career in Washington, where I met him again in the Bullets locker room at the Capital Centre. I could tell he didn't remember me from our failed try at making history, though he said he did. I was impressed but not surprised that he had matured into an elegantly dressed, quietly articulate, and cultured man of the world (marriage to the gorgeous model Iman surely helped the image).

Meanwhile, back in Knoxville, I had wondered in hindsight about a Plan B of my own. Why, I asked Coach Mears, hadn't he pursued Perry Wallace, a star at Pearl High School in Nashville, winner of the first integrated state tournament in Tennessee history. He was not only an exceptional rebounder with a huge vertical leap at 6'4" or 6'5" but an exceptional student as well. I might have helped in recruiting him because I had made contact with the Nashville counterparts of our local Human Relations Council and we might have promoted the idea of Perry being the right person at the right time to make a place in Tennessee history by integrating intercollegiate sports in the Southeastern Conference at his own state university. Wallace played his part in that drama anyway, along with Godfrey Dillard from Detroit's Visitation High School, when they were in uniform for the Vanderbilt freshman team. But Mears said he had looked at Perry and thought the kid didn't shoot well enough to be a star player and despite his leaping ability he might be too small to be a dominant rebounder (the only serious error in basketball judgment I am aware of Mears making).

U-T probably couldn't have recruited him anyway. Roy Skinner signed him for Vandy, where playing in his home town should have made the adjustment a lot more comfortable. Wallace distinguished himself on Skinner's very competitive Commodore teams, not only leading the conference in rebounds twice but becoming an effective scorer around the basket. Years later, as a successful civil rights attorney in Philadelphia, he made an inspirational appearance as a guest in my "sports culture" course at Maryland, and has since become a Professor at American University Law School. (Late in 2014, Andrew Maraniss published a biography of Perry, called *Strong Inside: The Collision of Race and Sports in the South,* disabusing me of any thoughts about "comfort." I wish I had been asked for my input.)

My mission to be instrumental in the process of athletic integration (and achieving a degree of fame as a result) had failed. But the issue had become moot. Tulane had fielded a Black baseball player, and LSU's signing of a Black football player had opened the gates wide throughout most of the South. Bear Bryant, who had made a practice of recruiting several Black players every year while waiting for someone else to lead the way, soon had a half dozen eligible athletes in Tuscaloosa. A big step for sports in the South; a small step for mankind; no credit to this would-be celebrity.

Perry Wallace

Spencer Haywood

With two of my basketball idols, Coach Ray Mears and Bill Russell

VII

HOLLYWOOD COMES TO THE SMOKIES

The Knoxville *News-Sentinel* broke the news and all of eastern Tennessee was astir about the movies. Columbia Pictures had dispatched its location scouts to find settings for a major motion picture. Folks were having pipe dreams about casting calls, star-watching, crowd scenes, and business opportunities. The timing was most propitious for me, coinciding as it did with what was becoming a primary focus of my attention: movies in general and film studies in particular.

The University of Tennessee was in the process of developing a plan for a new state-of-the-art theater building, and the development office was courting Clarence Brown for a major contribution to that effort, holding out the implicit promise that the building would bear his name. To sweeten the deal, they were hyping the potential for using the facility to house a film study program at U-T (which up to that point had no academic interest in movies whatsoever, with a traditional theater department that barely recognized the existence of the clearly dominant art-form in the culture).

How those university front office people got wind of me and cooked up a plan whereby I might be able to help their campaign I never knew, but I was summoned to a meeting of the suits. They had done due diligence. They knew that I had a connection with Jules Goldstone (father of my Dartmouth classmate and fraternity brother James Goldstone), who happened to be the agent for Clarence Brown. Brown had been a U-T undergraduate in engineering who made a fortune as one of the most successful Hollywood directors of his time. After proving his mettle in directing stars like Rudolph Valentino, Greta Garbo, and Norma Shearer, he became a fixture at MGM, with box office triumphs like *The Human Comedy, The White Cliffs of Dover, The Yearling, Intruder into the Dust,* and *National Velvet*. His handling of bright stars like Joan Crawford, Clark Gable, Jimmy Stewart, Gregory Peck, Jane Wyman, Mickey Rooney, and the young Elizabeth Taylor made him a particular favorite of the studio--and his real estate investments made him rich. Jules Goldstone had become more than a silver screen agent for Brown, had indeed become a trusted and wise investment counselor and close personal friend. It may have been an even more productive relationship than his representation of Elizabeth Taylor.

What the suits wanted was not merely my presence (with the Goldstone connection as my imprimatur) when Brown came for a visit to the campus and the building site, but also as an academic who could hype the potential of the theater itself as a mecca for film students. An exchange of letters between Jules Goldstone and me had paved the way and served as an introduction to Brown. So there I was, hawking my wares that were far from being mine except in my own head and in the pretenses of the hosts who were pitching a prospect they had no reason to believe would become a reality. Mr. Brown was a cordial, expansive, but remarkably modest acquaintance, and he listened politely to my spiel and apparently appreciated my enthusiasm. The Clarence Brown Theater, which he endowed to the tune of five million dollars, became after all the setting of my debut course in film study. The two following parts of this chapter will pick up other threads in the story arc of my career in movies.

As the reports came in about the Columbia Pictures production, the excitement grew. The locations that had been chosen included the historical Ayres Hall (which had once housed the English Department) on the U-T campus for a collegiate scene and Cades Cove in the Smoky Mountain National Park, perhaps the most beautiful preserved rustic area I had ever seen, with the resort town of Gatlinburg as a center of operations.

The movie was to mark the return of Ingrid Bergman to the American film scene, starring in a story called "A Walk in the Spring Rain." The script was in the hands of Stirling Silliphant, a pioneer and graduate of classy television drama ("Naked City," "Route 66") who had brought his genius to the big screen and was now about to embrace a new role as producer for this picture. Each further announcement kept the momentum of anticipation: Anthony Quinn as co-star, original music to be composed by Elmer Bernstein, Guy Green as director (known to me for his superb cinematography on *Oliver Twist* and *Great Expectations*, and whose American credits as director included *The Light in the Piazza* and *A Patch of Blue*).

The novella Silliphant was adapting was by Rachel Maddux, a name unfamiliar to most readers of literary fiction, but known in the region for her stories set in the southern mountains surrounding her home in the town of Tennessee Ridge. To me, she was the author of *The Green Kingdom*, a major work she had devoted almost two decades to, a well-reviewed but largely neglected masterpiece perhaps too facilely categorized as fantasy. When I hurriedly turned to *A Walk in the Spring Rain* I found it a thoroughly professional, carefully wrought piece of work, but hardly up to the level of her magnum opus, and since it is a story told entirely in the first person from within the consciousness of the protagonist, it did not have motion picture written all over it. Not that my opinion mattered: Ingrid Bergman read it and liked it, thinking the role of Libby would be a fine vehicle to carry her on her return voyage to Hollywood. Besides, in Silliphant, she had a writer who would do what was needed to translate it into a worthy screenplay.

And that was what generated my brainstorm. I called Steve Cox, assistant director and editor at the University of Tennessee Press, and we took a meeting. Steve was a bright, young, ambitious, energetic, and talented young man. He had taken two graduate courses with me, we had become friends, and I knew that film was an interest of his along with folk music, poetry, and history. He had, in fact, been the editor on my first serious scholarly book for the press and had done a great job. My suggestion to him was made in the nature of a gift, a favor, which might be a boon for the press and a boost for him personally.

Look, I said to him. This is falling right into our laps. Here I've been searching the literature for texts for film study, and the kind of book I'd like to use in a course I'm hoping to teach just doesn't exist. Why don't you see if you can get the rights to reprint Rachel Maddux's novella, secure the rights to publish Stirling Silliphant's screenplay, and ask him to write an analysis of the process of translating literary fiction into film? The novel-into-film framework is going to be very big in academic circles very soon.

Steve went right to work, writing to query Silliphant on his interest in such a project. He replied positively, suggesting that such a book could be a standard for the trade. Steve's superiors at the Press approved, the Maddux story was available, and a meeting was set up for Silliphant's next visit east to work out the details. I had done my part and was pleased to be invited to lunch at the Quarterback near campus. Silliphant was charming, affable, complimentary. and apparently eager for the book to happen.

Then, at the end of the conversation he dropped a bombshell. "The only problem is that I wouldn't have the time to do it; I have too much work on my plate as it is, too many projects beyond this one to give it the effort it deserves in the near future." And he turned to me and said, in a way that seemed casual but was not at all off-handed, "Neil, why don't you do it?"

Bob Leggett, probably the quickest wit among my colleagues, said, when he heard about this arrangement, "If there were a bus accident on Cumberland Avenue, Isaacs would get a book out of it."

Well, yes, if it were offered to me on a Stirling silver platter. I was in the right place at the right time, for a project that offered perks, possibilities, and both short-term and long-range goals to shoot for. I was promised unlimited access to the entire process: the shooting on location, the cooperation of all participants, the post-production in L.A., and even an invitation to the pre- release preview. Everything seemed to fall into place. I had already been granted a reduced teaching load for the spring quarter, clearing time to be on the set in the mountains, a half hour drive from home. Thanks to the National

Endowment for the Humanities, I would be on sabbatical the whole following academic year to travel and do research on my own schedule. The University chipped in through its Master of Arts in College Teaching Program to share the burden of my expenses with Columbia Pictures' Publicity Department.

Bus accident, indeed. I was going to meet, interview, and mingle with some of the big names in the business along with a large contingent of crew and crafts-people. I would be getting a hands-on education in movie-making that I might be able to use in a course. And five hundred students had signed a petition asking for the school to offer a course in the literature of film.

Maybe, just maybe, out of this venture I could get to be somebody, I could be a real contender for fame.

I plunged in with almost manic energy, and the rewards were plentiful. Rachel Maddux was generous with her time and discussed creative processes at great length with me. Guy Green was far more available than I ever thought a director on location could be and instructive in the style of Platonic dialogue. I caught up with Anthony Quinn for a brief demonstration of his own artistic ambitions. Fritz Weaver had been cast in an important role, and our conversations enforced my admiration for him as a conscientious objector. Only Miss Bergman, of all the principals, gave me short shrift, her time between shots being rather fully occupied with her reading of mass-market magazines, not at all the sophisticated lady I had conjured up from her film persona. Virginia Gregg, a character actress, whose face was far more familiar from myriad minor parts than her name, became a friend; she enjoyed dinner with my family at our home in Knoxville and made me promise to be in touch when I was on the Coast. And from start to finish, on location and at the studio, in person and by mail and phone, Stirling Silliphant played the role of godfather to the book, with his nephew Mark as adjunct facilitator.

For two days on the set, when the scene of a fist-fight in a lumber yard was shot, I was able to watch close up as the fight was choreographed by Silliphant's own martial arts instructor whom he flew in just for that action. It was Bruce Lee in just his second movie assignment, the first being an on- screen role in *Marlowe* (based on the Raymond Chandler character), which Silliphant had written for him. He had yet to become Bruce Lee, but in retrospect I am proud to be seen at the edge of a still shot of him at work-- one of my many souvenirs of that spring. In another still, of a large crowd scene at a fair, you can make out Chris Whittle, then still a student at U-T, who went from being an extra in a single scene to the most famous education entrepreneur of his time this side of Stanley Kaplan. [Footnote: Chris and I were both enamored, unrequitedly, of a beautiful redheaded graduate student in drama. She is also an extra in that crowd scene, and it's hard to miss her; the camera is drawn to her, like many pairs of male eyes.]

At the studio, where I was given my own little office, I was working too hard to go star-hunting in my old habitual way. I got a crash course in editing (from the great Ferris Webster) and tutorials on hairstyling (with the venerable Virginia Darcey) and on how a script supervisor guarantees continuity (with the slick Marshall Wolins). The sound editing led by Arthur Piantadosi was fascinating in itself, and I sat through the recording of the background music under Elmer Bernstein's baton. Bernstein graced me with an interview over lunch at the Beverly Hills Hotel, which I greatly appreciated (although the struggling academic, not the wealthy composer, picked up the check).

I stayed with Aunt Ruth and Uncle Lou while I was there, and they were gracious hosts. Ruthie worried that when I went to have dinner at Virginia Gregg's apartment I might be prey for a Hollywood seductress like so many star-struck innocents before me. It was just the two of us, all right, talking about interests we shared and laughing about my aunt's worries, Jane Wyman look-alike though she was.

Back and forth across country I flew for the sneak preview in San Francisco at the Vogue, a small art-film theater away from the center of town. That was an odd choice, since the typical Vogue audience was not likely to be favorably disposed toward what was essentially a traditional melodramatic offering. (Bosley Crowder in his subsequent review in the *New York Times* mentioned its "wholesome atmosphere.")

Nevertheless, there was heady optimism among the few studio executives and publicists in the small pre-screening entourage dining at Trader Vic's, while at the end of the table where the Greens and Silliphants sat the enthusiasm or hype was tempered with some expressions of anxiety.

The response from the preview audience, both while viewing and when commenting afterwards, was lukewarm. There were precious few raves and virtually no pans. With some minor editing adjustments, the movie went into distribution--with the same kind of moderate reception. Columbia Pictures broke about even on the deal. The hopes for a smash hit and Academy Awards went a-glimmering. There had been optimistic speculation that the industry would welcome Ingrid Bergman's return with an Oscar, but that hope was compromised by what I thought had been an error in judgment on the part of the studio. Columbia's deal with Bergman was for two pictures, and she had chosen Silliphant's project first. But then the studio cast her in *Cactus Flower*, which they shot and released first. There were rave reviews for that one--for Goldie Hawn, but Ingrid Bergman seemed out of her element. She had managed to retain much of her classic beauty (as long as shot from a favorable angle; a studio still photographer told me that she had been known to say to someone pointing a lens upward at her face and revealing an unflattering neck, "Get a fucking box"), but broad comedy was clearly not her forte. So the second of her films was compromised, not enhanced, by the first.

The movie had a modest run. It featured a good story, a fine script, a glowing cinematography, and widely praised performances by Quinn, Weaver, Gregg, and especially Bergman. Two young actors in key supporting roles attempting to boost them toward stardom, instead faced career collapse. But what about the book, *Fiction into Film: A Walk in the Spring Rain*, which I thought might be my own launching pad to some level of distinction?

The Press produced a handsome volume, scrupulously edited and brightly illustrated with more than two dozen photos (including several from my own amateur twin-lens reflex). And it more than earned its keep when Dell bought the paperback rights. So I got two books out of it (to trump Leggett's quip), but an embarrassment of petty royalties. It is an instructive book, and I think a model for the kind of book it was designed to be. But in order for it to have had a lasting shelf life as a text for academic courses, it would have had to be based on a much better movie. Even I couldn't see screening that movie as part of a fiction-into-film course.

So I had a wonderful time in the doing and a big nothing in the sequelae. I'd have to make my mark in the emerging academic discipline of film study through other means. My course was approved, however, and made its debut in the Clarence Brown Theater with a class of ninety (every seat in the house filled). The souvenir I most treasure from my Hollywood daze is a handwritten letter from Ingrid Bergman. She wrote to express her dissatisfaction with my remarks about *Cactus Flower*, but I have her pristine autograph.

On the set: Miss Bergman between takes

Guy Green showing Bruce Lee what he wants

Stirling Silliphant with co-author

Keep Thinking Sinking

Unlike almost all large gatherings of academia and culturati, the atmosphere is fairly festive in those where the common ground is in the movies--hence the term "film festival." Now Nashville will never be mistaken for Cannes, but the Tennessee Film Festival in 1968 was an eye-opener for me in more ways than one. It was easy to stay awake through hour after hour of original pieces of work of great variety and quality, testifying to a cultural awakening and bursting energy of young American film-makers. If there had been a *palme d'or* it would have gone without doubt to *Faces*, a new John Cassavetes film which, though heavily influenced by the French new wave, marked the maturation of an experienced American auteur.

I was there as a newly appointed member of the large board of advisors to the Tennessee Arts Commission, and I made the most of the opportunity to develop some skills in the art of networking, for which I had had little talent or patience. Two new acquaintances were the most intriguing to me and fortuitous for me. If ever I could have said "well met" immediately after shaking hands, I would have said it for Seymour Cassel and Mickie Coleman.

Cassel was the sole representative of the Cassavetes crowd, a long-standing featured player in what amounted to a stock company. After the screening of *Faces* at the Vanderbilt Theater, he and I engaged in a long conversation, more praise than analysis on my part, a lot of technical detail and back story on his, with the result of my enriched appreciation of what was going on in the director's radical approach to cinematic narrative. Seymour and I stayed in touch; he came to Knoxville for the movie's opening there, had dinner with us, and was impressed when I took him on a tour of the Clarence Brown Theater. Out of curiosity about what was happening in the mountains, he drove up to the Smokies with me for an afternoon on Silliphant's set.

Three screen artists and a cinema-wannabe

I got a kick out of introducing him to Virginia Gregg and Fritz Weaver, and an even bigger boot out of listening to them talk about acting for the screen. And finally it was my new friend Seymour who brokered a subsequent long- distance conversation between Cassavetes and me. (I do love using that phrase, "Cassavetes and me").

Like me, Mickie (Mrs. Nat Coleman, later Mary Jane or just M.J., of Creekside Farm in Greeneville, Tennessee) was a new member of the Arts Commission Advisory board. Her attractiveness and gregariousness, along with her husband's political pull, may have abetted her appointment, but the main element must have been her unbridled enthusiasm for the movies. With no illusions of any talent on her part, she seemed to be a natural-born patron of motion picture art. And she left Nashville with visions of her own film festival dancing in her brain. And that's how the Sinking Creek Film Celebration was born, and I was swept up in the moment to the point of agreeing to be an advisor on her nascent board.

Her plan was to bring the celebration to Knoxville in about a year and a half, with the Clarence Brown Theater to be a key venue for presentations. I couldn't help her with that. I tried, and so did Mickie with her far more influential connections, but U-T was very tight with its new treasure and declared a policy that the building would only be used for official functions of the university and the Theater Department. So the Coleman estate and nearby Tusculum College became the default setting for the festival.

The inaugural (called "first annual" in a bravura expression of its intention to become a fixture) was not without its rough edges; but festive it was, thanks in large part to the generous hosting of the Colemans. Mickie had used the American Film Institute as a conduit to Hollywood and lined up a pre-release screening of a feature. I had the dubious distinction of leading the discussion that followed the showing, where it was all I could do to muster up some provoking comments on *Norwood*, an ill-conceived Paramount production starring Glen Campbell (who'd shown some promise as an actor in *True Grit*) and Joe Namath (whose acting was a pipe dream in his agent's mind but who had star power as a Super Bowl champion quarterback). No matter. In the absence of studio staff or movie stars, I turned my attention to the process of converting written story to film, opportunistically plugging the book on *A Walk in the Spring Rain*.

Previewing the Sinking Creek Film Celebration, eastern Tennessee's most respected columnist Wilma Dykeman asked, "Was there ever a more preposterous--or provocative--title for an event in our region?" Many of the more than a hundred short films submitted were preposterous indeed; but, judged for prize money in four categories by a panel of distinguished film folks, some of them were truly provocative. For me, the highlight was not the homage paid to silent movies with screenings of a Valentino and a Chaplin movie, but a short subject by the brilliant independent filmmaker, John Hancock.

Based on a witty *New Yorker* short story by Gene Williams and backed by the American Film Institute, "Sticky My Fingers, Fleet My Feet" went on to be an Academy Award nominee, and many viewers thought it deserved to win. About a guy pushing thirty who plays in a weekly touch football game in Central Park, it takes us through a moment of self-recognition when a young upstart bogarts his way into the game. Virtually plot-less but a rare example of cinematic character study, it had all the makings of technical expertise one could expect of a maestro.

I got to spend considerable time with John and his wife Ann at the festival, and if I had had my wits about me (or was as quick on the opportunistic take as Bob Leggett cynically gave me credit for), I'd have made Mr. Hancock an offer he couldn't have refused. His movie was made to order for a handy textbook, a primer on fiction-into-film. No instructor would have been embarrassed to screen it for a class or assign the story to be read, and the AFI might well have contributed to the commentary that would round out the text following the story and the shooting script.

I missed that boat by a blind blunder of misdirection. Instead of focusing on the filmmaker, all I could see of book potential rested on the blond head of his wife, who happened to be an editor at Viking. I told her about an idea I had for a murder mystery set against the background of the PGA tour. (At this point I had the hubris to believe that I could do any kind of writing I set my mind on and my pen to.) She was clearly interested and made me promise that she'd get the first look at it when I had a draft.

With that kind of encouragement I went to work and filled my spare time (such as it was) with dashing off a first try at genre fiction. Here's the first paragraph of what I had on Ann Hancock's desk within a few months:

> The tenth hole at Augusta National is a par 4, 470 yards. Called the Camellia, it is one of the loveliest holes on this loveliest of courses, but although it is the longest of the ten par 4s it is very nearly the easiest. The fairway, which seems tight from most angles, widens out generously in the driving area, the gentle slope carries most tee shots down to a smooth and level lie, and the green is both ample and level.
>
> There are two large fairway bunkers, but they are no more than 200 yards from the tee, so that a whole Masters could be played without bringing these hazards into play. It was in the sand of the trap on the left-hand side of the fairway (golfers' left, as always) that the body was found.

Pretty good, I still think, after all these years. But, like the hole on the golf course, the whole manuscript went downhill after that. My idea was intriguing, that a series of bizarre and unsolved murders all across the country could be connected by a pattern discovered by Jacobi, not a detective but a sports historian. Each killing came on the heels of a colossal collapse by a star golfer in the final round of a big tournament. The climax would come at another tournament, where Jacobi has persuaded the authorities to monitor the galleries on every available TV camera in the hopes of spotting the killer whose insanity is the toxic extreme of a sports fan's obsession.

I couldn't bring it off. Jacobi was unbelievable and unappealing. There was no wit or charm in the dialog, and though the shifting point of view was a staple of the genre, I failed to approximate its other common devices, like quick sketches of people, their clothes and quirks, and their surroundings. Ann read it quickly, was disappointed, and let me down gently by asking, "Have you thought of writing straight sports?"

Indeed I had, if fleetingly, but I immediately decided to sketch out a proposal for a narrative of my lifelong love affair with the game of basketball. I sent it to Viking and a dozen other publishers. They all rejected it, though some said the idea sounded good but unless my name was a household word they'd have trouble marketing it. Ed Burlingame at Lippincott added another paragraph to his rejection. "We've just published a history of college football," he said. "How would you like to do a history of college basketball?" Did I take twenty seconds to jump up and down and then say yes and how soon do you want it? Anyway, that's how I got started down a track that led to a dozen books, many more periodical credits, and the great fun I had doing it. And all because of a film festival in Greeneville, Tennessee.

Sinking Creek grew and grew, until it overflowed its banks and had to move back to Nashville for its fourth annual. I got there for as many of those early renewals as I could, but had less and less to do with it. I played an indirect role in bringing the venerable Victor Trivas to the site and a screening of his long-forgotten and rediscovered 1931 masterpiece, *Niemandsland* ("No Man's Land" a.k.a. "Hell on Earth"). Shot mostly in World War I trenches, it ranks alongside *Dr. Strangelove* as the most powerful anti-war movies I've ever seen. I may have done a slow fade from the scene, but it was great for me while it lasted. The memories are strong, keeping the faith with its long- running motto, "Keep Thinking Sinking."

The Cassavetes Connection

The stars were aligned in such a favorable profile for my purposes that I could hardly believe how smoothly the pieces were all falling into place. It was like completing a jigsaw puzzle with my eyes closed. Dumb luck or just deserts? I didn't know or care. First the South Atlantic Modern Language Association approved my plan to introduce a new "section" on film studies at the 1970 annual convention in November, this one for a change in Washington, D.C.

With that encouragement I had hoped to plan a gala gathering for the inaugural, with a pre-release screening of a major motion picture and a panel of luminaries to discuss it. My association with Columbia Pictures from the Silliphant movie and my access to John Cassavetes through my acquaintance with Seymour Cassel paved the way, with perfect timing, to schedule the first big-budget movie of Cassavetes' career as a director, *Husbands*. The studio would take an active role in the occasion, promising that not only would producers Al Ruban and Sam Shaw be on hand, but two of the co-stars as well, Peter Falk and Ben Gazzara, with Cassavetes himself only a long shot to make it.

At the convention there would be two afternoon pre-release screenings of the movie at the Embassy Theater, just a short walk from the Washington Hilton, the convention hotel. On the evening following the second showing, there would be a panel discussion with a forum format including the kind of Q and A session that SAMLA had never seen or heard before. And the no-admission-fee showings would no doubt attract an unusually heavy turn-out. I had asked Bill Robinson, who had pioneered film studies at the University of Florida, to chair the panel. Bill was part of the gang of seven, including my friends George Garrett at UVa, Bill Free at Georgia, and Lou Giannetti, author of *Understanding Movies*, that formed the ad hoc committee to promote the idea of the new section. I had aimed high to get a leading film critic to take part, and to my great delight Joe Morgenstern, then *Newsweek*'s highly regarded movie reviewer (still going strong at the Wall Street *Journal*), accepted. Since he was married to Piper Laurie at the time, it was my tacit hope that her presence would decorate the occasion with added glitter and glamour.

Benny Gazzara was a no-show but his absence was more than compensated for when Cassavetes himself blew into town with Falk. I have to say that the two afternoons and evenings I hung out with John and Peter (we were on a first name basis after about thirty seconds) were a peak experience in my celebrity-hunting life. The three of us walked, ate, drank, and mostly talked. If we'd had a gym handy we might have shot some hoops as the three husbands do in a famous long take in the movie.

Cassavetes was clearly the alpha male in this threesome, but he was attentive when either of the others spoke. It amazed me that in a very short space of time he took my measure with precision: "Neil just wants to be acknowledged," he said. We talked of many things, fools and kings, movies and books, business and pleasure, life and death. Falk was much more reticent than I expected but his terse comments were usually telling. There were no mannerisms, no posturing, no diva behavior. Just three guys enjoying each other's company and talking the talk.

The movie was heartily applauded at both showings and the panel discussion got the biggest audience I'd ever seen at SAMLA. Again, Cassavetes had the lead voice, though Sam Shaw and Joe Morgenstern had their innings, while Bill Robinson presided capably and cleverly performed triage when questions came from the floor. I grinned my way through the whole thing, enjoying what my behind-the-scenes efforts had brought forth. And then we adjourned to a private VIP reception in the studio's suite.

Earlier I had been approached in the suite by a couple of suits from Columbia Pictures, who wanted me to back them up in their ongoing discussions with John to cut the movie by thirty or forty minutes. They knew of my work with Silliphant and had gotten the idea that my voice would carry some weight of authority as a film critic/scholar. Surely they knew that Cassavetes would ignore any such voice, authentic or not. But I opposed their view vigorously, supporting the length and pace that defined the whole enterprise of deep probing of character. I couldn't dispute their commercial sense, but I was on the side of the artistic vision.

At the reception, there came a surprising climax to my run of luck. I was having a private conversation with Joe Morgenstern, joking with him about how angry and disappointed I was that he hadn't brought Piper Laurie along, letting him know what a big fan of hers I was. And some little guy kept trying to interrupt and break into our private huddle. He wouldn't be denied, finally introducing himself, not so much to the prominent critic but to the unknown professor. It was Morris Freedman, chair of the English Department at the University of Maryland, College Park, who wanted to discuss the possibility that I would be willing to make a move. He was anxious to expand the department's already wide-ranging offerings to include film-as-literature, and he said he thought I'd be a good fit for what he had in mind.

That was not an offer, of course, just a "feeler," but it began a process that led to my last academic move. I had prospered and grown in many ways in my eight years in Knoxville, had achieved a local prominence of which I was proud, but I had come to a dead end. The department wasn't going to promote me, I knew, for at least a couple of years, and, about to turn forty, I was ready for a full professorship. My hopes for teaching film courses were dashed when I was told that my debut offering, though hugely successful, would be a one-time thing, that the Theater Department would maintain full and strict control over the Clarence Brown property (never mind how much the university's Development Office appreciated my efforts with Mr. Brown and Jules Goldstone).

My job, I had been patronizingly informed by my senior colleagues, was to continue the fine work I had been doing as the medievalist of record. Been there, done that, I thought, and proceeded to shop around for a better deal. Maryland was first in line and, finally, alone in offering me the kind of curricular freedom I craved. Besides, no one ever got famous for publishing articles and a book on Old English poetry and directing half a dozen dissertations by the future medievalists of the South. There was much I would hate to leave behind in East Tennessee, but much of the "new me" I could take with me.

VIII

MUSICMUSICMUSIC

In the late 'Sixties, roughly the second half of my time at U-T in Knoxville, I seemed to be living a kind of juggler's life with an ever-increasing number of Indian clubs spinning in the temperate air. There were, first, the now- completed nuclear family when my daughter Annie joined three maturing brothers and, second, the academic demands of teaching and scholarship and directing doctoral dissertations and masters theses. Already by that point I was trying to cut back on commitments to the inevitable committee assignments, even when elected to serve in the university senate.

My interests in "the movement" had taken me to an executive position on the Greater Knoxville Council on Human Relations (there being at the time in the Volunteer State no CORE chapter, which would have been my first choice of association because of my admiration for James Farmer) where as its vice- president I had planned and led a successful march on City Hall to support passage of a fair housing ordinance. I've already recorded here my efforts to push forward the racial integration of sports in the Southeastern Conference.

My growing interest, not just aesthetically but academically, was building to a major (pre-) occupation with movies, and I was toying with ideas for writing projects that went far beyond academic studies. On top of all this, I was keeping to my schedule of Tuesday night poker, my role of playing manager of a competitive slow-pitch softball team (The Knoxville Knicks, named not for the Madison Square Garden hoopsters but the reigning chairman of the U- T English Department), and playing whatever tennis I could fit in at the Racquet Club, especially when I could play in father-son doubles tournaments on both sides of the brackets with my sons Ian and Jonny. Could there be any time for anything else like, for example, sleep? The answer was yes, and it came in a surprising form: music. There had developed an active partying group to which I was welcome that featured, along with an ample supply of beer and home-grown cannabis, the playing of music of a mostly rockabilly beat. The star of these impromptu performances was my colleague Dick Penner, a dedicated academician by day and a guitar- playing and bold-singing trouper by night.

In his spent youth Penner had been a professional performer growing up in East Texas but playing as far afield as Memphis and recording with some of the Sun Records bands. Elvis was surely one of the main influences on his style, though Dick never played with the King, but his main claim to fame was his work with the immortal Roy Orbison. At some point during the usual raucous rounds, Dick would be asked to do a medley of his favorite hits, and he would gladly comply. Somewhere in my basement I have a tape I made of "Dick Penner's Greatest Hits," leading off with "Oh, Suzy-Q" and climaxing with Orbison's platinum 1956 hit "Ooby-Dooby."

What made Dick a hero in that crowd was the fact that, known at the time as Allen Penner, he was credited as co-writer of that song with Orbison. No wonder that when Dick played and sang it, he would himself "wiggle to the left and wiggle to the right." For me the true mark of that accomplishment was that he regularly received royalty checks for the song, amounts that were enriched by Creedence Clearwater Revival's cover of the song.

Dick Penner had thereby achieved the kind of fame that I only dreamed about, and I was jealous. I was also an opportunist, and once Dick had achieved the tenure that gave him the academic security he craved I suggested to him that we might collaborate on some songs. Why not? I thought, thinking of myself as a natural-born lyricist. Song lyrics were my thing, after all. As a child I had been a prodigy of song lyrics, able to remember whole songs from a single hearing of old-time favorites that predated my birth. My parents and grandparents were often dazzled by those displays, even when I misheard lyrics that at six or seven I couldn't understand anyway, so that "only a poor fool never schooled in the old rule" (from the Ella Fitzgerald hit, "My Reverie") came out as "poo foo" in my version.

Dick loved the idea, and we set to work. We composed a half dozen numbers so that Dick could record a demo tape, the way to go, he said, from his experience in the business. We were both real proud of one song, called "Sidewalk People," a mild social protest song about folks who deserved better than to be called "street people" by hard-liners antipathetic to their lifestyle. Sadly, no one bought it (if they even listened), though it became a staple of our local party crowd. We did, however, find an audience for one of our tunes, with a lyric that caught on, I thought, because it appealed to my well-nourished notion that the way to find fame is to associate with the famous.

Published by MusicMusicMusicInc., "Otis, Janis, Jimi and Me" was going to be our ticket. It was a swinging rock-and-roll eulogy to three idols we had lost recently--and of course prematurely. Simple in its language, structure, and chord sequence, it caught someone's ear up there in what was once Tin Pan Alley, and went like this:

> Who's gonna sing my blues for me
> Now that Otis is gone
> Who can say the way I feel
> Who can help me carry on?
> Nobody's gonna know and I just can't express
> The empty feelin' deep down sinkin' in my chest.
>
> Guess I'll have to cry a lot
> Sing some for myself
> But when I'm let-down low-down
> I could use some help.
>
> Who's gonna sing my loneliness
> Now that Janis is gone
> Who can say the way I feel
> Who can help me carry on?
> Nobody's gonna know and I just can't express
> The hurtin' feelin' deep down eatin' in my chest.
>
> (Chorus)
>
> Who's gonna sing my freedom cry
> Now that Jimi is gone
> Who can say the way I feel
> Who can help me carry on?
> Nobody's gonna know and I just can't express
> The prison feelin' deep down chokin' in my chest
>
> (Chorus)

Simple, right, but catchy, easy to remember and join in. The help/self rhyme still makes me smile, especially in the regional accent of its origin. The somewhat bouncy rhythm counters the desperate, dirge-like quality. Someone would surely pick it up in a musical climate chilled by the premature deaths of so many stars--a rock-and-roll heaven.

And somebody did! By this time I had moved to Maryland, but the long- distance wires hummed with our joyous sound when we heard that Mac and Katie Kissoon were going to cover our song. The Kissoons were a brother- sister act, Jamaica-born and England-raised, who had reached near the top of the American easy-listening charts with "Chirpy Chirpy Cheep Cheep." They were big back home, their single "Sugar Candy Kisses" having reached #3 on the British charts in 1975, the year they issued an album with our song on it. Actually, the album appeared on two labels, and only the Pink Elephant version from the Netherlands had "Otis, Janis, Jimi, and Me" on it (fourth track on the B-side), along with what passed for standards, "Games People Play" and "Love Will Keep Us Together". But never mind. Imagine my excitement when *Billboard* reported that Mac and Katie were among the top ten albums sold in Holland. Gave a new meaning to "Dutch treat," at least to my ears. And I must admit that hearing the recording of a song I helped write was a bigger thrill than any time I ever saw my name in print.

Q and A section:

Does anyone remember Mac and Katie Kissoon? Few.
Does anyone know that Katie, after the family pair broke up, sang backup for Van Morrison, Eric Clapton, Elton John, and George Harrison? Even fewer.
Does anyone remember "Otis, Janis, Jimi, and Me'? Probably a dozen, half of them related to me.
Does anyone think Penner and Isaacs alongside Rodgers and Hart or even Harburg and Saidy? Nobody.
And how much did the semi-hit album earn in royalties for its songwriters? Nary a farthing, not even a Dutch mark.

Jamming with Penner

Mac & Katie Kassoon

IX

COLLABORATIONIST

It didn't take the song-writing lark to teach me the value of collaborating with people who knew what they were talking about and agreed with what I wanted to write about. In a way I had already worked with Dick Penner whose critical studies of Alan Sillitoe's work led me to reassess some of that work in a published essay. But my collaborating ventures date back to my first book, which I co-edited with my fellow graduate student at Brown, Lou Leiter.

The three years I spent in Providence constituted a peak period in my life, a time of sustained enjoyment and satisfaction. Despite a near total lack of a social life (though perhaps in part because of that lack), I reveled in the time I could spend with my two young sons, usually from mid-afternoon until they were tucked away in the evening, with the hours before and after devoted primarily to my continuing education. On occasion I engaged in the action of Brown's weekly duplicate bridge tournament, winning a few master's points along the way, but this was an activity I gave up because it could have become a serious avocation and because it was a point of incompatibility in my marriage. But primarily it was the doctoral program that engaged me.

The Brown program was challenging and rewarding, but the general climate was one of camaraderie rather than competitiveness (the latter having been one of the least attractive aspects of my brief sojourn at the Harvard Law School). It was as if we grad students were engaged in a cooperative venture to clear the hurdles the program devised to test us. And the camaraderie extended to friendly relations with junior faculty, like Billy Axton, Dan Hughes, and Bob Creed (who directed my dissertation).

We played the game like teammates and sometimes were able to game the system. For instance, the German reading exam was considered to be one of the more difficult obstacles in the path of Ph.D. candidates. A shelf of books of literary criticism in German was set aside in the department offices, with the understanding that two passages taken from those books would constitute the exam. We figured out that in order to replicate the passages, the then primitive equipment for duplication would leave traces of clips or folds on the pages when they were reproduced. So we searched the books for such marks, finding perhaps sixteen suspicious pages.

My preparation for the exam then became a matter of carefully translating those pages, no guarantee of success of course, but in fact a good way to achieve the level of competence required. When I actually sat for the exam I was disappointed that not one of my thoroughly studied passages was on it. One was fairly easy because the terminology of the text was familiar, but the other was virtually unintelligible. In proper German type, all the nouns were capitalized, and "*Mittel*" und "*Pole*" were repeated several times. I assumed that this was part of a philosophical discourse contrasting "central" or "mean" matters with the "extreme." It wasn't until later, when discussing the exam with a faculty member, that I learned that Mittel and Pole were the names of German critics, and along with that discovery I assumed I would have to retake the test.

No, I must have satisfied the examiners on the one passage to make up for my imaginative construct for the other, because I was the only candidate to pass. Now, three of my buddies, Dick Robillard, Skip Delasanta, and Carl Stenberg, were scheduled to take that exam the next time around. We concluded that the test I took must have used passages reproduced at an earlier time, the trace marks faded into oblivion, and that the next test would likely use the ones I had studied. My three cronies banked on that conclusion and virtually memorized the translations I had labored over.

The exam, all languages combined, was administered in a large lecture hall with assigned seating so that no two students taking the same language test were seated near each other. Robillard's seat was down front, and when Delasanta and Stenberg were sitting down, he stood up and gestured to them with two fingers raised in triumph--not V for victory signs but an indication that both passages were those they knew almost by heart. They couldn't thank me enough and offered to treat me to a celebratory dinner.

When they knocked on my door, I was surprised to see that their wives were not to be part of the party. Esther simply turned back and said to her mother, who had driven down from Brookline to babysit for the occasion, that she wouldn't be going and didn't seem at all bothered by the change of plans. I did hear her mother, however, muttering a one-word reaction: "Goyim."

A postscript to the language-exam hurdle involves Lou Leiter, probably the brightest of our whole cohort of fellows, from whom I learned at least as much about the critical reading of literature as I did from any professor. It turned out that certain rules regarding the awarding of doctorates had to be waived for both Lou and me. In my case it was the requirement that a candidate spend a full academic year on campus following the successful completion of the comprehensive exams (both the three arduous written exams and the nerve-wracking orals before the full panel of senior faculty). Because I had so quickly (barely more than six months) and smoothly (the thing practically wrote itself from a cleverly constructed outline) completed a dissertation on Old English poetry and because my appointment at City College was premised on my completing the degree, that rule was waived. In Lou's case--and his appointment at Nebraska also was contingent on degree- in-hand--a waiver had to be applied because he had, by some bureaucratic oversight, never taken his required exam in reading Latin. Lou was fully competent to pass such an exam, but the solution was bizarre: he was examined, orally, by an appointed faculty member on the twenty-five-minute walk to the campus, fully dressed in academic regalia for the "hooding" ceremony.

Meanwhile, Lou and I had spent some time in our last year at Brown compiling a textbook called *Approaches to the Short Story* that was made up of familiar classics of the genre accompanied by critical essays on each (including one each by the co-editors). We had come to agreement about everything in the book--selections, contributors, format, philosophy; that was no guarantor of commercial success (didn't happen), but it was a good template for collaboration itself.

The next joint editorship was in Knoxville, when the editors of *Tennessee Studies in Literature* decided it would be a good idea to have a special issue devoted to Medievalist studies. My senior colleague Eric Stockton and I were duly designated as co-editors for this venture, but Eric was already slowing down from his struggle with multiple sclerosis and so the burden fell squarely onto my slender shoulders. With the loyal assistance of my colleague John Tinkler, we got it done with presentable results.

The contents included work by some of the leading lights in the field (Albert C. Baugh, Bob Creed, Ted Irving, Larry Benson, Fred Robinson, Jess Bessinger, Edgar Duncan, John Nist), and some of my friends (Rose Zimbardo, Paul Taylor, Bernie Levy) and former students (Walter Scheps, Hugh Keenan, Colonel Charles McClelland).

Two other U-T colleagues worked with me on scholarly articles, Dick Kelly for a piece on Browning and Jack Reese for one on *A Midsummer Night's Dream*. The former gave his poet's/Victorianist's cachet to my interpretation of a poem and the latter, a Renaissance scholar who rose through the administrative ranks to become Chancellor of the University, supplied bibliographical support for my innovative reading of the play.

Rose Zimbardo, whose enduring friendship made up for the struggles of my four years on the CCNY faculty, had been the one to introduce me to Tolkien's work, and she suggested that we work together on a collection of essays. We did so, once for a book with the University of Notre Dame Press (*Tolkien and the Critics*, 1968), again with the University Press of Kentucky (*Tolkien: New Critical Perspectives*, 1977), and finally with Houghton Mifflin (*Understanding* The Lord of the Rings: *The Best of Tolkien Criticism*, 2004). These were labors of love, in more ways than one. We traded roles back and forth, even traded feature billing on the covers, selected previously published classic treatments of Tolkien along with original contributions, including essays by Rose in each volume and introductions to each volume by me.

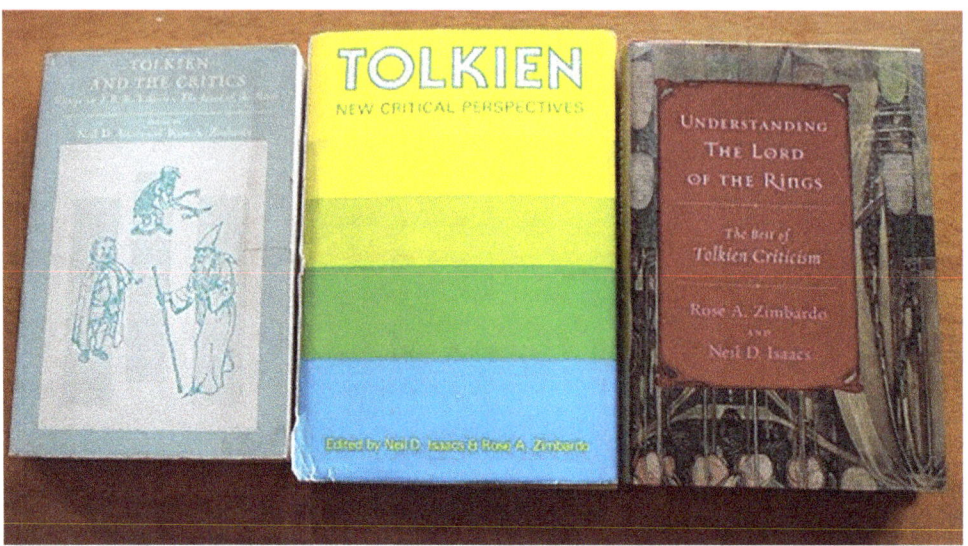

The titles of those introductions summarize the guiding principle of the sequence. The first was called "On the Possibilities of Writing Tolkien Criticism," the second "On the Need for Writing Tolkien Criticism," and the third "On the Pleasures of (Reading and Writing) Tolkien Criticism." Pieces by C.S. Lewis and W.H. Auden graced the first volume, by Paul Kocher and Verlyn Flieger the second. One otherwise admiring reviewer of the latter took me to task for the carping tone of my intro-- and he was right. I had tried to counter some of the silliness evoked by the publication of *The Silmarillion* and the cottage industry of fanzines, video games, and the like. Aside from choosing what we conscientiously regarded as "best" for the third volume-- which included, without false modesty, selections from the first two--and clearly enunciating our criteria for the rest, we commissioned an essay by Tom Shippey, widely regarded as Tolkien's foremost analyst, to chart the monumental translation of the trilogy to the screen by Peter Jackson. This brilliant piece alone made the volume indispensable.

The question remains of why the book failed to earn out the advance the editors were paid. The publishers, for reasons partly petty but generally unknown, buried the book, sometimes even excluding it from their own comprehensive catalog of Tolkien material. My best bet is that they had only bought our project so that some other publisher would not get it, promote it, and cut into HM's virtual American monopoly on the subject. Publishers are infamous for such thinking (like the Yankees of old for stockpiling available pitchers), and authors and editors (like the rest of the American League) victims thereof.

Another U-T connection provided for a wonderful collaboration. My student, battery-mate, and faithful friend Jack Higgs proposed that we do a textbook for Harcourt Brace (where our old friend and first baseman for the Knoxville Knicks was an editor) to serve the emerging needs of "literature of sports" courses. Jack, as one of the founding fathers of the Sport Literature Association and a mainstay of its journal (originally called *Arete* and later *Aethlon*) was well situated to promote it. Jack, who has always overrated my qualities, insisted that my name on the project would be a selling point, and I went along with it--if not with his thinking vis-a-vis his collaborator. The result was *The Sporting Spirit: Athletes in Literature and Life*, 1977, which did pretty well for us and for Harcourt, and all because it was the best kind of collaboration, one where Jack did the lion's share of the work all the way through and I was in the executive position of signing off and then endorsing the royalty checks.

Jack Higgs with my son Daniel

I've already detailed a major joint venture from the Knoxville days, where my name appeared on a book jacket as author along with Rachel Maddux and Stirling Silliphant. Not quite a collaboration, except in the spirit of a mutually desirable project, because we were writing--or had written--disparate parts of the whole. And then it was on to College Park, where I had the honor of collaborating with two distinguished figures who were at the peak of their respective sports-related careers.

The first was Gerald Strine, sportswriter for the Washington *Post*, whose successful predictions on the outcome of NFL games in his column "Playing Football" had put him on record as one of the premier football handicappers (as betting analysts are called) in the country. Gerry's fellow horse racing writer and friend at the *Post*, Andrew Beyer, had written a successful book on handicapping thoroughbred horse races. His editor at Random House, Grant Ujifusa, proposed that he and Gerry put together a guide on football betting. Andy declined, citing his wish to focus on horses, and Gerry made me an offer I couldn't refuse. "I write columns," he said, "but you write books. I'll tell you how it works, you have the complete run of the column to show you how well it works, and you structure it and write it."

That's how *Covering the Spread* (1978) was conceived, though Gerry hardly gave me carte blanche. He closely edited every inch of the writing. And he also led me through a gestation period that took me far afield--to Las Vegas and the Churchill Downs sports book in particular--to meet and pick the brains of Bob Martin, then the "head linesman" who set the point spreads for bookmakers across the country, and a colorful array of sports betting insiders, who chose to be "deep background sources."

The book was an immediate success. Alas, the day after a glowing review by Christopher Lehmann-Haupt appeared in the *New York Times*, a huge newspaper strike closed down many presses--and Random House's proposed advertising campaign was scuttled. As for using other promotional media, they had chosen to use their entire sports-minded budget for their runaway best-seller, Jim Fixx's book on running. Gerry and I made a couple of appearances on Larry King's radio show, but we soon learned that our audience was very interested in getting specific tips on games and not at all in buying a general how-to book to study. The Gamblers Book Club in Vegas bought up all the used copies it could find. Gerry got many calls and offers-- until new policy at the *Post* canceled the column. And I got a few calls as well, including a message from a big bettor named Norman Mailer--but I never got through to him when I called back (another dropped call on the celebrity-contact quest).

Gerry and I had worked well and harmoniously together, leading to a few later efforts: a report for the "Style" section on the opening of the first legal casino in Atlantic City, a report on a new facility for betting in Connecticut, and a model issue of a slick magazine to celebrate the advent of the Breeder's Cup event in thoroughbred racing. It was Gerry's hope as editor to make this an annual publication and named me his "literary editor" (I did manage to secure a Maxine Kumin poem), but the folks who made the decisions for racing proved unwilling to pay the price for a high-class celebration of itself. So much for a dying industry.

Not long after that venture, my agent hooked me up with Harper & Row, which was publishing a series called the Sports Illustrated Library, elementary texts on individual sports. I would be the basketball writer and would have a big-name hoops maven as co-author. My first choice was Dick Motta, whose work I first admired when he led unknown Weber State to college basketball prominence. Jumping to the NBA he soon had the pre-Michael Jordan Chicago Bulls contending for a title with an offense riding on the shoulders of two sharp-shooting forwards, Chet Walker and Bob "Butterbean" Love. With Tom Boerwinkle (a product or project of my friend Ray Mears at Tennessee) at center and the tenacious guards Norm Van Lier and Jerry Sloan, he had them within one shot of playing for the championship.

Now Motta was coaching the Washington Bullets and had led them to an unlikely NBA title. I had a nodding acquaintance with him and was delighted when he agreed to lend his name to the project. Dick had always been a cordial, engaging, funny source for basketball writers, and we worked easily together--though he took it seriously. He spelled everything out for me, diagrammed plays, outlined his theories, and in general gave me a cram tutorial on the game.

Reader, I wrote it, it was published as *Sports Illustrated Basketball* in 1981, and it's still in print (now subtitled "The Keys to Excellence"), my name getting top billing. Any success that it has had, however, is owed to the well- recognized name of Dick Motta on the cover.

A few other collaborations came my way. An article called "Winning" in *Washingtonian Magazine* was a virtual ghost-writing job (though my name appears first in the credits) in which I related Tim Temerario's tales of working as an assistant NFL coach under the legendary leadership of Paul Brown, Vince Lombardi, and George Allen. There followed a number of items for the *Encyclopedia of World Biography*, six of them in the Twentieth Century Supplement of 1988 and four more in the 1990 Supplement. My collaborators here were my son Jonny for the first six and my daughter Annie for the following four; what a pleasure it was to act as a kind of executive supervisor for the research and writing of two of my talented children.

I did not expect that this phase of my writing career would end two decades ago. It had had, after all, its share of success, though it never resulted in even marginal celebrity. As an example, when Pete Axthelm wrote glowingly about Gerry Strine's accomplishments as a handicapping writer, he never even mentioned my name. Pete later wrote me a kind apology, but that hardly lit my name in lights. The number of projected collaborations that ended up buried in a round file or on a cutting room floor could earn me the title of "collaborator Manqué," but to list them would be as tiresomely unfunny for me as for the readers. I would, however, mention here what can only be considered a collaboration in the broadest sense of the word. The book is *Reciprocities* by my friend and colleague Jack Russell. My role was relatively slight, and yet it is clear that without my efforts the book would never have seen the light of day.

Its subtitle "Studies in the Nonfiction Novel" indicates its subject, which was the last enthusiasm of a brilliant teacher and substantial scholar. We had discussed the project often, and I was privileged to have read several sections in draft. We didn't always agree, especially about his relative evaluations of the works he was studying (and I strongly objected, on philosophical rather than strictly artistic grounds, to his inclusion of Celine alongside Dinesen, Cummings, the Koestlers, Ondaatje, and Primo Levi), but I had a clear understanding of what he was doing and where he wanted to go with it.

Jack was almost done with a draft fit to submit for editorial consideration, though he was at a loss about what publishers to try. Even with the careful editing that he was accustomed to doing, he probably had no more than a few months' work left--when he was suddenly unable to work at all. He had been struck with rapid-onset Alzheimer's. And once the diagnosis was confirmed and while he still had most of his wits about him, I asked him if I could take on the task of placing the work for publication.

I was honest with my approaches to university presses, saying that there was some work left to be done, but that a few of Jack's friends and colleagues would do whatever needed to be done to round off the manuscript and see it through the press. The good people of the University of Georgia Press, especially senior editor Malcolm Call, familiar with and respectful of Jack's earlier work, agreed on the value of this book, and I found ready assistance from John Auchard, Bob Coogan, and Mike Olmert to help me with the finishing and editing touches and checking of citations (with Gayle Swanson and Jennifer Comeau adding excellent support at the Press). I even got to write a "Foreword" (originally an "Afterword," until Jack Bryer and others persuasively argued for the change) that expresses our profound respect for the author, and thanks for the privilege of carrying his final major work across the finish line.

Jack's son Ryan, a very talented painter, three of whose works adorn our dining room wall, has told me this story. He and his mother Bette, along with two old friends, were visiting Jack just weeks before his death in a nursing home in Harrisonburg, VA. *Reciprocities* had just come out, and Ryan and

Bette were waxing enthusiastic about the book. Jack took it all in and said, "That sounds interesting. I'd like to read that book." If that doesn't make me proud, as well as sad, of what I'm presuming to call a collaboration here, I don't know what would.

X

LEFTY GETS COUNTED OUT

Probably what brought me the most notoriety in College Park was my long-running feud with basketball coach Charles (Lefty) Driesell. He preceded me by a year at the University of Maryland, though I already knew a good bit about him from my ongoing research of college basketball. He had attained some prominence through his success at Davidson College, even more so by announcing at his first press conference in College Park that he would turn the campus into "the UCLA of the East."

No doubt Lefty was a champion recruiter in his early days in the big leagues. His first coup came as a shock to me while I was still in Knoxville. The competition for Tommy Roy had come down to a choice between Tennessee and Maryland. Roy had been an all-time record-breaking schoolboy scorer in the state of Connecticut, and great things were expected of him wherever he chose to play. As a big man (6'10" or 6'11"), he might have taken a look at what Ray Mears had accomplished with Tom Boerwinkle, a very large, relatively immobile center, who seemed to lack the athletic abilities that could develop into a productive career. Four years under Mears, and big Tom became a force, not only on defense at the center of a 1-3-1 trapping zone, but scoring and rebounding with steady improvement--enough so that he became instrumental in the NBA as a center on Dick Motta's surprising Chicago Bulls team.

But Tommy Roy bought the Driesell hype and came to Maryland, where his skills deteriorated over four years and his pro prospects went up in the smoke and mirrors of the lefthander's reputation. I could easily chronicle several other failures of players' talents being wasted, underdeveloped, and even eroded under the coach's tutelage. Nevertheless, I had a contract to produce a history of college basketball and determined to leave no stone unturned in my pursuit of first-hand testimony to athletic development. Besides, I felt that as a matter of courtesy I would have to include, among my scores of interviews with active and former players and coaches, a session with my "colleague."

We met in his office at Cole Field House, and I dutifully recorded forty-five minutes of rather desultory hoops conversation. I learned nothing that was of any use to me. His knowledge of and appreciation for the history of the game was virtually non-existent, to all intents and purposes limited to an idolization of John Wooden. I did learn that, as a player at Duke, Lefty had played in a double-post offense, that he had imposed that offense on his high school teams and his Davidson teams, and that by golly he would have the Terps play it too. The results of this limitation with the extraordinary talent he recruited were typically underwhelming and sometimes calamitous, both for the teams and individuals.

I knew that I would run afoul of Lefty (and probably the overwhelming majority of the American basketball establishment) when my treatment of Coach Wooden in the completed book, *All the Moves: A History of College Basketball*, published by Lippincott in 1975, was less than worshipful. The timing was hardly likely to go unremarked in College Park, because publication preceded by a matter of weeks a visit to the campus by the legendary coach, an occasion to honor him and by his presence the Maryland basketball program and its coach, despite the often-mocked pronouncement that he, Driesell, would replicate UCLA's success on the East Coast.

As far as iconoclasm goes, my treatment of Wooden in the closing section of the book hardly ranks up there with Christopher Hitchens's book on Mother Teresa. (I am a fan of Hitch, full of admiration for his powers of witty intellectual argument in progressive and iconoclastic causes, but I've never been able to play in that league: see Chapter XV below where I describe my indirect contact with Hitch). Nevertheless, the more I researched the entire Wooden career the more dubious I became of his sainted image. His trademarked "pyramid of success," for example, when viewed in the context of that career, may well be perceived as narrow-minded and self-serving hypocrisy passing for modest piety.

The records, as sportswriters are wont to say, speak for themselves, pointing to an excellence derived in large part from a style of play, precise game-time adjustments in strategy, and remarkable practice-time discipline as much as the extraordinary talent he (and the financial supporters of the program) brought to Westwood. In these ways, Wooden was indeed a wizard. But the adulation attendant on the person seemed to me misguided, especially when aspects of his personality and history were taken into account, like his dogged pugnacity as a player and his strategic harassment of officials in his early (losing) years as a coach.

When the book came out, my friend Gerry Strine was asked by his editor to write something about it. Gerry suggested that instead of a typical review, since his column would appear in the sports pages, that we do an interview about basketball at College Park and particularly to expand on my lukewarm comments about the coach. I felt comfortable doing that, particularly since Lefty had a high-ranked team in action and continued to have trouble with rivals like Dean Smith and his Tar Heels. So I made some specific criticisms about his strategic inflexibility, his misuse of talent, and his slowness to react during games, along with a suggestion that his behavior and language were embarrassments to an institution of higher learning.

By chance, the report of that interview appeared during the week that North Carolina would arrive to complete a season sweep of the Terps. At his weekly news conference, when he had said that he wished he could sit back and enjoy the upcoming game, a reporter suggested that Neil Isaacs would be happy to sit on the bench in his place. After calling me "just a ama-toor" Coach Driesell said that he had never met me but that when he saw my picture he "couldn't tell whether he was either a professor or a hippy, one." Among other remarks, he also said that he wouldn't mind trading jobs with me, though he wouldn't want to trade salaries, and he finished with a prediction: "He won't be around here much any more."

The sportswriter who reached out to poke Driesell's sore spot was Bill Tanton of the Baltimore *Sun*, an occasional guest in my classroom, and he got a fine column out of it. Lefty probably thought he'd settled my hash with his witty responses, but Tanton's faithful reporting of what I'd said and what Lefty had said left me on the high road of accurate observation. And then, in his columnist's mode he made sport of the coach by advising him that if he really wanted to take over in my classroom he'd have to quit saying things like "Depth ain't hurt me yet" and "Clubs better start getting a-scared of us" and(in response to a question about a protester who threw a cup of oil on the floor when Maryland hosted a visiting Russian team) "If they'd a-throwed two cups I'd a-had to call the game" (all taken verbatim from the reporter's notebooks).

Round one to Isaacs. If I'd a-taken him to court in a libel suit all I'd a-had to do was play the tape of my interview with him to prove he had lied publicly to the press about never meeting me. But how had I been hurt by his performance?

I'm not sure what he meant when he said I wouldn't be around there much. He may have meant Cole Field House, because he gave orders that no matter how much I was writing about basketball I was not to be allowed into his locker room after games. I shrugged that one off because I continued to have access to his players, some of whom took my courses (although at one point he ordered them not to) and others who'd stop by to chat. Maybe he meant that I'd be denied the privilege to sit at the press table for games, an edict that came down from on high after I'd done a halftime interview on Tar Heel Radio, on which I praised Dean Smith at the expense of you know who. But Jack Zane, the capable Sports Information Director, told him he couldn't do that because of my legitimate credentials as a writer.

A few years later, another possible meaning emerged. Driesell wrote a letter to then-Chancellor Gluckstern suggesting that I be fired. His reason was that my published remarks criticizing him and his program were hurting his recruiting, that other coaches in competitive pursuit of the same talent would have prospects read my stuff. Can the pen really be mightier than the whistle and the pep talk and the jive and the promises? Maybe so. In any case, Gluckstern did not dignify the letter with a direct response, but he instructed an aide to convey a message to the coach: "Isaacs has tenure; you don't." Round two to Isaacs.

In 1983, a valuable player (and generally thought to be a decent guy) named Herman Veal was rumored to have sexually abused a coed on campus. In fact, a WRC TV newsman who happened to be a friend of mine taped his interview with Veal in which the player confessed that he had raped the young woman. Veal was never charged, though he was "disciplined" by the Athletic Department in some undisclosed way. The tape has never aired.

How had the cover-up been accomplished? Coach Driesell, to his credit unfailingly loyal to his players, had taken matters into his own hands. He barged into the woman's dorm, told her what to expect if she did not withdraw all charges, and was relieved when she withdrew from school. She just went away, and so did the scandal. The Women's Center on campus published a statement denouncing a pattern of sexual misconduct on the part of scholarship athletes. Asked at his next press conference what he thought about the statement, Coach proclaimed that **he** was the "Men's Center," and that Herman Veal (whose name had not been published in connection with the report), was the real victim in the incident.

I thought that Driesell's egregious intimidation of the woman student was clear grounds for dismissal, but he was never so much as reprimanded, never mind fired. I made no secret of my views on the matter but they fell on deaf ears on campus, while my friend the reporter could not or would not tell me why his scoop was buried or what actually happened to the tape. Years later, in a novel, *The Doaker's Story* (Drinian Press, 2009), I had a Driesell-like coach take similar action when one of his players (with the unlikely name of Bruno Lamb) is similarly accused. The title character is loosely based on the reporter I knew, and that incident initiates the whole action of the novel. Of course I changed the chronology and masked the location, and the novel got no attention anyway.

So my little act of private outrage and vengeance had no practical effect. The coach made a clean getaway. Round three to Driesell.

In the decade of the 1980s, I became seriously involved with long-distance running, with two marathons, a half marathon, a dozen ten-mile and fifteen kilometer races, and scores of 10 k's. One of the last was a campus-based event called The Terrapin Trot, and I thought of a way to call a truce in my feud with the coach. I wrote to him, challenging him to join me as a participant in the race, that we would compete head-to-head and the loser would make a contribution to one of the charities that benefitted from the race. Getting no response, I tried to reach him by phone to follow up, or at least to confirm that the offer was genuine and that he had received it. But he never took the call.

Then, in 1986, the tragic death of Len Bias took that feud to a new level. Part of the aftermath was the termination of Driesell's employment at the University. I was glad to see him go, but I thought his departure was long overdue and that the proximate cause of it was all wrong. He had been made a scapegoat, cynically thrown under the bus for something he had no direct responsibility for, something that caused him great grief and to which he responded with admirable consideration for the Bias family.

Nevertheless, the ensuing investigations presented me opportunities to have a public forum for my views on the athletic program and the administration that supported it, a relationship that seemed to me to be a model of what was wrong with big-time revenue-producing intercollegiate sports throughout the country. CBS News taped an hour-long interview with me on the same day that Chancellor John Slaughter's memo to faculty appeared in my box, asking faculty "to direct all media inquiries" to the director of public information. That was not, I thought, appropriate; the faculty of a public institution of higher education must clearly be free to voice its opinions, particularly when its intellectual and philosophical convictions diverge from the policies of its administration.

The Baltimore *Sun* asked me to write a piece for its Sunday "Perspective" section, and I was happy to do so--happier still when I was given the lead space on page one. Headlined "Business as Usual at U. of Maryland," the column led with the following sentence: "The University of Maryland athletic department, when it acts as if it were accountable only to itself, simply reflects the attitudes and values of the university's administration." The piece carried over to page three, where it was accompanied by a sidebar headlined "Tenure for Lefty: A Matter of Ancient History." Never mind that my primary target was Chancellor Slaughter's administration and the way it parroted in general the NCAA's hypocritical regime of protecting the interests of intercollegiate athletics, how officials advocated "reforms" that would only serve to entrench the hierarchy of power and control (add "financial" before both nouns). The arrangement of the columns drew attention to the coach-as-fall-guy rather than the larger issues, and I cannot fault the *Sun* for stirring up the waters with a ready-made controversy, since I referred to my long feud with the coach as an egregious example of what ailed the system--hardly a cause of the toxicity, but surely an annoying symptom.

Responses came in a torrential downpour, or--foully to mix the trite metaphors--the shit hit the fan. And, given the large number of Driesell fans out there among the less educated denizens of sports fandom, it was no surprise that I sustained many palpable hits. I suppose the *Sun* was obliged to print one such response because it came from an apparently official source, Robert Armbruster, the Director of University Relations at the Baltimore campus of the University. With a nod toward my "good writing" (he cited "an athletic program running wild under the big top, while a benevolent, blinking administration plays both barker and absentee ringmaster"), the overwhelmingly snide personal attack elicited this headline by the *Sun*: "Spoiled, Rude Know-It-All."

This, in turn, evoked a terse rebuttal from Howard Altstein, a distinguished faculty member of the School of Social Work at UMAB. In "attacking the tenure system and the academic freedom it carries with it" Armbruster had unintentionally applauded the system that allowed a faculty member to challenge his administration without fear of retribution. "Perhaps," Altstein concluded, from an "untenurable position, Mr. Armbruster is not just a little jealous of a system he cannot understand and a status he cannot attain." (Full disclosure: Prof. Altstein was an instructor of mine in a program that awarded me an MSW degree less than three years after this letter was printed.)

Another letter, which the *Sun* chose not to print, was forwarded to me and to Lefty. It made some telling points, arguing that some of my charges against the coach's character might more accurately be used against me; I resented the description of "vitriolic sarcasm" to characterize my tone, but I found the writer's rhetoric to be effective and some of his points rather chastening. (I cannot, without his permission, use his name; he is not, to my knowledge, a public figure.)

What bothered me most in this Lefty-admirer's letter was what, for me, justified the sidebar in the first place. Lefty had often argued that he had as much right to and justification for the award of tenure as, say, a Professor of English. So what I did was analyze his credentials according to the standards employed across the board by the university: the three categories of teaching, publication, and service. Allowing for some parallel criteria for coaching, I presented and documented a brief that demonstrated Lefty's failings in all three categories.

When, several months later, Driesell's "tenure" had been terminated by the University in the major fallout of the Bias tragedy, riding to the rescue of the coach's reputation came one of his biggest celebrity-fans, the syndicated columnist and TV talking head, the late Robert Novak, a man often referred to as "The Prince of Darkness," ironically in the guise of "White Knight." "Lefty, They Done You Wrong" was the title of Novak's lament appearing in the Washington *Post*'s "Outlook" section. He praised Lefty as a coach and a man of moral integrity, citing Chancellor Slaughter as the villain who made the coach a scapegoat, and he blamed the media for taking sides against the coach when they had consistently defended his cross-town rival, John Thompson at Georgetown.

Right about Slaughter, Novak had been wrong about too many things for me to sit with idle pen and stew about it, and the *Post* saw fit to print my response less than two weeks later. (I was glad about that, sorry only because Novak's wife had been a very good student in a course of mine some years earlier.) One mistake of Novak's I decided not to correct. Asserting that he "happen[s] to know some details" about the Herman Veal case "that convinced me that intimations against Veal were exaggerated," he praised Driesell for his efforts "to save the boy's reputation." I don't know what Novak claimed to know (he never documented that claim), but I have shown above that what I knew contradicted his conclusion.

I did call attention to other mistakes. His claim that Driesell is "an excellent bench coach," for example, was supported only by his season ticket's proximity to the bench, while I could cite chapter and verse to show that the claim would be greeted by derisive laughter from many of Lefty's peers and other knowledgeable basketball folks. I also had to point out how media attitudes toward Driesell and Thompson were much alike, particularly when both coaches assumed a posture of "they're out to get me and it's us against them." Finally there was Novak's notion that Slaughter's recent appointment of Bob Wade was ironic because "everyone knows that [Wade] effectively barred Driesell from the rich lode of talent" at Dunbar High School and elsewhere in Baltimore. Good luck to Coach Wade, he offered, ever a loyal Terps fan; but "he is John Slaughter's man, which Lefty never was."

He was right about the irony, but for the wrong reasons. I noted that Wade's appointment without adequate search or even the pretense of a consultation with a search committee would never qualify as due process or due diligence. (This came as no surprise to me: here was a chancellor who overrode decisions of his own admissions office to reject applicants who were promising African American athletes, a pattern of executive behavior that led African American members of the admissions board to resign their positions.) The irony is that Wade and Driesell were both coaches of the legendary Ernest Graham, a player of enormous natural talent and NBA potential, "who was never taught the adequate fundamentals or the appropriate attitudes" by either coach.

"Finally," I said--and say again, if Wade was Slaughter's man, which Lefty never was, "how come the chancellor rewarded Driesell with a ten-year contract at a time when many--perhaps most-- administrators would have fired him? That makes Wade, even with his colossal five-year deal, only half the Slaughter's man that Driesell was. Wade's pitiful performance as coach showed he was less than half the coach that Lefty was, and the series of violations that contributed to his firing after three years made him, perhaps, less than half the man as well.

As for John Slaughter, while I was criticized for sharing my views on network television, his appearances and the pious posturing with which he accepted responsibility (without having to pay any concrete penance, and never mind his way of misrepresenting the scholarly performance and graduation statistics of scholarship athletes) may have helped him win appointment as President of Occidental College in Los Angeles after six years in College Park, not to mention his many other honors and positive public recognition.

I call round four even, because Lefty and I both were battered in the final go-round. The decision, however, was Isaacs by TKO. I didn't knock him out; heavier hands were at work. I deserve neither credit nor blame, though some would enshrine me in a hall of infamy for my behavior in the ring. In effect the joke is on me after all, given that whatever celebrity I gained from the feud has been short-lived. When Coach Driesell returned to be feted by the campus and the community, not even the reporters who remembered these old battles asked me for a sound-bite. I wouldn't have had to chew over any such invitation for very long.

XI

THE WISDOM OF SOLOMON

Andrew Beyer, Gerald Strine, Dave Kindred, Thomas Boswell, Ken Denlinger, John Schulian, Barry Lorge, Robert Fachet, Sally Jenkins, Jane Leavy, Tony Kornheiser, Michael Wilbon, Richard Darcey, David DuPree, Jack Mann, Dick Schapp, Leonard Shapiro, Bob Addie, Angus Phillips, Mark Asher--the names come rolling off the tongue like a roll call of honorees, and I've probably missed a bunch of others who should not be forgotten. I hope they'll forgive me the unintended slight. This is but a sample list of those whose bylines appeared on the Washington *Post* sports page under the editorship of George Solomon (along with the occasional piece by the revered Shirley Povich). Only in the days of my youth when I was a faithful devotee of Stanley Woodward's *Herald Tribune* sports page has there ever been such a distinguished cast of ensemble reporting and editorializing. They could observe, they could judge, they could entertain, they could provoke thought and argument and appreciation, and could they ever write.

In the spring of 1975, when my course called "Sports Culture, USA" made its debut appearance with an enrollment of 140 students/fans under the rubric of "special topics" endorsed by Morris Freedman's open-minded, big-tented, progressive English Department, Solomon was among the very first guests invited to appear for an interview/presentation--and one of the first to accept. He took the opportunity to inform the class (and its instructor) about the way a major newspaper functioned, how important the "fun and games" section was, and how he saw the function of its editor. Meanwhile, that instructor, impressed with the guest's wisdom, modestly suggested that he'd be glad to contribute to that best of pages whenever invited to do so.

If I needed some journalistic bona fides to supplement my scholarly writings, the *New York Times* graced me in the first week of 1976 with a twelve- column-inches extract from *All the Moves: A History of College Basketball*, in which I critiqued the way basketball was televised at the expense of its inherent appeal for spectators. Solomon never mentioned if he had been influenced by that piece, but shortly thereafter he commissioned me for a feature assignment: preview the March madness of the upcoming ACC basketball tournament with an assessment of Maryland's chances. The whole top half of a page was devoted to this piece, labeled "Commentary" and including a Dick Darcey photo of Coach Driesell with his three-guard array of Brad Davis, John Lucas, and Mo Howard, a head-swelling thirty-six inches of type under my bold-face italicized byline.

I was all pumped up to write it, given my opinion of the coach as coach, my relationship with Howard and Lucas (who were taking the course), and my confidence in my own hoops expertise. So I studied the draw, evaluated the likely match-ups, anticipated some strategies, and sketched a recipe for the Terps to succeed. My strategizing was sound, but my clouded crystal ball meant that there would be no chance for Driesell to do things his way and not succumb to Dean Smith's four-corner offense (instead of following my suggestions of ways to break it down, playing to Maryland's strengths). Playing in their own virtual backyard at the Capital Centre in Lanham, the Terps squeaked by Duke in overtime in the quarter-finals and then were unprepared for Virginia, surprising winners over North Carolina State. At least I was right that the Phil Ford-Walter Davis-Mitch Kupchak Tar Heels would prevail.

Having so generously opened the door for me, Solomon left it open for me to make him an offer he would be unwise to refuse. The Olympic Games were just a few months away, and the limited accommodations in Montreal put sports editors in a bind. Even a major newspaper like the *Post* was allowed only two sets of credentials, and in Washington, Sally Quinn, then an elegant "Style" section writer, had dibs on one of them. That left Bob Fachet, who covered track and field as well as hockey, to work round the clock on all events and related news while she wrote atmospheric pieces on the "scene."

I had long since planned to go, a once in a lifetime opportunity with the Games within reach of a day's drive from New Haven, where I had planned to visit my dad en route, bring him some cheer now that it was a little more than a year since my mom (his "sweetheart-wife") had left him to mourn his remaining years away. My colleague Jackson Bryer had rented a house for the occasion to take his three children on a unique vacation trip, and I was promised a couch to sleep on at a token charge for the eight nights I would be there. So I spoke to my now good friend George and said, "How about this? I'll be there anyway, and I'll report on what I see and hear. I'll see as many events as I can scrounge up tickets for and while I won't do 'game stories' I could make many other kinds of observations. Call me 'The Fan in the Stands' and if you use any of it you can decide what it's worth."

"Done," he said. He worked out ways I could get copy to him, and, behold, I was on my way north to be a foreign correspondent, sort of freelancing in terms of the open-ended nature of my assignment. By the time I got there, Quinn was packing up to leave, and I just barely had time to hear her dictate her departing story, marveling at the way she could deliver flawless prose without benefit of notes or rewrite. Fachet, for his part, was a whirlwind, working round the clock to cover events and attendant incidentals, though the versatile Ken Denlinger was on his way to inherit Quinn's credentials.

My first posting was datelined July 21, and I was thrilled not only to see my name with the legend, "Special to The Washington Post," underneath but also the specially designed "Fan in the Stands" icon surrounded by a solid oval line. The headline was "If the Price Is Right, a Fan Can Always Find a Ticket," and it ran across the top of the page, six columns wide, twenty-one inches altogether. Most amazing to me is that it appeared exactly as I had wired it in.

I started with acknowledgment of some of my biases, first that I do not love a parade and have no interest in Opening and Closing Ceremonies, second that though sports and show business may have been "wedded in a ceremony performed by the media (with Howard Cosell trying to catch the bouquet)" I think of them as close cousins so that a marriage is taboo. "So let not the mass promenade and dos-a-dos detract from the competition," I said, and got on to the subject of ticket availability.

I had joined with Jack Bryer in early applications and had secured two seats each for the basketball finals and the last four days of track and field, the extra ones to be used for barter. At the swimming venue on my first night, scalpers were asking $50 for a $9 ticket, and then I found a crowd gathered around three members of the American basketball team (Phil Ford, Quinn Buckner, and Scott May, if you must know) selling the same item for $25 and quickly unloading their whole stock.

I described some of the techniques used by buyers and sellers and commented on the varieties of fan behavior. I even got to talk some about women's and men's basketball games. With great seats for the diving next night I was able to note the subjectivity of the judging, how the perception that a diver is doing well raises his scores despite actual performance (I called it the "Jimmy Carter syndrome" from the media reporting on the primaries). And I closed with my determination to score a seat for the gymnastics starring Nadia Comenici.

Two days later, "The Fan" was back in print, with a collection of a half dozen snippets, observations and comments about a kaleidoscopic scene. My third posting, consisting of four short components, featured two personal profiles. The first was of a man I recognized from more than a decade earlier, when I knew him as John the Egyptian, hustling around Wonderland, the greyhound track in Revere, Mass., betting the dogs on a system based on whether they were tugging at the leash in the post parade. Here he was trying to make it as a scalper. But I saw him apprehended by one of Canada's finest and given a choice of arrest or selling everything he had at face value. The other was a man in a clown costume whom I interviewed at some length. The punch line came when he sold at face value some basketball tickets he'd paid scalpers' prices for. Some folks, he predicted, would go home and say, "Some clown sold me a ticket at cost."

The Fan's final communique from the front got feature billing again, six columns across the top of the page, twenty-five inches of type, under a headline that read, "Rx for Olympics: Leave Flags Home, Return Games to Athletes." It was a lament for the way world-class sporting events were undermined, delayed, interrupted, and diminished by shows of patriotic fervor, by the ceremonial pomp, and by the insistent self-importance of middle-aged officials. The response was warm and positive, Solomon told me. I was delighted. And I got paid for living out a dream.

But my summer in the sun wasn't over. The PGA championship was coming to Congressional in August and I offered to do a feature previewing the tournament from a fan's perspective. I had never published anything about golf before, but I told George about my experience at major tournaments. In 1955, taking time off from my M.A. studies at Berkeley, I saw every shot of Jack Fleck's upset playoff win against Ben Hogan in the U.S. Open at Olympic in San Francisco. I told him how I started to drive to Hanover for my tenth college reunion in 1963, only to turn east at Hartford and head for Brookline where I saw Julius Boros sweet-swinging his way to the Open championship. I told him about my week in Augusta watching some inspired play by Hogan though Gay Brewer won that Masters in 1967. And I told him about taking my two oldest kids, Ian and Jonny, to Minneapolis in 1970, where we stayed with Ted and Jerry Wright and saw Tony Lema win the Open at Hazeltine.

"All right, already," he said, got me my credentials, and sent me out to walk the course with a greens-keeper, see some practice rounds, and write a guide for those who would brave the crowds for the event. It was my longest feature ever in the *Post*, six columns across the whole top half of a page, fifty-two column inches. I suggested strategies for making the most of being a spectator at a golf tournament, which I touted as the best fan experience in all sports because of the ability to stay close to the action where and when it mattered, almost a spectator-as-participant deal and a physical challenge as well if properly pursued.

The sports editor was not done with me yet. Apparently I had carved out a niche. When a local team was having trouble, Dr. Isaacs was called in for a diagnostic report. When the Bullets were struggling under K.C. Jones after reaching the NBA pinnacle in the Dick Motta years, I wrote a long feature in which I defended the coach against the common charges of his critics but questioned his employment of a traditional seven-man rotation when, given the increased population of outstanding players in the league, there was a new trend toward a nine-, ten-, or even eleven-man rotation, exemplified by Al Attles's champion Golden State Warriors. Players like Dave Bing, Wes Unseld, Elvin Hayes, and Phil Chenier, I argued, would be more likely to function at an all-star level playing thirty-five minutes a game rather than forty-five, while Kevin Grevey, Truck Robinson, Jimmy Jones, Nick Weatherspoon, Mike Riordan, and Tom Kozelko all deserved opportunities for productive minutes. Another feature piece said the obvious: that NBA basketball is head and shoulders above the college game, especially because the 24-second clock speeds the action up while college coaches often enforce a slower pace or outright stall.

My recent publication of *Checking Back: A History of the NHL* must have given me a kind of "ice cred" at the paper, because Solomon asked me to assess what was wrong with the Capitals. Headlined "'System' Lacking for Caps," this feature went past the cliché that they were just two or three star players short of being a genuine playoff contender. "Coaching in hockey," I said, "is the most ineffectual and archaic of all major team sports." I spelled it out by giving examples of what an innovative coach can accomplish while most teams, however remarkable the individual skaters, play an undisciplined, chaotic style. Pointing to chronic problems both in clearing the puck from the defensive zone and in scrambling in the neutral zone rather than following a pattern of contingent plans, probably made me no friends among the local Zamboni zealots. And yet, more than three decades later, my analysis still clarifies an often-cloudy rink scene.

And that is almost a complete summary of my "tenure" on Solomon's page. Note that I was never allowed to venture onto the sacred turf of the Washington Redskins, that premier reservation of D.C. sports fans and sportswriters. Never mind that I was collaborating with Gerry Strine on a book for

Random House about how to bet pro football or that I would co-author with Tim Temerario a feature for *Washingtonian Magazine* on Tim's years as an assistant coach under George Allen, Vince Lombardi, and Paul Brown; the gridiron was off limits.

Yet George would be instrumental in the next departure in my mini-career as a sportswriter. The Montreal experience of writing columns on deadline (if four pieces in nine days could be called that) suggested to me that I could offer a regular column of my own. Including much of the material I had put together from my course and the contacts, themes, attitudes, values, and methods I had developed. I would call it "Jock Culture, USA," the same title as I used for the book which grew out of the course itself.

George liked the idea and encouraged me to pursue it, but alas would not agree to find regular space in his pages. I had expected that. I thought he had too many good writers on staff to squeeze out space for someone who was no more than a part-time dilettante stringer. But he would provide me with a list of sports editors who might be interested and he'd support my approach with a personal endorsement. I duly wrote to the half dozen he suggested. Four responded negatively, all citing the lack of space and wishing me luck. Bill Dwyre of the Milwaukee *Journal*, however, wrote me a letter that seems appropriate to quote, in part, here:

> I read your letter with deep interest and I can candidly say that, if George Solomon suggested that you contact me then there must be a certain quality to your work that goes well beyond the ordinary.
>
> I have two problems. First of all, the book that you said you would send along, JOCK CULTURE USA, never arrived. With it, I would have a better handle on exactly where your head is and what you might add to the Journal sports page. And second, I have a young and aggressive sports staff that is currently generating at such a pace that I have days where Ernest Hemingway himself wouldn't get three paragraphs in the paper.

He went on to keep open the possibility of working with me and asked for the book and perhaps some sample pieces. I include these remarks, however, for two other reasons: to indicate the respect for Solomon in the field, and to pass on the warning that books sent to a newspaper press room rarely reach the addressee.

By the time I received this letter, I had already signed on with Vince Doria of the Boston *Globe*. The short but hardly tragic tale of the column will be told in the next chapter, but a couple of postscripts testify to the fact that I was not yet finished with Olympic Games commentary. The first includes another one of those brief brushes with the red-carpet world of the famous. In a symposium on sports and society at the University of South Florida in May of 1980, I was scheduled for a debate on "America and the Olympics" with the great Dwight Stones.

An Olympian medalist himself, Stones was one of the most prominent track and field athletes of his generation, American record-holder in the high jump, handsome, articulate, and at the time a successfully self-promoting commentator on all things athletic. He was also a flag-waving supporter of Jimmy Carter's edict that the United States would boycott the Games as a gesture of Cold War hostility in the absence of effective diplomacy against the Soviet bloc. I was an outspoken opponent of the boycott, not because I had been looking forward to my friend Skeets Nehemiah competing for the gold in the hurdles, but because of my long-standing and frequently expressed distaste for the way jingoistic politics intruded upon sporting ideals. Besides, I wanted to lament about how the United States Olympic Committee, with contemptible hypocrisy, opted to violate its very charter and support the boycott in return for a financial-support package to prepare for the next Olympiad. So I was prepared to refute all of Stones' arguments, and I thought I had a favorable time slot as second speaker in front of a largely academic audience.

Stones must have thought so too. There was no moderator to heed and no ground rules to follow, so in the hour allotted our place on the program, Stones belted out fifty-five minutes' worth of bombastic arrogance and narcissistic balderdash, presenting himself as the avatar of appropriate competition in the land of the free and the home of the brave. Moreover, he appealed to the hero-worship of his audience instead of any pretense of intellectual engagement, receiving thunderous acclaim even without any accompanying drum-rolls or soaring anthem.

What could a thinking man do in five minutes? Well, he could present a brief and, I thought, overwhelming argument that to compete on the world's most prominent stage in athletic competition, each individual athlete in the greatest bastion of freedom on earth should be allowed to make a conscientious decision about whether to go to the Games wherever they might be held. I won't say I won that debate; quantity triumphed over quality. And no American, traveling without benefit of a visa, would or legally could compete. And Skeets decided to try professional football as a wide receiver for the Forty-Niners.

But thanks again to the wisdom of George Solomon I got the last say in the Washington *Post* in a column that appeared on June 25th, 1984 just as the 1984 Olympics were about to begin in Los Angeles. The Soviets, predictably, had decided to return Carter's favor and, as Sam Goldwyn would say, were staying away in droves, depriving fans of, for example, six of the world's best pole-vaulters, the best women's 400- and 800-meter runners, and a whole bunch of likely medalists in basketball, hockey, boxing, and swimming. The Games were being meanly diminished in significance by political posturing and patriotic pique. Still, with the summer off, a scheduled performance at the SLA meetings in San Diego, and a chance to visit my two West Coast resident sons, I had long planned to drive cross country.

The headline for my fifteen inches of sour grapes was, "Olympics' Closing Ceremony Could Be for Real." I had invested more than $1,300 on tickets, including typically hot items like six of the eight track and field days and three of the six swimming finals nights, with extra seats to use as barter, plus the always-in-demand closing ceremony. Alas, one incidental casualty of Cold War pettiness was the slumping market for scalpers' wares. There were, of course. some priceless moments to celebrate, peaking with Joanie Benoit's historic win in the first Olympic women's marathon. But the bitter point of my carping column was that this time I, no fan of the colors-bearing parade, would stay in town for the final evening's spectacle. Why? Because I was predicting that this would be the last Olympics as we knew them, a mournful playing of "Taps" to put period to the anthems of a world fallen to the spiteful sacrifice of free competition and to the lust for national pride.

No one called me chicken when I had the guts to say it in print, but in the event, I was more Chicken Little than Cassandra. In a trade-off that was not entirely to my benefit, I got one of my best short stories out of the experience of the return trip east after the Games, but none of the above got me any closer to that old goal of fame.

XII

JOCK CULTURE, U.S.A.

What I didn't know at the time that I accepted Morris Freedman's offer to come to College Park as a full professor (and it was several years before I got it straight) was that he had put the appointment over on my colleagues, the senior staff on his faculty, under false pretenses. I had thought that my job would be to inaugurate film studies in the department, and to show that he was taking that curricular expansion seriously he had also hired, at junior rank, Bob Kolker, a freshly minted Ph.D. from New York whose promising research focused on movies.

When I came to the campus for my final round of interviews, the paper I delivered before the gathering of the whole department was a tour de force on how a class might study a movie. I used *On the Waterfront* as my showpiece and I made it sound like the model of Elia Kazan's work as an auteur. Never mind that in my zealous recreation of the artistry involved I unconsciously invented a sequence that never appears on film--but nobody caught me on it (and Kolker wasn't there to set me straight). It went well, so did my meetings with administrators, and the offer was soon forthcoming. I had the resumé, the published credentials, and the work ethic.

What I didn't have was the understanding that half my assignment was to be the senior medievalist on the staff, exactly what I was eager to escape from the dead-ended drudgery of repetition in Knoxville. My film publications, one book and half a dozen articles, hardly qualified me for senior rank, but Morris was cannily persuasive that my scholarly book on Old English poetry and another dozen articles made me a valuable, versatile double threat.

With a fresh group of graduate students I was starting the traditional sequence of seminars all over again, and I found it tedious and stultifying. The quality of minds in my classrooms was not up to what I had enjoyed at U-T (in large part because the better students at Maryland were not interested in that area of study), and I began campaigning for them to hire someone who'd take that load off my back. In fact, I was disenchanted with graduate programs that I believed were training a generation of people for jobs that did not exist in the real, changing world of academe.

I was stuck with a bad case of teacher's block. I knew that I had moved into a slot that seemed uniquely suited to my accomplishments, so that there would be no next academic move available. I considered leaving the profession and trying something else, but as marginal as my financial status was (I had four children to support, two already in college and struggling to get by without much help from home), I couldn't gamble on trying to begin a new career.

What I did was find a way to refocus my pedagogical energy on undergraduate education. I began to invent courses, to have a course number of my own where I could change what I offered every semester and be satisfied with the students' responses. One experiment was called "The Uses of Literature," in which I would assemble a reading list on such topics as Madness, Love, Death and Dying, The Drug Experience, Alcohol and Alcoholism, and Baseball (!), and attract students who were interested in the topic itself and willing to see how literature illuminates the subject at hand. It worked for them and it worked for me. Students often repeated the course when the topic changed, and I found that their writing, not untutored attempts at traditional literary criticism, was richer by far and surely more pleasurable for their instructor to read.

The other course was "Sports Culture, USA." Somewhere below the conscious threshold of this invention, or deeply buried in my heart of hearts (though I've never made a public confession of it before this), I must have believed that it would make me a proverbial household name. It was an idea that was floating around in the intellectual atmosphere of the time. I didn't invent it, I had no copyright or registered trademark, but I was going to present it in a way that suggested I owned it. I would make it mine in a way that demanded my name be associated with it. Essential to this innovation was my belief that academicians owed it to their constituency to teach courses associated with the professional writing they were doing, and I had been as actively a publisher of sports-related writing as I continued to be an analytical commentator on literature.

The core idea was that our society had become a (jockocracy), that not just sports themselves but an omnipresent sports-mindedness pervaded American culture to the virtual exclusion of any other set of values. I didn't coin the word, and it was Howard Cosell who made its usage current. He only began to use it, however, after I had given him a copy of my book. Alas, he neither credited me nor thanked me.

The Course

The course, as I conceived it, would be very appealing to an undergraduate population, not just because of a widespread interest in anything with "sports" in the title or description, but because of my plan to have guest appearances by well-known people whose names would be familiar to readers of sports pages and watchers/listeners of sports shows on TV and radio. For me, there would be the added attraction of conducting public interviews with these guests, a kind of Zelig-gets-up-close-and-personal-with-the-stars gig, a fertile field for a frenzy of name-dropping.

In its debut semester the course took advantage of its host campus to bring in Maryland's outspoken, colorful Athletic Director, Jim Kehoe; its savvy Sports Information Director, Jack Zane; the chief fund-raiser of its biggest booster organization, Tom Fields; and two of my closest friends and colleagues in the English Department: Jack Russell, son of the legendary basketball coach and three-sport professional athlete, Honey Russell; and John "Hezzie" Howard, who coached the Maryland lacrosse team for several years after his own Hall- of-Fame playing career at Washington College. I knew they all would have interesting things to say, from a variety of angles, and I felt comfortable with challenging them with questions on controversial matters. Bear in mind that I had no budget to pay the guests any appearance fees, so their willingness to appear testified to their public-spirited interest in matters they found important.

I also took advantage of my contacts at the Washington *Post* to welcome George Solomon, the Sports Editor, and several of his leading writers: Andrew Beyer, the horse racing guru; Gerald Strine, the canny pro football handicapper; David DuPree, the smooth hoopster turned writer; and Steve Hershey, at that time still with the Washington *Star*, but hired by Solomon for the *Post* when the *Star* folded, before moving on to *USA Today*. Best of all in terms of prestige, we were graced with the presence of Shirley Povich, one of the most honored sports columnists in American journalism. (I know Shirley enjoyed the visit because, when his son Maury was hosting a local TV show, I was invited to appear on a panel discussing American sporting heroes that was aired along with a one-on-one interview with Muhammad Ali.)

Dr. Stan Lavine, who happened to be my orthopedist, who had quarterbacked Maryland's Gator Bowl football team in 1948, and who was the team physician for Maryland's football and basketball teams along with the Redskins and Bullets, faced questions about the sometimes-questionable ethics of sports trainers and doctors. Shelby Whitfield, distinguished baseball writer often featured in *Sports Illustrated*, put in an appearance. Jerry Sachs, number two man in Abe Pollin's organization that owned the Bullets and the Capitals franchises along with the Capital Centre, spoke carefully about issues facing management of pro sports. Donald Dell, tennis champion and partner in an important agency that managed many star athletes, talked candidly about the growing importance of agents in professional sports and the possible consequences of that development.

From East Tennessee State University, we were enlightened and amused by the wit and wisdom of Professor Jack Higgs, whose backcountry humor and detailed citations of Emerson and Thoreau highlighted as rich a presentation of a philosophy of sport that anyone present might ever have heard. Jack is my age, but after his time in the service as a graduate of the Naval Academy he was a student of mine in the graduate program at UT-Knoxville (where he was also my battery mate on our softball team and rugged lineman on our touch football team). Jack's contributions to the subjects of sport literature and the relationship between religion and sports are seminal works in those fields, and as a friend I love him dearly.

At the end of the semester, I wrote a thank-you letter to what I called "A million-dollar supporting cast of guest stars" featured in the course, which I trumpeted as a "most rewarding experience for me and 140 students." I called it a success "in its announced intentions--raising consciousness about the pervasiveness of sports and sports-mindedness in our society and examining some of the implications of that pervasiveness (implications concerning our literature, our heroes, our media, our rituals, our institutions, our priorities, and our values)." I also called it one of my own most satisfying educational experiences for what I had learned from them all.

What I didn't say was how much I had also learned from that large body of engaged students. Their primary assignment was to keep a journal in which they would respond to readings, to the interviews, and to my occasional lecture, but also to record if they wished their own personal experiences in and with Sports World. The latter category chronicled the exhilaration, the satisfaction, the frustration, the disappointment, and the anger of their experience, whether they were scholarship athletes (there were at least a dozen in the class) whose recruitment had been embarrassing or whose coaches had "destroyed their love of the game" or who were appalled at the lack of equity for women's sports or who, far from being encouraged, had been discouraged or even prevented from pursuing strictly academic goals.

Others recorded their treatment as second-class members of a student body that catered to, idolized, or were somehow disadvantaged or even victimized (socially, academically, sexually) by the powerful clique of jocks.

I had tapped a rich vein of information and emotional attitudes, and I was convinced that the course was performing a useful educational service and should be repeated. I also persuaded the department to assign a few graduate assistants to help with the grading. The enrollment had grown to 170 and reading so many journals, most of which deserved the attention I gave them (not least because of the energy that went into them) was a heavy burden. Two of those assistants deserve special mention: Mary Beth Hatem, who teamed up with me to win the university mixed doubles table tennis championship (see the photo of the cool paddlers), and Rich Drozd.

The tall staffer who ran the tournament is Olympic high-jumper Paula Girven

Richard A. Drozd
February 21, 1949 - June 30, 2010

Rich became one of my closest friends. He went on to an acclaimed teaching career at Georgetown Prep where he served as head of the English Department and was All-Met coach of the cross-country team (he was, incidentally, my training partner for the 1985 Marine Corps Marathon and became a regular host for the Tuesday night poker game). His sudden death, at 61, from a brain aneurysm, left all who knew him sorely bereaved.

The course's enrollment peaked for that second go-round, but after a sabbatical it ran for three more seasons, with some variations in format. The essential concept remained, however, and so did the featured visits of various informed guests. The experience must have been worthwhile for these gratis visits because more than a dozen returned for encores. Among fresh faces and voices from the media were such writers as Jonathan Yardley (book reviewer of the *Post*, baseball fan, and critic of sports literature); John Steadman (Baltimore *Sun* columnist, chronicler of every Super Bowl until his death, winner of the Red Smith Award); Dave Kindred (columnist for the *Post* and later the *Sporting News*, a professionally generous colleague and mentor, author of a great dual biography of Cosell and Ali, and chronicler of the saga about the decline of the *Post*); and Jane Leavy (*Post* columnist, beneficiary of Kindred's nurture, a writer of great wit, and subsequent author of biographies of Sandy Koufax and Mickey Mantle, in my view two of the top ten sports bios of all time). And among the broadcasters were Pat Summerall of NFL fame, Nick Charles (then sports anchor of WRC-TV), Frank Herzog (great favorite on local radio and TV), Johnny Holiday (versatile play-by-play man and frequent star of local theater), and Mel Proctor (among the best baseball and basketball voices in the business).

Added to the roster of athletes and coaches were Wes Unseld, Kevin Grevey, and Bob Ferry of the Bullets, John Thompson (who wouldn't bring the Hoyas in to play Maryland; but then Lefty Driesell wouldn't even deign to appear in my classroom), Lacey O'Neal (three times an American Olympian runner and a dynamic commentator on the burdens carried by black women in sports), and three former class members who returned in a tutorial role--Mo Howard, John Lucas, and Skeets Nehemiah.

Some guests are mentioned elsewhere in this memoir, but a few deserve individual attention here. Abe Pollin, for example, came himself (instead of his deputy), an indication of some approval by management of what we were doing. And we had an illuminating session with Peter O'Malley, a prominent local political figure who had an interest in the professional teams but who was a member of the university's Board of Regents (later its chair), with the subject of potential conflicts of interest as its major focus.

Don Ruck, Deputy Commissioner of the NHL (and an old college chum of my brother), flew in from New York to give us the inside scoop on hockey management. Mike Trainer, lawyer and confidante of Sugar Ray Leonard, forcefully shared his views with us. And in hindsight there was an amusing appearance of sorts when Donald Dell made a return visit, accompanied by a young associate, who actually carried Dell's briefcase into the class. It was David Falk, later known as "The Vulture" after he contentiously departed from Dell's firm to launch his own very profitable venture, operating in a way that seemed to violate most of Dell's admirable principles.

Finally, during the course's closing season, came Larry Harrison, a college classmate and good friend. Larry had been a high school tennis and track star, a varsity squash player in college, and had achieved high rank as director of several Latin-American missions of the US Agency for International Development. Later, as author of several books, including *Underdevelopment Is a State of Mind: The Latin American Case* and *The Central Liberal Truth: How Politics Can Change a Culture and Save It from Itself*, and director of the Cultural Change Institute of the Fletcher School at Tufts University, he had become an influential if controversial voice in matters of diplomatic policy. He was in my classroom, however, because he was a strong opponent of the negative view about sports in America that pervaded my book. A fan and booster of the positive values of sport in this society, he gave eloquent testimony to his love and respect for our games, to which I could only give grudging approval followed by a "yes, but...."

Larry Harrison at my son Ian's wedding

The course had had a good run and it was time to move on. The book was already out, and I was hardly finished with the subject; still, I felt that the pedagogical aspect had run its course--so to speak. I asked this final group of students for specific comments on a final paper about "how their attitudes and values were changed, developed, enriched, or modified by the experience of the course." By and large they were very appreciative, and nothing gladdens a teacher's heart more than being gifted with such reviews in large numbers.

And so it ended, with nary a whimper and perhaps a bit of a bang. Not surprisingly, perhaps, the column that grew from the class and the book came to an end about the same time. In fact, it was the book that came closest to achieving a degree of public attention beyond a limited and perhaps provincial audience.

The Book(s)

Without any immodest commentary about the book itself, I may be indulged in taking some pride in how it came about. When I had received an offer to write a history of college basketball, I felt the need for professional representation and was referred to the Curtis Brown agency. There I was assigned to a young agent just beginning in the business after serving an apprenticeship as a publisher's editor. Ellen Levine not only took over the negotiation with Lippincott but began to work vigorously to expand my potential and enrich my opportunities as a writer. With *All the Moves*, she managed to get an excerpt published in the *New York Times*, which in itself demonstrated her skills of representation. When she left Curtis Brown and established her own agency she became in short order a major player in the trade, and I take some pride in being one of her first clients.

While Ellen had some doubts about the commercial appeal of *Jock Culture, USA*, the sports-related book I had in mind as a follow-up to the basketball history, she tried to interest W.W. Norton in the project. That effort led not only to a contract with one of the country's most distinguished book publishers but to a senior editor there, Eric Swenson. When he took me to lunch at the stately old New York Yacht Club, where I felt totally out of my element, appreciating that for me in that milieu there was some irony in the cliché of "fish out of water," he boosted my ego by generously applauding what I had done in the basketball book. But he was a hockey, not a hoops, fan and wondered whether I'd do a similar job with the game of his fancy. He thought the critique of sport I had in mind was interesting and thought I could carry it off successfully, but he wanted a commitment to a hockey history. Ellen Levine then went to work and she and Eric worked out a two-book contract for me with Norton.

I was ecstatic at the prospect and immediately set to work on the NHL because Eric clearly wanted that done first before Norton would issue *Jock Culture, USA*, though the latter was much further along at the time. What I had brought to college basketball, however, I lacked on ice, that is, a broad view of the evolution of the game and some well-defined notions of how and why that process had evolved. My early interest in hockey had waned when the sport's excellence had waned--or been diluted--with expansion, with the dismal example of the Washington Capitals as an immediate case in point. What I produced, I'm sorry to say, after a concise summary of the game's origins and an eloquent tribute to its inherent beauty, was a tedious account of games and stats and Stanley Cup results, tributes to stars, and a territorial expansion that I thought of as over-extension. Well-produced but lacking the illustrations that might have made it more attractive, the book did not do well. Eric said he liked it, praising the writing, but I felt that I had disappointed him.

It wasn't until almost twenty years later, September of 2006 to be exact, that I received a vindication of sorts for *Checking Back*, a book the best part of which, I thought, was its title. A letter from the Society of North American Hockey Historians and Researchers (SONAHHAR) informed me that I had received the first annual "Sun God Award for Outstanding Hockey Research" (named for the sun god religion of ancient Mesopotamia, in the accounts of which, circa 2500 B.C., are the first records of a stick and ball game with curved sticks and a ring. I thought at first that the letter was a joke, until a subsequent mail brought a package containing an engraved 11 ½- inch wooden obelisk with my name and the award in gold print. Maybe I hadn't done so bad after all and I needn't rank the rink-book as the least of my written accomplishments.

Jock Culture, USA followed shortly, and it quickly began to draw some attention. Bob Edwards came calling, and I had a short interview with him broadcast on NPR, and so did Larry King. Not Billie Jean's ex-husband and not the author of "The Best Little Whorehouse in Texas" but the host of a late-night radio show that was reputed to be the next best media thing to promote a book after "Good Morning America" in those pre-Oprah days. I would have been more excited about that invitation if I hadn't appeared on the show earlier that year with Gerry Strine, to promote *Covering the Spread*.

That topic was a natural for King, given his keen interest in sports, football, and betting. And yet, in spite of his own enthusiasm and the flood of calls from listeners who wanted to pick Strine's brain (I just wrote the book, but the betting strategies were all Gerry's), and in spite of the apparent interest that led to an encore appearance for yet another hour of discussion and call-ins, there was no apparent effect on a book-buying market. Disappointed in the sparse sales I could at least take some dubious consolation from having an excerpt printed in *Penthouse*.

The second time around I learned to appreciate King's interview technique, the key to his syndicated success and the subsequent triumph of his prime-time TV show. Not only did he not read the book under discussion, but he steadfastly avoided any pre-knowledge of what it had to say. His questions, then, came from an inquiring mind, from someone who wanted to know what the author was about and what he had to say in his book. In other words, he spoke *for* his audience, people primed to be informed. Because the book was provocative and challenged some widely held cultural attitudes, with King's probing questions I was able to highlight the issues I had addressed in a bold, uncensored, common-sense, and I hoped non-pedantic manner. King himself seemed intrigued and again asked me to come back--which I did (he also honored me with two visits to my classroom, where we traded roles as interviewer and guest), and now that the reviews were starting to come in I knew that there were some problems with my presentation that I had to address.

I am a great admirer of Terry Gross, whose interviews of authors on NPR's "Fresh Air" seem to me to be quite evocative of the substance of the book in hand (which she clearly has read insightfully) and perfectly pitched to a culturally sensitive audience. Larry King's pitch, however, seems to me more productive with a mass audience. Speaking of a degree of mutual admiration, in the three decades since I last was heard on the radio with him, I have only encountered Larry King once--when he presented me with a signed copy of a new book of his, inscribed personally to me and saying, "I admire you very much." In all those years, however, he has never admired me enough to respond to messages I've left for him, but I can understand how heart trouble, multiple marriages, and prime-time prominence can cause old admirations to fade.

Whenever interviewed, I would typically confess to a love/hate relationship with sports. I love the competition, the striving for individual excellence in the context of fair play, the beauty of teamwork, the endorphin rush of participation, and the vicarious thrills of watching; I hate the over-emphasis, the bureaucratization, the commercialization, the media manipulation, the cheating, and the corruption. No wonder the typical tone of most reviews was "mixed," whether "damning with faint praise" or praising generally only to take issue with specific points, phrasing, and the occasional exaggeration. When a fussy, nitpicking reader in a review of several sports-related books singled out my writing for praise, I felt slapped (it was George Core, who replaced the great Andrew Lytle as editor of *The Sewanee Review*; I'll take the accommodating wisdom of the old school over narrowly careful pickiness any time; and the same goes for *The Virginia Quarterly Review*, where the openness of Staige Blackford, who generously published me several times in various formats, has been replaced by the grandiosity of Ted Genoways).

Having published, not long before the book's appearance, a long op-ed piece in "Outlook" addressing some of the central issues of *Jock Culture, USA*, The Washington *Post* honored me by excerpting passages in three successive sections. And then I was off on a self-promoted book tour that took me to all of two stops. The first was at the University of Minnesota, where my dear old friends Ted and Jerry Wright, hosted me and got me sufficient publicity to have a large audience for an appearance that was more of a lecture than a reading. Reviews were good, the student paper was flattering, and I went west to Vermillion, home of the University of South Dakota.

Two of my graduate students at Tennessee, Tom Gasque and Alice Tealey, had established themselves in the English Department there, and again I was warmly welcomed, honored at a festive party, and went on to face a hall packed with an interested student audience. I had not been forewarned, however, that there would be a group of hostile critics of my work, despite my disclaimers that my presentation would be less scholarly than journalistically sociological.

I was shocked, as perhaps only an East Coast provincial might be, to find that there was a group of radical feminist lesbians in Vermillion, then shocked again that they would loudly voice their objections to my whole approach. Would I have to explain to them that I was an unlikely target of their accusations of sexism, that I was a staunch supporter not only of Title IX but also the Equal Rights Amendment? (I was reminded of how little effect I had in defending myself against a graduate student's claim of racism by offering my credentials as an activist for integration in the "movement.")

And why did they rain condemnations on my head (I quickly repressed the impulse to call the attackers a coven of cursers)? It was because of my use of the word *jock* as a synonym for *athlete*. I could hardly argue for an innocent choice of a commonly accepted term, whether slang or not, when

I was informed that this band of sisters called themselves "radical feminist lesbian *linguists*." I had to acknowledge that language is often the vehicle of indirect or buried bias, as the usage of words like *hysterical*, *sinister*, *Redskins*, and *black* demonstrate.

I left Vermillion a chastened but wiser man. At least sometimes, if not often, I would screen my own language for the hidden vestiges of someone's prejudice--no matter how earnestly I rejected the thinking underlying it. But when I finally was able to entice a newspaper sports editor into running my stuff, I reverted to the original title of the course, and "Jock Culture" was restored to its pristine form, "Sports Culture."

Cosell, Gifford, and Exley; Molinas and Me

On a cool night in early November, I attended my first and only Monday Night Football game. The date was November 6, easy for me to remember because it was the birthday of my Grandma Braun, sixteen years gone at the time but never forgotten. (That it is also the anniversary of the death of Arnold Rothstein, the man who fixed the 1919 World Series and the model for Fitzgerald's Meyer Wolfsheim in *Gatsby*, is purely coincidental.) The Washington Redskins were at Memorial Stadium to face the Baltimore Colts, but convenience wasn't what brought me there, nor was whatever local recognition I might have had what earned me credentials for the press box that night.

I had set up a pre-game interview with Frank Gifford, my brother's old acquaintance from his McCann-Erickson days on the Westinghouse account for whom Gifford was their leading celebrity flack. My business with Gifford, as he knew, was that I wanted to write a column about his relationship with Fred Exley. Since Gifford was a main "character" in Exley's novel, *A Fan's Notes,* I wanted to know about any real-life connection they might have had, when it had begun, what it was like, and how Gifford felt about Exley's idolization of him. It was my intention to interview Exley, too, if I could track him down.

Of course I could have arranged to talk to Gifford any old time. It didn't have to be face-to-face, but I had a hidden agenda for orchestrating the meeting in this way. I wanted to meet Howard Cosell and present him with a signed copy of *Jock Culture, USA*, which was fresh off the press. I had high hopes that he would read it--I knew he agreed with much of my take on the role of sports in our culture--and give it a plug on his radio show. More than being a publicity hound, I had considerable admiration for Cosell as a journalist who, in the phrase he made famous, kept "telling it like it is." I placed him in my pantheon of those who wrote intelligently and critically about sports, along with Leonard Koppett, Frank DeFord, Pete Axthelm, John McPhee, Bill Barich, and Robert Lipsyte (the latter's book, *SportsWorld*, came out just before *Jock Culture*, and while its foreword very closely anticipated my own, his was a personal narrative of how his close associations and eye-witness observations as a sportswriter led him to his socio-cultural conclusions). And I appreciated the satirical edge of Cosell's language, much as I enjoyed Hind's and Millar's syndicated comic strip "Tank McNamara" and the long- running *Sports Illustrated* feature called "Signs of the Apocalypse."

That night I had two encounters with Cosell. The first was when I introduced myself and gave him the book. He thanked me, glanced briefly at the cover, and proceeded to pontificate--largely I thought for the benefit of the three or four other people within hearing distance of his inimitable voice. The other was later, after the game, when I had a chance to talk with him in private. What a difference! Without the audience, he was understated and respectful, engaging me in a frank if brief discussion of some of my main points.

There was no follow-up to that meeting and no direct benefit to me or my book for having Cosell read it. But I know he did, because he soon began to use the word "jockocracy" that I had used as a kind of shorthand refrain throughout the book to encapsulate the central significance of sports and sports-mindedness in our society and culture. I cannot claim to have coined the term, nor can I remember where I first saw or heard it. To my knowledge, however, Cosell had never used it in public until then, and shortly thereafter it became a stock figure in his grandiose vocabulary, popularizing it--and never citing his source for it. That omission did not make me any the less proud of a meager contribution to the lexicon. (It is worth noting, I think, that in subsequent work of his own following our roughly contemporaneous books, Lipsyte also may have adopted "jockocracy" as a rough synonym for his "SportsWorld." And according to later reviews of Lipsyte I see that he has also used "Jock Culture"--without an attribution that I may or may not deserve--particularly in a recent column that uses the phrase as a headline.)

I found Frank Gifford to be in person exactly what he appeared to be in any other medium, straightforward, unassuming, good-natured, and personable if humorless. He told me how he had first learned that he would be featured in a novel, when Bennett Cerf (a personal friend of his who had his finger on the pulse of American book publishing) called to tell him about its forthcoming publication. He read it with interest and seemed unaffected by the hero- worship with which Exley had regarded him as an icon. He and Exley eventually met (though Exley maintained that they had had a nodding acquaintance at USC) and there ensued a relationship in which the worshipper would call the icon, usually long distance and always collect from as far away as Key West, London, and Hawaii, sometimes sounding drunk, and often asking for favors like tickets to a game. He didn't really understand the guy, Gifford said, always accepted the calls just as he routinely accepted the adulation, and his only reservation was the quiet wonderment about "how a guy could publicly pour his guts out like that."

To complete the work for what I thought would be a fascinating column, I had to get Exley to talk to me--and that took a major effort. In truth, the 800- word piece that was the result was hardly worth all I went through to prepare for it. If anything the effort was worthwhile in itself for what I learned about the novelist, whose book I admired greatly and often included on course reading lists (I mean *A Fan's Notes*, not the two succeeding books, *Pages from a Cold Island* and *Last Notes from Home*, that demonstrated a precipitously declining talent; that first brilliant work of genius marked Exley as a prime example of a one-book writer).

At this time, Exley was triangulating his quarters among upstate New York, Key West, and Hawaii. With a little help from friends in New York I was able to reach him by phone only to have him say that instead of a live interview I should write out some questions to send him, and he'd tape his responses extemporaneously. I followed his instructions and waited weeks and then months without hearing from him. I used my contacts again and was guided to a Key West telephone number where he was staying. Someone there gave me a number at a bar where he might be found, the bartender there said that he'd gone on to another bar, and that's where I heard his slurred voice.

"Did you ever get my questions?" I asked.

"Yeah, I got 'em," he said, "but it was too much like a fuckin' essay exam." I laughed and told him he was right, and then he proceeded to give me his version of his post-publication relationship with Frank Gifford. So I had my column after all, and you could look it up in a Boston *Globe* archive. Much more important for this narrative, however, is that I was inspired by the connection between Gifford and Exley that I had focused on, a connection that in Exley's own words led to his bitter, lugubrious, mawkish, and probably alcohol-driven conclusion that "Gifford was my fame."

Coincidentally, the precise period when I was engaged in the trivial pursuit of this column, I was also trying to frame an approach to my next book project. I had told Eric Swenson at Norton that I wanted my next book to be about Jack Molinas, a boyhood hero of mine as a high-IQ, brilliant basketball player who went historically off the tracks mentally and legally as the "master fixer" of the college point-shaving scandals. Eric advised against it, saying that no one cared about a forgotten figure of a faintly remembered scandal, while I argued that in my view Molinas could be seen as a seminal figure in the recent cultural history of an American generation. Pointing out that this was an idiosyncratic view of my own, he then suggested that I write it as fiction, and I had leapt at the challenge that a fictional memoir presented.

I began work right away and Ellen Levine, still my agent then, enthusiastically supported the concept and the early fragmentary drafts I produced. She persuaded Eric to have Norton give me a (token) advance to support the effort--and give them the right of first refusal. The essential conceit of my approach was the creation of a character, Jesse Miller, upon whom I projected much of my own experience and attitudes, to undergo a passage from hero-worship to disillusion, while in alternating chapters I told Molinas's story through his own warped view. The title was to be "The Great Molinas" but the echo of Fitzgerald's Gatsby is less central to the focus and approach of the book than that of Exley's Gifford. From the very beginning I was intoxicated with the idea that, finally, Molinas would be my fame.

You would have thought that the kind of exhaustive research I did on this project meant that I was preparing a detailed biography of an important figure. Well, I thought Molinas was important in his crooked way and I was determined to be scrupulously honest about the details of his life. But in order to do that, I needed the protective pretext of a novelist's vantage. Many people who would not have given me the time of day for a journalistic biographical approach were willing to talk freely as long as the result would be *fiction*. And so I found a growing chorus of voices, people with first-hand knowledge of my subject, from his boyhood, his basketball-playing years, his involvement with organized crime, his gambling exploits, his hide-and-seek game with law enforcement, his time in jail, and his "second act" of post- prison life in California.

For example, one of my informants was an investigator from New York's District Attorney Hogan's staff who was part of the team building the case against the conspirators of the basketball fixes. He happened to be a friend of my brother and spoke extensively about the case and about the whole context in which it occurred, naming names, describing characters, and providing inside information without the filter of bias so far as I could tell. He had no axe to grind. But he also demanded confidentiality because he had become a private contractor in the security business, and so to use the data he supplied I devised various fictive ways of shifting his knowledge to the awareness of several characters of my invention. In other cases, where the demimonde of gambling overlapped with a criminal underworld, my informants claimed to be taking great risks in talking to me at all, but under the cover of artistic license I gave them the opportunity to indulge their taste for embellishing anecdotes.

The final result, several years in the making, was a hybrid "historical novel" that gave an intimate and accurate portrait of its title character while constructing a wholly imagined parallel narrative. Never mind the bits and pieces of my own personal experience that I borrowed and revised for Jesse Miller; Jesse and I shared a boyhood idolization of the rising young basketball player, Jack Molinas, for example, but Jesse eventually meets him in person and I never did. Nevertheless, I maintain that I came to know him as well as or better than anyone else ever did.

Norton was not enthralled with the manuscript I submitted; Eric Swenson praised it but said that it raised problems for him both as a reader and as a publisher. The result was an offer to publish but with such a small advance that it was destined to appear below even the rank of a "mid-list" offering on a distinguished roster of books. I was nevertheless pleased: to be anywhere on a Norton list was an accomplishment for a "first novel." My agent demurred. It's an insult, she said, and we can't accept it, but don't worry, I'll place it elsewhere. To her credit, she believed in what I had created and worked hard for it--but exhausted all her contacts without success. Two years later I was no longer her client and began the frustrating process of finding a publisher on my own.

Almost at the end of my fame-seeking tether, *Molinas* was rescued from the filing cabinet of abandoned manuscripts by two friends, p.r. guy Jim Walczy and printing company guy Tom Dolan, partners in an ad hoc publishing company called WID (you may guess what the "I" stood for), along with a generous grant from the Sport Literature Association. It was Jim's and Tom's feeling that they could gamble on producing, promoting, and distributing this book because the long-range payoff would be a movie deal. We all agreed on the cinematic potential of the story and began casting the characters in our fuzzy heads. Good blurbs came in from chosen readers (Irv Faust, Sam Jones, Chet Forte, Jerry Klinkowitz, *The Gold Sheet*'s editor and publisher Mort Olshan, Gerry Strine, and Tony Kornheiser), a distributor was engaged, books rolled off the press, and some went out to prospective reviewers. The notices were mixed, some readers thinking the Jesse Miller narrative a distraction from the Molinas story while others admired Jesse's cautionary tale while minimizing the cultural-historical importance of Molinas. A few were generously impressed, most notably Dave Kindred, who devoted an entire lead column in *The Sporting News* to the tale.

Out of the woodwork came people who had known Molinas and had bits and pieces to add. Some praised the accuracy of my portrait, while others claimed I'd missed some vital points or fudged others. A few live-radio interviews involved both those points of view. One Boston radio host devoted a whole hour to the book, but asked me very few questions while mostly bragging about his own knowledge of the scandalous doings I'd narrated. The bottom line never approached black print; the book just didn't sell.

As for its power as story material, it might be validated by the fact that several other novelists tried their hands at retellings and that at least two film projects wrestled with it, one by Spike Lee who never got a script he could work with, another by my college classmate Dave Picker who wanted to produce a bio-pic for Paramount and had gone so far as to commission a script by an established writer (I believe it was the late Avery Corman, but never had that surmise confirmed) but never got to the shooting stage.

Nevertheless, the legend lives on. In 2001 there appeared what purported to be an actual biography, clumsily called *The Wizard of Odds*, written by Charley Rosen, with the assistance of Jack's younger brother Julie Molinas. In fact, the main sources of this version, beyond newspaper archives, were a set of taped interviews that Molinas had prepared for the fine sportswriter, at first.

Milton Gross who was preparing an as-told-to autobiography (which Molinas at the last moment blocked from publication) and my own novel.

The troubles were with these sources was that the former was the property of the Gross family estate which never gave permission for its use and that the voice on the tapes was that of a pathological liar with a flair for self-dramatization. In the case of the latter source, Rosen, who had received personal encouragement and cooperation from yours truly, couldn't tell the difference between fact and fiction and went on to cite as historical evidence scenes and dialogue that were my original inventions--and quoted them verbatim and without attribution. At least four other sources cited by Rosen, who had been led to them at my suggestion, subsequently told me he had totally distorted what they had said.

Rosen's phony biography had sufficient success to justify a paperback follow-up from Seven Stories Press. Out of respect for the publisher, Dan Simon, I chose not to pursue a lawsuit for copyright infringement though intellectual property attorneys confirmed that I had a solid case. Mr. Simon and I worked out an agreement in which considerable revision would be done for the new edition, dropping some material and paraphrasing certain plagiarized language and including an amplified acknowledgment of my work. Rosen never made an apology to me, public or private, asking instead why I wanted to "destroy" his "career." (My carefully annotated case against him is documented in the journal of the SLA, *Aethlon*, Spring 2003, under the title "Charley Rosen's Game: A Basketball Biographer Fouls Out.")

The story, at least my version of it, has legs, as seen by the fact that Rob Smith, of the small, independent Drinian Press, chose to release a revised second edition in paperback in 2010. But has my Molinas brought me fame? No, but I'd like to say not yet.

Jim Walczy, having retired from his p.r. firm to pursue a second profession as a playwright, has been at work for some time on a screenplay of *The Great Molinas*. If I am deceiving myself with false optimism, I guess you could call it the mendacity of hope.

I should add that Drinian was the publisher I found, at Tom LeClair's suggestion, for my novel, *The Doaker's Story*, a book that played fast and loose with some Lefty Driesell material for a larger purpose than petty payback. Dave Kindred's blurb notes that "it says all the right things about sports in America, and says it memorably." That was quite gratifying to me, just what I had hoped for, but the very modest sales suggest that Kindred was a voice crying in a wilderness of non-readership. So what else was new?

Still, the lure of sports-related books persisted. Some aspects of the material below continue the tale of this enchantment.

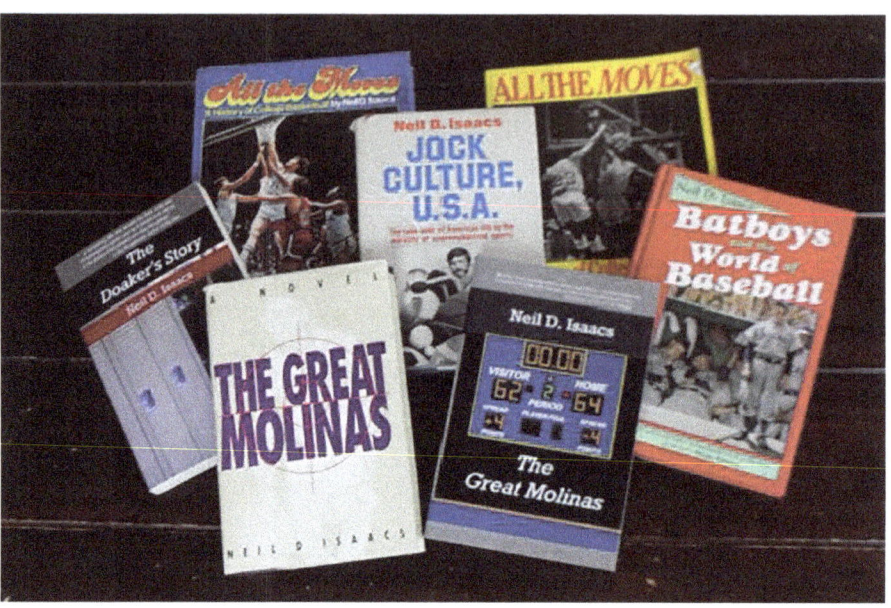

The Column

Over the course of these hands-on experiences with athletes, their media coverage, and the management "teams" that are both the support systems and the true beneficiaries of a system that is a jockocracy, I had warehoused my memory bank with enough material and contacts, I thought, to fill years' worth of newspaper columns. At George Solomon's suggestions, as I've said above, I wrote to selected sports-page editors to offer up those wares. Typically, the response was that lack of space and an existing staff that was ambitious enough to plead for more space made my otherwise attractive proposition impossible.

But then Vince Doria of the Boston *Globe* said that they were planning a new weekly section called "Sports Plus" where he thought my column idea would work nicely. Well, the eight-hundred-word essay once a week turned out to be harder than I had anticipated (never mind the low rate of recompense) and I acquired a new respect for the journalists who work on deadline several times a week. It was work but I truly enjoyed it, notwithstanding my lack of comfort with the demands for concise, punchy writing.

The little vignette, the capsule review, the iconoclastic attack, the touching if brief human interest story, the caustic critique, the ironic observation--these were my new preoccupations. I wrote about players like the guy I met on the beach at Harwich Port during a summer visit to my colleague Jack Bryer's place, a lacrosse star at Amherst whose ambition was to be the first African American on the US. Olympic lacrosse team--and didn't know that lacrosse was not (and still is not) an Olympic sport. I wrote about a gallant basketball fan whose season tickets for the Bullets was what sustained him through arduous recovery from a severe accident and who earned an ovation from the crowd when he returned to his familiar spot. I wrote about friends like Jack Higgs and George Graboys whose determined play and sense of competition and sportsmanship, maintained through middle age, augmented their professional success as academic and banking executive. I wrote about books and movies that exalted sports or ridiculed them. I wrote about the relationship of Frank Gifford and Fred Exley (as described above).

I wrote about some of the absurdities that radio and television sportscasters used to mask their ignorance, misdirect attention, and mangle the language. And always I tried to keep a focus on the ways that I found to illustrate the lengths to which a sports-minded society can go to make fun and games central to its functions and rituals and most strongly held beliefs. But in all candor I have to say that I got very little attention from readers. Still, when the editorship passed to Dave Smith in Boston, he chose to keep the column going, saying that it gave a touch of class to his page. And when he moved on to the Washington *Star* he took "Sports Culture, USA" with him (and appeared as a guest in my classroom). Alas, the *Star* soon folded, and I would lament its absence while bragging that my column must have been the straw that broke the old standard's back.

The column reinvented itself some years later when I was hired to write a regular piece for a fledgling quarterly, *SportsFan Magazine*. launched from an office in Bethesda by Jimmy Patterson. I signed on as a contributing editor for the fourth issue, Winter 2001, and was allotted space for a column that I called "The Fan on the Couch," an allusion to the running head for my 1976 Olympics coverage. The point, as I asserted in my first column, was that in the six Olympiads that had passed, an aging sports fan had concluded that the best place to watch almost any event (except a baseball game) was on TV. Despite poor production decisions, especially for basketball games as I lamented in another column for that issue called "And Another Thing," the view is always better and the only distractions are of one's own choice.

As a paid gig, on a much higher scale than any newspaper work I'd done, this was a welcome assignment. I could choose my topics, playfully argue my takes, and only have to perform four times a year. It was too good to last, and I should have had an inkling of that when, in the second issue with my name among the cast credits, the format changed from glossy 8 x 11 magazine to 11 x 14 rough paper tabloid. In the succeeding seven issues, through Summer 2003, it survived, struggling to break even with advertising and subscriptions, until it folded into an exclusively online publication--with no budget for contributing writers.

Great fun while it lasted, though. I got to devise a twelve-step program for recovering golf addicts, to critique the "other" opening day for baseball in the annual onslaught of new books on the game, to attempt a definitive definition for "most valuable player," to reminisce about my ten greatest experiences as a fan in the stands, and to deride the sports fan's assignment of the "hero" designation to repugnant figures like Pete Rose and Bob Knight. I also got my ass off the couch to do three "road" pieces. For one I toured several ballparks (extolling the virtues of Comerica in Detroit and the Jake in Cleveland while calling SkyDome in Toronto an engineering marvel but a lousy place to play baseball). For another, I did a participant/observer survey of the Super Senior tennis grand prix tour in Florida. And for the third, my brother and I traveled to Montreal during the Expos' final season, to praise and not to bury them, and to muse on what to call the new D.C. franchise (my bottom-line suggestion: the Washington DosEquispos).

No longer a columnist, I sometimes wistfully fantasize a new piece. Most recently I have been toying with the idea of advocating a new way of televising baseball so that the game on screen is at least equal to a live visit to the ballpark. It calls for the use of the evolutionary developments in telecommunication technology to give viewers a view of the whole field and the options to zoom in on any particular area in close-up and to replay a play from several vantages. It will happen eventually, but why not now, in my lifetime?

XIII

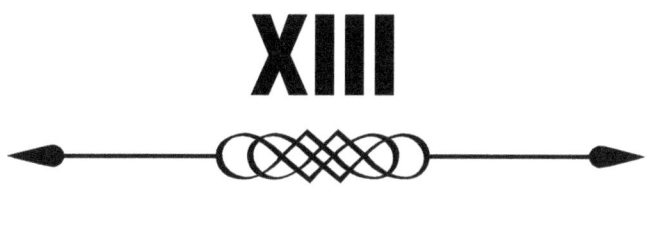

IN THE TANK

Now, I admit that I might have been slightly more paranoid than the average Jewish academic, but still I can tell when people are looking at me funny. And on Monday, the 6th of June in 1977, I kept having the fleeting sensation that someone or other was looking at me funny.

One of the perks of senior rank at UMCP was a parking sticker that entitled me to use the lot just outside Taliaferro Hall, where my office and classrooms were located at that time. Unfortunately, it's a small lot, with about a quarter of the spaces needed to accommodate all those of senior rank in the building. You had to get there early, which I typically did not, or else use the nearest overflow lot--all of about fifty yards away.

It was a Monday, the first day of a summer session and my seventy-five- minute class started at ten. Nineteen undergraduate students had registered for a course called "The Uses of Literature," an invention of mine based on the premise that literature is a culture's best way of recording its thoughts and feelings about what seems important to it. Then, each semester (and I taught this course for more than fifteen years), I would choose a topic I considered important. Some of the topics (Literature of Madness, of the Drug Experience, of Baseball, of Alcoholism) always attracted maximum enrollment. Others (Literature of Love, of Death and Dying, of The Absurd) not so much. That summer it was "Death and Dying," chosen because for a summer session I welcomed a smaller class that would meet every weekday for six weeks.

I was somewhat preoccupied that morning, because, as was the case every time in forty-four years of teaching that I met a class for the first time, I would get nervous--a mild form of performance anxiety that I tolerated because it always passed before that first meeting ended. Besides, I assumed that some of these students would be enrolled because they were experiencing or anticipating some kind of traumatic loss.

No sooner had I stepped out of the car and shouldered my classic green baize book-bag when I felt eyes upon me. From both the right and the left, people-- apparently a colleague I didn't recognize and a graduate student who looked vaguely familiar--were looking, indeed, frankly staring, in my direction. I use a general term, but I thought they both were deliberately softening the gaze toward acceptable mildness rather than offensive concentration.

What's going on, I thought, and then as I walked along the path to the concrete-and-brick front steps of Taliaferro, it happened again. And again. I caught several students glancing my way, something unfamiliar students never do, and a couple of junior colleagues greeted me with grins and a heartier hello than was customary, accompanied by a kind of gleeful, knowing look. Something is up, I thought, something I should know about and that they think I do know about.

Instead of passing through the main office and checking my mailbox, I went straight up the flight of stairs to my office, dropped my bag on the desk, and went down the hall to the men's room. There I took a rare long look at myself in the mirror but found nothing remarkable or in any way out of line. The hair was fairly long but neat, the beard trim if full, the checked shirt clean and unwrinkled, the fly of my jeans zipped.

Get a hold of yourself, I thought. Put it out of your mind and get ready for your first class. The trouble was that for the hour and a quarter of that introductory session I could sense that my students were looking at me with a degree of attentive curiosity and something that looked more like amusement than admiration that I found not just surprising but disconcerting. Paranoia? No, I thought, there's something different about me--and noteworthy--and I don't know what it is.

Walking from the classroom back to the office, I got the answer to my questions. My friend Larry Mintz accosted me in the hallway and rushed over with hand extended. "Congratulations," he said. "You've made the big time."

When I shook my head in bewilderment, he quickly saw that I didn't know what he was talking about. "Haven't you read the paper yet?"

I shook my head, with a sudden fear that notoriety of an unwanted sort had befallen me, but Larry beamed his pleasure at me and said, "You're in today's 'Tank McNamara.'"

Larry Mintz was the perfect person to tell me about this. He was the humor maven of the American Studies Department, housed in Taliaferro just down the hall from my office. Moreover, he was a knowledgeable sports fan, whose cynical views of our national pastimes were very much in agreement with mine.

I got hold of a copy of that morning's Washington *Post* (the "morning miracle," as Dave Kindred calls it in his wonderful book on the paper's struggles to stay afloat when most were sinking), and there I was, hair, beard, checked shirt, and jeans, addressing a meeting of faculty representatives to the NCAA. I thought it an uncanny rendering, especially since I'd never met either Jeff Millar, the writer, or Bill Hinds, the artist, the creators of Tank.

Not that I hadn't tried. My original concept for "Sports Culture, USA," was that I would invite guests to talk to the class about the ways that sports and sports-mindedness impacted virtually every aspect of our society. I compiled a wish list of athletes, coaches, agents, sportswriters, broadcasters, sports physicians, sports attorneys, etc., and began to send out informal feelers in advance of actual invitations. Miller and Hinds would be among my most sought-after personages, their strip a less than gentle satire of the flaws and the foibles, the hypocrisy and half-baked ethics, of American sports. I had no budget to pay for appearances or travel, but I hoped that if such folks happened to be in the D.C. area they would enjoy the classroom experience.

I wrote to them at their home base, the Houston *Post*, praised their enterprise without having to fake my appreciation, and Millar was kind enough to respond. They rarely strayed far from Texas, he said, but thanked me for asking and said they'd keep it in mind. When, eventually, the course and its whole *raison d'etre* provided the material for my book, *Jock Culture, USA*, I sent them a copy. And now they'd more than returned the favor, making me a character in the strip.

The first panel shows a closed door with a "DO NOT DISTURB" pinned up and a posted sign next to it that proclaims, "NCAA FACULTY REPRESENTATIVES IN CONFERENCE." Above the door is a balloon indicating someone speaking behind it and saying, "SPORTS LIKE INTERCOLLEGIATE FENCING AND GYMNASTICS AREN'T BIG BOXOFFICE, BUT…" In the central panel, there "I" am, on my feet and boldly challenging NCAA policies as counterproductive to the ideals and goals of higher education and the concept of student-athlete. I look just like what I saw in the mirror the day the strip ran--fairly long dark hair, full beard, prominent nose, checked shirt, jeans, jean jacket. Finishing my point to a visibly bored or disgusted audience I say, "…BUT DOES SPORT HAVE TO BE BOXOFFICE? ISN'T THE BASIC IDEA TO PROVIDE CHALLENGE AND CHARACTER ENRICHMENT TO THESE YOUNG STUDENT- ATHLETES?"

In the third panel, the balloon indicates that I am off-screen, saying, "I MEAN, AREN'T OUR PRIORITIES OUT OF LINE WHEN WE…" A group of three good ol' boys are whispering at the end of the conference table. The three-piece-suited one asks, "What does that clown teach?" The bow-tied one says, "Ethics." And the pipe-smoking one gets the strip's last word: "Figures."

The next day, this mini-satire continued. The first panel has the same drawing of the closed door, and the balloon says, "FOOTBALL, BASKETBALL, THEY MAKE A **MINT**." In the second panel, with "me" slumped two seats from the chairman, he says, "SOME OF OUR INTERCOLLEGIATE

SPORTS--YOUR SWIMMING, YOUR GYMNASTICS--COST MEMBER SCHOOLS A **FORTUNE** TO SUBSIDIZE." The third panel has me in close-up, looking like I'm about to explode with rage, vomit, or both, while the two men flanking me are smirking. Panel four shows the chairman in a one-shot, saying, "WHICH BRINGS ME TO AN INTERESTING PROPOSAL FROM THE UNIVERSITY OF SOUTH CAROLINA, ABOUT INTERCOLLEGIATE STOCK CAR RACING."

I wrote a note to Millar, asking, "How did you know what I looked like?" "Bill's psychic," he answered. A couple of weeks later I received a blown-up copy of that first day's strip, signed by both beneath a handwritten message that said, "To Neil Isaacs, whose resemblance is entirely coincidental."

"I" disappeared from the strip after two days, never to reappear. The satiric joke ran for two more days, with Tank interviewing A.J. Foyt, asking where he'd find recruits when tennis and basketball players may be seen on their respective courts, and the punch line is "TRAFFIC COURT." And on the fourth day, Tank reports that the new sport will be introduced with "the whole traditional treatment," including marching bands and cheerleaders chanting, "Put th' pedal to th' metal for yew ess ceeee!!!"

Two questions echoed in my head for a long time afterward. Is this all there is? And, Is this what Warhol meant by fifteen minutes of fame? Whatever the answers might be, I framed the drawing and had it hanging in a prominent spot over my desk for more than a decade. My son Josh, answering my query about what keepsakes he'd like to have from the home, put that drawing at the top of his list. What he's done with it I have no idea. (Note: as I write this in December of 2011, Miller and Hinds have just finished a week's strips that lampoon the idiosyncratic mores of the "JOCK CULTURE.")

XIV

CROSSING THE BAR

At the risk of upsetting any pretense of chronology, I return to an account hinted at earlier in a mention of time spent at Harvard Law School. For a period of four or five years in the late '30's, we shared a two-family house on Edgewood Avenue with the Winnick family, they on the first floor, we on the second, and the attic space divided between us. It was a comfortable arrangement. We were well-matched, two sons each, cordial parents, respectable and respected middle-class folks, politically allied, and members of the same conservative synagogue. We each had a dog, too, but they didn't get along. Our Boots was a quiet, friendly, well-trained Boston terrier; their Spud was a short-hair mixed-breed who barked incessantly. The pets notwithstanding, we all got along famously, Al and Birdie with Mory and Florence, Gil and Eddie with Phil and me.

Al Winnick was a bright lawyer on the rise in New Haven and Birdie a forceful political activist. At some point early on, there arose a fantasy future that focused on a firm called Winnick, Winnick, Isaacs, and Winnick. I was to be the Isaacs in the bunch, a dream of sorts that my parents took to heart, though in their unassuming way they never pressured me about it. Somehow I internalized the idea that the law would be my future but I took no practical steps to get there. And by my senior year at Dartmouth, though signing up to take the LSAT, I had virtually abandoned the whole notion.

I was, however, at a total loss as to what would replace it, and in that frame of mind I almost missed that exam. Walking downtown with my roommate Jack Kiernan for breakfast and nursing a hangover, I noticed a crowd assembling in front of Dartmouth Hall, and Jack said, "Diz, aren't you supposed to be taking that exam?" I was and I did, hungry and head-achy as I was, and my testing skills came through for me big time. I scored in the 97th percentile and on that slim reed was accepted at Harvard despite my mediocre undergraduate record. Mother and Dad were elated, but I told them honestly that I really didn't want to be a lawyer after all. They said they understood, but Dad said, "Don't you think, with the aptitude you've demonstrated, that you owe it to yourself to give law school a chance?"

So that was the premise on which I headed Cambridge-ward, though I had a couple of other less logical reasons: I had nothing better to do and I would be in the neighborhood to pursue my courtship of the elusive Esther. A bonus incentive was that I would not be drafted. The only other application, besides law school, that I had pursued was the Naval Air Cadet Training program. But for that I had been rejected. I passed the physical exam, the night blindness test, and two of the three written exams; my vision and reflexes were superior, and I dreamt of being a carrier-based fighter pilot in Korea.

When I failed a "mechanical comprehension" test, however, I was declared ineligible. In later recruiting periods, the rules were changed so that the written test scores were averaged, and I would have cleared that hurdle. No doubt that the timing of my failure saved my life, given the survival rate in battle of what I had hoped to do. And with that decision came the spiteful determination to avoid serving in the armed forces at all since they wouldn't let me serve the way I wanted to.

From day one at the law school, I hated it. I developed psychosomatic symptoms, couldn't read a page of a text or even a paragraph of a case without being felled by a severe headache. But I was fine when I read what I wanted to read, viz., literature. The realization had grown over the summer that what I really wanted was an education, what I had neglected to pursue in my four Hanover years. So I was starting to fill in gaps in my reading and was working my way through Kafka for starters. I had to laugh when a law school classmate saw a copy of *The Trial* in my desk next to his in our Procedure class, smiled at me, and made a note of the title and author. But when the next week he saw me with *The Great Wall of China* and asked whether that wouldn't be more appropriate for an engineering student, I knew conclusively that I was in the wrong place. That was my last Procedure class, followed quickly by my sudden breach of Contracts.

By the first of November my only presence at the law school was for some Criminal Law classes, because the professor was a histrionic performer, and the moot court where I enjoyed researching my case and trying it. Of course I lost because my argument on behalf of a client was based on a search for justice, while my winning adversary argued from precedent. That was all I needed to know about the law, I thought. Meanwhile, I was planning a marriage for December, applying to graduate schools, reading literature, and demonstrating my knack for testing on the GRE.

I waited until April to submit my formal resignation for a very practical reason. Until I had an acceptance into a graduate program I'd lose my educational deferment and be swiftly drafted. But when I was admitted to the English program at Berkeley, I was free to make my absence known. As it happened, the faculty advisor for our class was also my Contracts professor, the legendary Kaplan whose text was the gold standard for the course. I must have sensed that his celebrity would soar when the character based on him won an Oscar for John Houseman in *The Paper Chase* two decades later, which might account for the prescient excitement I felt as I went to his office to tell him I was leaving.

"Why not stick it out for another month and take the exams?" he said.

"Sir, I haven't been in your class since October. Do you think I could pass Contracts?"

"If you know the principles and can write cogently, you can indeed." And then I delivered a smartass remark that I have regretted ever since.

"Well, I wouldn't want to beat anyone out of a seat on the Law Review."

He didn't laugh, and I was through with law school-- though in typically bureaucratic fashion, based I suppose on precedents, I have never been able to get them to remove my name from the mailing lists for alumni.

And yet. And yet. I have somehow maintained a dilettante's fascination with the law. It has nothing to do with the fact that my son Jonny became an attorney. I think he did so in part to prove he could do something I couldn't, but I am proud of his accomplishments anyway. Now this leads me to the real subjects of this chapter, the occasions when my interest led me to action and that action could even have proven a pathway to fame.

I don't mean to say that I sit around watching Judge Judy on TV, but I do find that novels and movies with climactic trial scenes are powerful for me, in a way similar to the most exciting sporting events. In fact, I think the appeal of both kinds of spectacle involving infinite varieties of outcomes within the rules of engagement often pass beyond cliché to brilliance. The familiar tropes, language, conventions, and the like only serve to heighten the rewards of the unexpected. The resolution of conflict, whether in practical or symbolic formats, is a compelling fulfillment of human aspirations.

So the emergence of Court TV became for me a welcome addition to the pleasures of, say, *To Kill a Mockingbird* or a Super Bowl or a John Lescroart novel or the *Oresteia*. At best, a sensational trial would inspire my active participation. The trial of O.J. Simpson had particular resonance for me because I had used his persona as a prime example of a media-enhanced hero-figure whose athletic feats induced an image of imagined nobility of character and who actually was led to believe that he could get away with anything. That was in my 1978 book, *Jock Culture, USA*. Now here he was, seventeen years later, getting away with double murder.

I actually wrote a letter to Marcia Clark with three suggestions for her closing argument. First, anticipating that Johnny Cochran would make a big point of how much time the prosecution took to make its case in chief, she should respond with an account of how much of that time was occupied by the defense in a deliberate strategy of distraction, dilution, digression, and delay. Second, if O.J. was so distraught when he returned to L.A. the day after the murders, as characterized by the defense, how come he thought it was so important to call Chicago to make sure his golf clubs were being taken care of? Was there something in the bag that was important for him to get back into his possession--or did he have an early tee time? Third, please point out that there was an egregious example of inventing evidence in Barry Scheck's testimony. Purporting to read C.S.I. Dennis Fung's notes about the location of the glove at the Simpson estate, he repeatedly inserted the words "of the" before the word " fence" when the word "fence" was actually used to remind Fung where the glove was found and could mean "at the fence" or "near the fence" or "in the vicinity of the fence," etc. Scheck therefore was misleadingly distorting a report that was assumed to be hard evidence. Then I added a footnote, reminding her that the night before he signed on with the defense's dream team Alan Dershowitz appeared on a TV panel where everything he said assumed Simpson's guilt. Therefore; a review of a tape of that discussion might be useful in confronting Dershowitz on appeal. No acknowledgment, never mind answer; advice ignored. All in vain. Was I motivated out of a wish for justice, or perhaps the wish to secure a walk-on role in one of the great media dramas of its time? Was I acting out my bitterness about Dershowitz whose success in cultivating celebrity put my own failed efforts to shame? In any case, I was bitterly disappointed.

Four years before that, I had been so engrossed by the trial of William Kennedy Smith on a charge of rape that I detected a fatal flaw in the defense's case and wrote a piece about it that appeared in the Baltimore *Sun*. The Kennedy nephew's exculpatory story involved a detailed scene of consensual sex at the family's Palm Beach compound. 0ne concrete detail was the beach towel on which the alleged action took place. But no such prop was ever offered in evidence. Either the investigators failed to recover it or one of the involved parties had managed to disappear it; either way, that piece of material could have provided dispositive testimony. My bias against privileged elite suggested which of those alternatives I believed. Smith's acquittal, like Simpson's, only served to sharpen that bias with cynicism.

In three separate and distinct cases, I was involved in providing testimony of my own as the proverbial expert witness. One took place in Family Court in Montgomery County, where I appeared to present my views on a contested matter of child custody. I happened to be the therapist assigned to work with a troubled family, so my notes on the case would weigh heavily in the judge's decision. I won't rehearse any of the particulars here, but I argued persuasively in favor of limiting the father's access to one of his four children. Unhappy as the whole situation was, it was the isolated opportunity for me to be on the "winning" side, though of course no public acknowledgment could ever be made.

In 1980 I was contacted by a defense attorney from Tampa (Cacciatore, by name, a colorful courtroom figure whom no one ever called "Chicken") to see if I could testify on behalf of a client charged with being an illegal bookie under the Florida RICO statute. He had found my name in a search for scholarly publications, where he found listings of books, chapters, and articles I had written on gambling. I could, indeed, I said, and after reading his material on the case, I found it to be a no-brainer, that this man was no more a professional bookie than the host of my Tuesday night poker game was running an illegal casino. So I appeared for the defense in the Hillsboro County courthouse.

I was not challenged regarding my qualification as "expert" and proceeded to give my testimony, addressing the jury directly with detailed explanations of what constituted the profession of bookmaking and how it was clearly distinguishable from the activities of an inveterate gambler. The defendant was clearly the latter. He was a well-known presence at the local race track, while his sons ran his chain of furniture stores, and the proprietors of the track had at times urged him to accept wagers from punters who otherwise might throw off the parimutuel figures for the track's payoffs to their disadvantage. The defendant also made frequent trips to casinos in Nevada and New Jersey, and he enjoyed the football season when he would accept bets on NFL games from perhaps a dozen of his cronies. He used the newspapers for the point spreads and never laid off his action with professional bookies but risked taking losses when his handle was unbalanced. It was the latter aspect of his habit, however, that drew the attention of the sting operation that had led to his arrest, even though such behavior flew in the face of the state's claim that his gambling was within the statute's definition of racketeering.

I thought I had made the distinctions so plain that the jury couldn't convict a man for a bad habit of his that was not in my view anywhere near criminal behavior. Yet convict they did. The dice were loaded, the deck stacked against him. This RICO sting operation that had occupied a task force for a couple of years had produced several dozen indictments, the better to justify the expense of the operation. Cacciatore's client was the last to come to trial, and every other defendant (none of whom had been charged with illegal gambling) had been found guilty. The jury knew that and gave the prosecutors their perfect game.

Chronology is inverted again because my best chance of gaining some fame through my amateurish involvement with the bar came early on, about midway through my eight-year sojourn in Tennessee. The news came clear across the state from Memphis to Knoxville that a large selection of books had been seized from a prominent bookstore and the owners charged with dealing in pornography. It was one of those periodic outbursts that seem as indigenous to the Volunteer State as the Great Smoky Mountains. I thought of the Scopes trial and wondered who would play the Clarence Darrow role this time around. More to the current climate in the state, I thought of the way Miles Horton of the Highlander Institute had been viciously persecuted and his progressive haven of adult education had been run out of its home in Monteagle near the town of Sewanee.

The lawyers for the defense contacted their colleagues at U-T's law school and asked for someone on the Humanities faculty, someone with a reputation for supporting progressive causes and expert in contemporary literature, to consult with them. If they were forced to go to trial in this matter, that someone would appear as an expert witness. And that someone, thanks to my law school acquaintances, would be me.

I relished the assignment--without consciously thinking of its potential for notoriety--and when I was sent a list of the titles that had been seized I produced a memorandum to report on the relative literary merit of the novels, several of which had appeared on reading lists for courses that I had taught or was planning to teach. To suggest the ignorance displayed in this police action, three of the works labeled pornographic in this seizure were Bellow's *Herzog*, Donleavy's *A Singular Man*, and Baldwin's *In Another Country*. That is a clear indication of how far beyond the usual suspects in the seizure (Genet, Henry Miller, D.H. Lawrence) this police action had stretched the envelope of its philistine taste.

After examining the full list of titles seized, I wrote a fifteen-page report, "Sex in Literature and Obscenity," based on twenty-one titles, finding no example of pornography anywhere. Crucial to the case was Terry Southern's *Candy*, which, I said, "is designed not to corrupt the morals of readers or even to titillate already corrupted readers, but to point up comically and satirically the foolishness of a sex-obsessed society and its literature." "*Candy*," I concluded, "provokes laughter, not prurience."

There is no way to know how persuasive my arguments were, since the State became convinced that it could not successfully prosecute the case. There was, however, one concession. The bookseller involved, a large department store in Memphis, agreed not to sell *Candy* any more, a minuscule loss to them but a surrender of First Amendment rights to free speech.

The news that the charges had been dismissed came as a relief to the progressive community in general, though there was some residual grumbling from supporters of free speech in particular. I may have been the only one to suffer a serious disappointment. I was happy for the result, but unapologetically missed the opportunity to have a day in court, have the media report the elegance of my testimony that was to be instrumental in an acquittal, and have someone say to my children, "Stand up, all you Isaacs kids, your father's passing by."

XV

MAN OF LETTERS

Like Saul Bellow's great protagonist, Moses Herzog, I often respond to what I read or hear or happen to think by writing "letters of the mind." Unlike old man Mose, though, I invariably sit down, write the letters, and send them off. It is not, I assure you, to see my name in print that drives me letterward. I've had many tiny frissons of satisfaction from all I've published and would never list a letter to any editor on my c.v. (as an occasional colleague has done).

Instead, what inspires my inveterate letter-writing is the opportunity to enter into a dialogue with the prominent, the famous, the recognized authority, the public intellectual. or anyone else of note whose "errors" of fact or judgment or logic I can correct, never mind the frequent occurrence of faulty grammar. My vigor as part of the grammar police has waned, however, in the face of the growing tsunami of solecisms that engulfs the eyes of any newspaper reader. King Canute is not my model, and I tend to be more querulous than quixotic. Sometimes, even now, I cannot hold back my dismay at a vulgar error, like the daily crossword in the *Post* assuming that "kudo" is a singular form of *kudos*. That is like calling a member of Jeff Bezos's family a "Bezo," I wrote. Even though Bezos now owns the paper, my bit of wit went unpublished.

In the early days, my letters were primarily concerned with politics and social policy, beginning with my undergraduate campaign against the kneejerk editorial practice of the *Daily Dartmouth*, traditionally manned by what I had to call limousine liberals. Wherever I was in the dozen-odd years after college, I would ply papers like the Providence *Journal,* the New York *Herald Tribune*, and the Knoxville *News-Sentinel* with views about local, national, and international issues. The usual targets are all there: Nixon, Kissinger, Reagan, Bork, Clarence Thomas, just about all the Bushes, Cheney, and right-wing religious zealots by the dozen. In Providence, I took to task the state Supreme Court for its decision to invalidate, on a dubious technicality, all absentee ballots in an election that would otherwise have elected a Republican governor. In Knoxville, tongue in cheek, I congratulated the City

Council for its collective contemporary wisdom, what I called "a brilliant demonstration of conspicuous ostrichmanship," in rejecting a proposal to establish a human rights commission. In all fairness, I must add that the very same council did pass a fair housing ordinance for the city--on a day when our non-official Human Relations Council (during my proud tenure as its vice-president) organized a march on City Hall--the only time in my life that I ever carried a placard.

Certain issues were quick to trigger my typing fingers. About Israel, I could be defensive or vitriolic or passionate or, at my best, coldly analytical. I talk elsewhere here about my series of exchanges in the pages of the War Resisters League publications, finally resigning when their pro-Palestinian stance became so extreme that they began to call Hamas and Hezbollah "freedom fighters." But my clearest statement of policy came in the pages of *Harper's Magazine* in response to an essay by Edward Said, a brilliant Professor of Comparative Literature at Columbia, whose scholarship I much admired, but whose fanatical support of Palestinians led him off the deep end into fanciful historical constructions as the foundations for rather vicious policies that smacked of the "final solution" (which some of us can never, never forget). *Harper's* gave my considered response full expression, though in general as revealed in its monthly "Index" it tends toward an anti-Israel bias itself. Where Said states "facts" which aren't as support for a rhetoric that goes beyond the "moral equivalency" argument, I place the conflict in a context where, even while finding some aspects of Israeli policy abhorrent, I see many Arab governments wary and resentful in non-support of Palestinians. Where the pressure of Israel's enemies reflects a sworn siege unto death, and where deliberate targeting of innocent Israeli civilians includes the barbarism of suicide bombings, I have some sympathy for preemptive Israeli strikes against military targets. I fear that the voices who share my views are becoming more and more isolated, resulting in shriller expressions of anxious outcry. And I wonder if the vision of a Jewish homeland (a Zionist utopia which I never strongly supported) will vanish along with the democratic if flawed society that looked like the mythic "miracle in the desert" I thought I saw twenty years ago even while buses were being bombed in Jerusalem.

I will often weigh in on many of the mistaken notions I see and hear in the media regarding gambling. The hypocrisy, for example, of our professional sports leagues (and I include the NCAA under that rubric) opposing legalized sports betting to "protect the integrity of the game," will often push my letter-writing buttons. The NFL's rise to preeminence was largely implemented by the betting, while the Las Vegas interests became the most important protectors against corruption. To leave the billion-dollar enterprise in the hands of those who operate illegally is to encourage scandals, coups, and fixes, as well as serving to support other criminal activities. Governments, I believe, should not be in the gambling business, but should use their authority in the appropriate practices of licensing, taxing, and rigorously supervising private, transparent enterprises. (Kudos to Adam Silver, the new NBA Commissioner, for his progressive stance on this issue.)

Another arena in which I feel called upon to challenge the media's expressed attitudes is the problematic forum of ideas about mental health, especially in areas where my twenty years as a practicing therapist have given me some confidence in my views. For example, the ongoing debate about the relative merits of medication versus therapy in the treatments of mood disorders (depression, anxiety, et al) will get a knee-jerk response from me about either-or thinking. The most thorough and elegant studies of the matter conclude that the best treatment is almost always likely to be a combination of medication and therapy. In my four years of service on the NIMH's Institutional Review Board, I was amazed at how many protocols crossed my desk with research designs that assumed either-or approaches, neglecting the option of combinations of competing treatments.

As primarily a couples counselor, moreover, I would often have to rise to the occasion of defending my kind of practice against those who advocate marriage-saving as the be-all and end-all of treatment; those who confuse computer-generated matchmaking with science (instead of the cross-listing of self-measured superficialities that they are); and those who conflate couples counseling with eugenic thinking. Such *bêtes noire* may irritate me to the point of crying out against them but those cries are typically voices in a wilderness of the unheard and unpublished.

Finally, among the pet peeves that elicit mail from me, there is the academic issue of confidentiality. In a legal, spiritual, or therapeutic context, honoring confidentiality has significant value. It is fit and proper that the patient, client, or confessant own the privilege--though there are exceptions when risks to innocent people are involved. But in the higher ranges of the groves of academe, confidentiality becomes something else entirely. Faculties make decisions on candidates and manuscripts while being protected against revealing their votes or their reasons for them--this from a profession that aims for the publication of its ideas and theories. Peer reviews thus become disguises for cronyism and supports for exclusivity. Even where faculties are open about their proceedings, their administrations will choose to reverse decisions without answering to anyone about their methods, reasons, or biases. Correspondence on this topic fills the pages of faculty papers, and I have had my say repeatedly therein. But the so-called "black boxes" in which academic decisions on personnel and publication are made remain in the controlling majority.

As the letter-writing habit developed, I began to alternate the missives of developed argument with what I thought were clever one-liners. I consoled myself that though most of the gag-lines would get no ink, at least they'd get some laughs from editors. In one case, the joke was passed on to its butt and evoked a response. In 1961 (on my son Daniel's first birthday, as it happened), I wrote to the *New York Times* Drama Editor, as follows:

> Caroline Burke Swann's note on closing nights was interesting, reflecting a popular point of view. But I don't think any "last-nighter" ever saw "lesser roles...played with Matthew Arnold's 'hard gemlike flame.'" If Arnold had one, he wouldn't have known to call it that until Walter Horatio Pater used the phrase in the famous Conclusion to *The Renaissance*. In Pater's context, it is the equivalent of what he called "Cyrenaicism"--the spirit of intensity of the Renaissance. The phrase occurs in the first sentence of the penultimate paragraph: "To burn always with this hard, gemlike flame, to maintain this ecstasy, is success in life." In Pater's usage it is a highly commendable characteristic; in Ms. Swann's, it has a pejorative suggestion (the preceding conjunction is "and," not "but"); and as for Arnold, well, one can only guess.

Ms. Swann had the good grace to respond, under the letterhead of Brendan Behan's *The Hostage* at the Cort Theatre:

> Thank you for your kind and correct words about BROADWAY'S LAST NIGHTS. You are perfectly right, and I know why I attributed "hard gem-like flame" to Matthew Arnold. It's because of Santayana's essay on Shelley which has always stood out in my mind, in which he quotes Matthew Arnold saying that Shelley is a "beautiful, ineffectual angel beating his wings in a luminous void in vain." In the same article he speaks of burning with a hard gem-like flame and somehow I unconsciously associated it with Arnold. I am going to stay after school and write Walter Pater on the blackboard 500 times!

More than an explanation, this seems like an effective and good-humored display of intellectual superiority.

In a few other instances, my attempts at epistolary wit got printed. The *Herald Tribune* liked this 1960 submission: "The Connecticut State Police have overlooked one important slogan for their highways: LESS SIGNS ON ROAD--MORE EYES ON ROAD." *The Dartmouth Alumni Magazine* went for this 1966 quip: "I was amused at the pun in the February 'Undergraduate Chair': 'hundreds of students [got] a peak at the porn.' At least I assume it was a deliberate pun and not an egregious

Freudian slip. In either case, the Alumni Magazine must be careful, for pornography is erecting its loathed head all over; and I wonder if it should ever be sent through the male."

In 1974 the Washington *Post* got it, with this: "As a grand-nephew of Morris Green, its original producer, I am always happy when *Desire under the Elms* is revived. But what a surprise to find a reviewer referring to Abbie's desperate act (and Medea's) as matricide. Uncle Morris would have laughed with scorn, O'Neill might have scorned to laugh, and Freud would probably have referred the slip to unresolved Oedipal conflicts. Infanticide or filicide, Mr. Coe; matricide is Orestes' number."

Here's one quickie that didn't make the *Post*'s editorial cut: "A headline on p.2 of Metro today reads, 'Women Urged to Take Caution After Attacks.' Shouldn't women be urged to take caution before attacks?" Another one, however, was passed on to the public for a laugh: "In the front page 'Campaign Journal'…Dan Balz wrote of the tastes of baby boomers being 'pedaled by Madison Avenue,' raising some questions. Is this a new sort of ad campaign, biking door to door? Is it like the soldier who either medaled in his sergeant's business or tested his metal in battle? Speeding on the highway, does Balz put the peddle to the mettle? Is there an editor about to be recycled?" I'm afraid I rode that one into the dust.

Obiter Obits and Provoked Connections

I would take delight in following up on obituaries of recently deceased celebrities with tributes derived from personal anecdotes. Ted Straeter comes to mind, along with Dick Darcey and Bob Fachet (see Chapter XVII below for a reprise of these tributes). Then there was Orbison, whom I'd never met but had some inside info about (see Chapter VIII above). Candidly, and obviously, these letters were motivated by the wish to be associated with the departed, while in other cases there was a desire to show off knowledge that the obit writer didn't have. On the one hand, to be mentioned or remembered in the context of those who achieved fame is to achieve a secondary, reflected fame oneself, a kind of fame by association. On the other hand, to add some inside knowledge in the context of a remembrance is a kind of one- upmanship that suggests a familiarity with celebrity. As an example of the latter, I raised some questions about the obit for Wellington Mara:

1. He "learned of the Japanese attack on Pearl Harbor while at a game between the Giants and the Washington Redskins." How long did it take for the news to reach him? I ask because on December 7, 1941 the Giants were losing to the Brooklyn Dodgers in the Polo Grounds.
2. "His father, a legal bookmaker, bought the fledgling New York Giants when the NFL was struggling for a legitimate place in the sports landscape." What makes a bookie "legal"--or was

he some kind of printer/publisher? Did he operate in London? Las Vegas, without the benefit of taking action across state lines? Did the legality end with new legislation that more precisely defined his activities--and did he then close the book? Did it help the NFL's struggle for legitimacy to have a bookie for an owner? Were other "sportsman" owners similarly employed? Was that perchance the beginning of the connection between betting and the NFL that persists as a prime contributor to the success of both ventures?

A little healthy cynicism there, along with the skinny.

Another motivation stands behind those letters that succeeded in drawing a direct response from their targets. To prompt persons of fame or prominence to become pen-pals, even if in a single exchange, may pave one's own way to celebrity. I treasure my responses from Senators Mikulski, Ribicoff, Baker (two of them), and McGovern that bear their cherished signatures. When I wrote to praise William F. Buckley, Jr. for his essay on anti-Semitism while taking issue on a few points, he graciously responded in some detail. When I wrote to Joseph Frank to praise an essay of his and suggested a way to strengthen part of his argument, it triggered a respectful interchange.

Other letters, inspired by the kind of admiration that produces "fan-mail," brought the intellectual richness of connection with the likes of novelist Thomas Berger, book reviewer Carolyn See, and linguist Deborah Tannen. Jerry Klinkowitz (see the John Barth item in "Brief Encounters" below) fits this category, along with three brilliant psychiatrists who are also wonderful writers: Irv Yalom, Gordon Livingston, and Kay Redfield Jamison. My expressed admiration for four other writers initiated correspondence. One is Jay Neugeboren, whose admirable fiction includes one of the best basketball novels I know, *Big Man*. The second is Jerome Charyn, whose series of "Pink Commish" novels are just some examples of his amazing versatility, along with *The Seventh Babe*, arguably the greatest of baseball novels (which I persuaded the University Press of Mississippi to reissue--and for which I wrote an "Afterword") and his book on Joe DiMaggio (which I was proud to vet for Yale University Press). Third, Tom LeClair, whose critical work on post-modern fiction has been justly acclaimed, was a primary inspiration for my course, "Literary Hoops Dreams," with *Passing Off*, the first novel in an accomplished trilogy. Our correspondence led to an amusing exchange of essays in *Aethlon*; to an extended exchange of views and reviews and war- stories; to an introduction to his last publisher who then issued two of my books; and to reports of his current escape from the world of academe as "Professor Ping-Pong" at Susan Sarandon's table tennis emporium cum nightclub in New York. Last but far from least, Alan Lelchuk, one of our most under-rated novelists, whose *Brooklyn Boy* and *American Mischief* are modern classics of the *bildungsroman* and whose *Playing the Game* also elevates the subgenre of basketball fiction, keeps challenging me to come to Hanover for a tennis match (where I might get even with him for sharply critiquing my own efforts at fiction).

In one case, a correspondence began when I was on the receiving end of the admiration. Matt Bruccoli, a prominent literary academic and publishing entrepreneur, wrote to compliment me on a review-essay of the fiction of Irvin Faust (another neglected master). That correspondence ended with an exchange with Matt's widow and the coincidental discovery that he and I were born on the same day in 1931 in the same hospital in the Bronx.

Back in 1963, I was intrigued by a Burton Rouché entry in *The New Yorker*'s "Annals of Medicine" series which discussed déjà vu under the heading, "An Emotion of Weirdness." I wrote words of praise in response but expressed surprise that there was no mention of two seminal if poetic contributions to the subject, Lorenz Hart's lyric for "Where or When" (from *Babes in Arms*, 1937) and Wordsworth's "clouds of glory" passage from his "Intimations of Immortality" ode. The magazine responded that my remarks would be forwarded to the writer, but he, alas, never made acknowledgment.

Let me mention one other letter, though it was a personal one, that I wrote with two hopes of a response (slim and none). Towards the end of my eight- year stay in Knoxville, I wrote to the president of the university. "Dear Andy," I had the temerity to say, "if we have to have an invocation before every football game, why not honor our distinguished studies in the liberal arts by having an invocation to the Muses?" Well, "Slim," of course, had already left town before I did.

The Critics' Critic

By far the preponderance of my letters to editors have to do with a discouraging habit of reading what critics, reviewers, and assorted hacks have to say about the arts, especially literature and movies. Also, by far, the percentage of these letters that go unpublished is the largest in my corpus of correspondence. There are, I believe, two reasons for this relative failure: that the most prominent of critics seem to be regarded as sacred cows by their host publishers (unless there's a contractual obligation that their critics get a pass from hostile criticism); and that my outraged responses to critical misunderstanding, ignorance, and bad taste are among my most vitriolic responses. My wrath runneth over into the most excessive language I can dredge up; no cultural superego restrains my egoistic blasts.

The "Book World" section of the Washington *Post* has been a frequent addressee of my outbursts, but I think it took almost three decades of rejection before its letters column printed my tribute to Joyce Carol Oates in response to a niggling review of *I'll Take You There*. The review (by one Martha Southgate) began with what had become cliché remarks about Oates's prodigious output, as if the quantity of her published books somehow automatically implied a lack of quality. After addressing that illogic, I offered a detailed account of the factual errors in the review, of which there were many. The book may be fiction, I argued, but it is the reviewer's responsibility to be accurate about the factual matters in the fiction. Errors of fact, logic, and omission, along with misguided attempts at establishing contexts or standards of taste, have for more than forty years been staples of my problems with reviewers. And on those grounds I have attacked such movie reviewers as the *Herald Tribune's* Paul V. Beckley and Judith Crist, whose reviews I usually admired but who evoked my rage in a *New York Magazine* review where she resorted to what I called "that cheapest of all journalistic ploys--distortion for the sake of half-assed parody." Nor was the great icon Pauline Kael spared from my spleen. She may have "lost it at the movies" but I had occasion to lose it at her movie reviews in *The New Yorker.* when I found, for example, that her essay on *The French Connection* included many mistakes and that her assessment of it "seems to have been based on some of those mistakes." Five fairly long paragraphs detailed those assertions, and I concluded rather mildly with what I thought was an inarguable point, that a movie must be seen accurately and clearly before assessment can justly be made."

The New Yorker didn't publish that letter. *The New Yorker* has never published a letter of mine (and there have been many). All the way back in 1962 I wrote to the "Department of Corrections" to point out that in the seven sentences given to an anonymous review of Dorothy Baker's *Cassandra at the Wedding* (in "briefly noted"), there were no fewer than five "errors of fact or distortions of material, to say nothing of false assumptions based thereon." I then listed the factual errors, the distortions, and the false assumptions, moving on to opinions I rejected. All this was framed by my argument that reviewers have one responsibility they share with any reporter, that of accuracy.

Half a century later I can list six recent failed attempts to break through what is a kind of magnified glass ceiling. I cite one in full to indicate that even wit, the staple of the magazine's aesthetic, goes unheeded--at least where my target is the unedited prose of a regular contributor:

> Not the least of the many pleasing revelations in Daniel Zalewski's thoroughly detailed and enjoyable profile of Ian McEwan is that during the preparation of the piece Zalewski had moved into McEwan's home. The epiphany arrives in the sentence, "On the first of several visits to Fitzroy Square, McEwan greeted me at the door in a state of genial distraction."
>
> Even more astonishing is the implication that the novelist had moved out and returned only on the occasion of visits to the profiler. McEwan's geniality is apparent in

the exchange of places, but no wonder he was distracted when he had planned to host a party at the home and had to impose on Zalewski to help with the arrangements.

No higher tribute to the civility of the Anglo-American community of writers can be paid.

Nice try, Isaacs, but to no avail. A year later I tried an approach that was both complimentary and complementary, in a short letter praising Peter Schjeldahl's review of the Metropolitan Museum's exhibit of Bronzino's drawings. It gave me the opportunity to discuss the artist's portrait of Lucrezia Ponciatichi, which so entranced Henry James that he made it a centerpiece of his own portrait of Milly Theale in *The Wings of the Dove*.

Cultural edification didn't work either, but two months later I was back on my high horse to protest Jill Lepore's description of couples counseling in the context of a discussion of eugenics. Announcing my bona fides as a licensed credentialed family therapist, I corrected at least four major misconceptions promulgated by Ms. Lepore in what I called "a sad, cynical view of human behavior." Mine was an informed, literate, and professional corrective piece, but found no public audience in the big city.

Finally, most recently, I took exception to Nancy Franklin's review of the dramatic television serial, "The Killing." Ms. Franklin was honestly trying to account for her distaste with the production. Unfortunately, though she noted that the show is a faithful translation of a Danish production, transplanted to the Pacific Northwest, she failed to place the original in its immediate context of Scandinavian crime fiction. I mentioned the international best-sellers of Stieg Larsson, Henning Mankell, and Peter Hoeg, and added the popular work of K.0. Dahl, Karin Fossum, Anne Holt, Camilla Lackberg, and Jo Nesbo. My point was that the genre has "a firm set of conventions that has found a warm, receptive audience abroad. Against the backdrop of forbidding climate and societal angst, flawed and conflicted protagonists struggle with their own messy lives while pursuing variously perverted perps." The TV show seemed to me to have fluently translated the central elements of atmospherics and complex characterizations and could have been acknowledged if not praised for that.

Again, no recognition. Lepore and Franklin, as staff writers, may be immune to correction, but why, I wondered, was Jonathan Franzen similarly privileged? Just a week before the "Killing" letter, I had strongly reacted, barely short of regurgitation, to Franzen's long piece called "Further Away." "Bad enough that he trades on his friendship with David Foster Wallace, a far better and much more important writer," I wrote, "to enhance his own reputation, he makes his response to Wallace's suicide the center of that devastating event." I called such a display "toxically Boswellian." And I went on from there to attack the content of the display, the darkness to which he retreated, the remote refuge named for Alexander Selkirk, Defoe's inspiration for *Robinson Crusoe*. Franzen's Wikipedia-like summary of English prose fiction focuses on that novel as a model of his own stranded struggles, using Crusoe's experiences to frame a report on how he wrestled with such trials as homesickness, ordeals with weather and terrain, boredom and depression, the failures of his expensive camping equipment, and above all his heroic efforts to mourn Wallace, to find some balance between his adulation of and anger at his friend.

One of my problems with Franzen's artifice is the confusion over whether he fancied himself playing the part of Crusoe, presenting his "true" adventures as "written by himself," or put himself in the place of Defoe, who was pressured over time to acknowledge his fraudulent invention. In other words, I said, "in *either* case, can one accept the accuracy of what Franzen narrates as taking place when he is alone on the island (if he actually was)? The best descriptive writing in the whole piece happens to be found in these very passages, which suggests the conclusion that it is, in fact, fiction."

I was led to the reasonable conclusion that Franzen, as an escape from the burdens of his fame and a relief from the wearisome whirlwind book tour, had sought a place where he could write this very "essay" (presumably handsomely underwritten by the magazine). "*The New Yorker*," I said finally, calls the piece 'Reflections.' Indeed, what Franzen sees in the glass of his narcissistic gazing is the overblown balloon of his ego."

I was not surprised that it was not published, not just because of my track record of losing entries, but also because I was questioning the magazine's own editorial choices. On the other hand, I was disappointed, because I thought that I had got it exactly right and that it was something that should be said and heard, a kind of truth to power and a diatribe against the sense of entitlement that privileges the most arrant form of self-aggrandizement. Franzen continues to confirm my diagnosis. In a recent blurb for Alice Munro, he says, "Reading Munro puts me in that state of quiet reflection in which I think about my own life: about the decisions I've made, the things I've done and haven't done, the kind of person I am, the prospect of death. She is one of the handful of writers, some living, most dead, whom I have in mind when I say that fiction is my religion." This is as flagrant a demonstration of pathological narcissism you could find: two sentences containing nine first-person references about another writer who apparently has value or even exists only in relation to that fully advertised self.

Somehow, though I've been so persistently scorned by *The New Yorker*, I feel worse about my rejections by *The Atlantic*. What makes it worse is that the latter reserves more space for readers' commentary, allows for longer missives, and more often includes responses from writers and editors than the former. I even began one letter by praising *The Atlantic* for publishing a statement of its rationale for publishing reviews. The occasion for my observation, however, was my astonishment at finding, sandwiched between a pair of "unusually long" reviews concerning Proust and Cervantes, a segment devoted to the self-titled "Dr. Laura." I was reminded, I said, "of the Woody Allen character, the poet Manqué Sean O'Shawn, who disdained his mother's deathbed plea that he renounce his calling in favor of selling vacuum cleaners, but who climactically, at an international poetry conference, sold a Hoover to both W.H. Auden and Wallace Stevens."

I went on to lament in general the standard of "popularity" as justifying certain reviews and in particular the attention paid to this advice maven. "Her hypocrisy aside," I said, "it is the judgmental mean-spiritedness and Procrustean closed-mindedness that make her anathema to psychotherapists. She serves as a poster-person to remind us why we are not in the advice business. Our offices are filled with people who are depressed, damaged, even dumfounded, as products of marriages marked by animosity, antipathy, addiction, anxiety, and anti-social behavior--but who stayed the course 'for the sake of the children.' And we all know people who have thrived in homes of parents who have given marriage and family life a second chance. Granted that stability, structure, continuity, and security are important for children, how can one listen with respect to someone who constructs best-case scenarios for *all* maintained marriages and worst-case scenarios for *all* second, 'step-, or blended families?" Popularity alone, I argued, should not outweigh a lack of wisdom, decency, and fair-mindedness, not to mention a total lack of clinical experience.

Was I too harsh? Is it possible to say so in defense of a magazine that published a rave review of Dale Peck's *Hatchet Jobs*, a collection of the incomparably nasty attacks on writers that have made Peck notorious? Benjamin Schwarz embraced Peck as "Mencken's heir," which I judged as elevating "sophomoric if not puerile *merde*-slinging to the level of mordant iconoclasm." There followed a detailed listing of Peck's obscene attacks on major literary figures, including his indictment of much classic American fiction as "narcissism." This led to my conclusion, in which I warned any prospective Peck readers of the critic's revealing display of his own clinically diagnosable Narcissistic Personality Disorder: "...a passage in which Peck rejects the notion that *The Age of Innocence* and *Moby-Dick* may 'exist in any but the most obvious relationship to each other (the relationship in this case being that they both happen to be sitting on my desk).' The solipsism is apparent, the pathology flagrant. Caveat lector." Peck and Franzen: what a pair!

An *Atlantic* reviewer named Sandra Tsing Loh (whom I couldn't help thinking of as "Sweet Chariot") provoked my ire on more than one occasion, for her unfortunate phrasing (e.g., "Talmudic awe," "Falstaffian airspace," "literally falls in love"), her misplaced embrace of popular culture, and her ignorance about writers' cultural frames of reference. She was at her most revealing in printed responses to other letter-writers' corrections, but was never given the opportunity to answer unpublished me. But among the *Atlantic*'s featured reviewers my favorite target of letters was Christopher Hitchens.

I have always had great respect for this most formidable of iconoclasts. I admired his wit, his debating skill, his erudition, his rhetoric; I enjoyed his take-down of Mother Teresa, applauded his indictment of Henry Kissinger; and I couldn't help but be impressed by his stalwart allegiance to atheism in the face of his own terminal cancer. Even when I deplored his shocking support of our Iraq war (as did most of his friends) I accepted that aberration in the context of his personal integrity and loyalty (as in his providing sanctuary for Salman Rushdie after the fatwa).

And yet some of his literary judgments cried out for angry ripostes, especially his denigration of the fictions of Philip Roth and John Updike, main pillars of my literary generation. In one case, when I fully acknowledged that I shared his delight in Nabokov's *Lolita,* I took him to task for extolling the "many pleasures" he found in reading Alfred Appel's annotated edition. I confess that my reluctance to honor Appel dates back to his first book, a study of Eudora Welty's work that was rushed into print to secure tenure for him at Stanford. It failed to do so primarily because, on further review, it proved to be largely plagiarized from Ruth Vande Keift's seminal volume (not to mention other borrowings from Robert Penn Warren and even from yours truly). His academic career nevertheless prospered at Columbia and Northwestern, and he earned his scholarly reputation for his studies of Nabokov and such broader cultural interests as American jazz.

His annotations of *Lolita*, a close reading based significantly on personal interviews granted him in Switzerland by his former Cornell professor, were extensive, detailed, often derivative, and occasionally illuminating. But sometimes obtuse, misguided, naive, or just plain wrong! I listed many of these in my letter, concluding that Nabokov must have enjoyed putting on his acolyte "with naÿve assertions, knowing they will be taken as gospel, masking a god-like George Burns irony with Gracie Allen simplicity."

Even Hitch gets fooled, as when he accepts as a "discovery" (via Appel) that Nabokov didn't know that Girodias published "erotica" at the Olympic Press. Sez who, without tongue in cheek? As a final example of Appel's misses, I point to the last annotation in the book, regarding "the native illusionist, frac- tails flying...." Appel notes that *frac* is French for 'dress coat' and that Nabokov is here wittily demonstrating "that the 'native illusionist' is now an internationalist" and that it is "just that Nabokov (and this edition) should conclude with a joke...."

On whom is the joke? "The homophonous frock-coat," I wrote, "is standard American for several garments, including a conventional costume for vaudeville comedians. Nabokov may never have seen Irwin Corey, but the image of vintage Groucho Marx, frock-tails flying, is clearly seen in this passage."

There was no action at the magazine and no word from Hitch. Some seven years later, I contrived to get a copy of the letter put into his hands by my wonderful wife, who in the course of treating him in her role as oncology nurse had become his friend. He read it, Ellen said, and reported his entire comment: "Very interesting." However cryptic, it was gratifying to me; I took it as praise from Caesar.

Unlike *The New Yorker* and *Atlantic*, *Harper's* has been kind enough to give me space among its printed letters. Maybe I've earned some attention as a repeat winner of the contests to solve Richard Maltby's unfailingly clever monthly creations of cryptic puzzles. In any case, the letters editors have published on occasion my differences with the magazine's reviewers. When I took exception to Jennifer Szalai's negative take on Ian McEwan's *Saturday,* a carefully edited version of the letter appeared, along with Ms. Szalai's response. My harshest language had been edited out, while my commendation for a reviewer's impulse to be iconoclastic remained. The response took issue with my assertion that when she said McEwan "creates worlds in which ambiguity is banished" she missed the prominently ambiguous--or at least ambivalent--features of *Saturday*." She then claimed that her point referred to form, not content, which was surely not a distinction made in her global assertion. "Ambiguity...might be everywhere in *Saturday*, but...unambiguously paraded about for everybody to see."

I wrote again, thanking *Harper's* for allowing the exchange to go forward, but had two crucial points to assert. One was to parse her chop-logical distinction between form and content. The other was that they had edited out a major objection to the review: the claim that all those who jumped on the bandwagon of praise for *Saturday* "hadn't really...*read* it (her emphasis)." In my view, a blanket claim that all who disagree with the reviewer are less intelligent readers should *always* be unacceptable in a review.

The magazine had given enough space to the issue, however, and my second go was a no-go, unprinted and unacknowledged. Similarly, on a subsequent occasion, I wrote to take slight offense that David Thompson, whose high regard for the movie *The Night of the Hunter* I happened to share. Yet I felt that he had significantly downplayed the contributions of James Agee, whose screenplay was used by Charles Laughton as an explicit guide on how to shoot the whole thing--and I got in a plug for Davis Grubb's original novel that was the basis for the script.

I was pleased to see the letter printed in full. But here's the rub: I had added a postscript to point out a remarkable flaw in another piece from the same issue of the magazine. It was Vince Passano calling Pat Cooper "the only Italian- American comedian I ever heard of." "It seems a mistake," I wrote, "to make a public confession of ignorance. I thought of Charlie Manna and Jerry Colonna, not to mention the half-paisanos Lou Costello and Jay Leno. But is it possible, even at this late date, never to have heard of Jimmy Durante?"

I suppose enough is enough when it comes to indulging a regular reader and correspondent with column inches. I count my blessings, as my Grandma Isaacs often advised. And now, even when I have virtually given up on political letters and playing the grammar policeman and tossing out one- liners, I am likely to continue the occasionally gratifying compulsion to critique the critics. Maybe, in some fantasized hall of fame for writers of letters to editors, I might win an iota of celebrity.

XVI

BURT AND BROOKS; THE TOSH AND DOLLAR BILL

The justification for these pairings will become clear as the chapter unfolds. It all began at a regular Tuesday night poker game in Silver Spring, though it sounds like a scene from *The Graduate*. My old friend, Burt Dietch, knowing that I had finished my Grace Paley book, asked me what I was planning to do next. I said I didn't know.

"Back to the world of sports?" he said. He had been a sportswriter for his college paper at UConn and was proud of my work in the field. "How about baseball? You haven't touched that, and it's the game you know best--except for poker."

"I don't think so. Everything worth doing on baseball has been done and done again."

"Well, I have one word for you." Dramatic pause. "Batboys."

I had known Burt since fourth grade in Mrs. McQueeney's class at Roger Sherman School. We had moved from Edgewood Avenue to Boulevard that summer, and my walk was usually down Whalley Avenue and then over Norton to the school. Since Burt lived on the Goffe Terrace side of Norton, we often walked that last block and a half together. Joel Leibling lived on Ellsworth near Maple, and I sometimes walked down Elm Street and met up with Joel on the way to school. Burt and Joel were already good friends, and by the time we started junior high we were a regular threesome.

Augusta Lewis Troup Junior High was several blocks further down toward the center of New Haven, and when Burt, Joel, and I walked together we were a sight to behold, two precociously full-grown six-footers flanking a scrawny little kid. Our friendship extended past school hours to the playgrounds, usually either grassy Edgewood Park or the larger dirt-covered park at Goffe and Winthrop. We played lots of baseball, some touch football, and no basketball. Playground basketball was a thing of the future in New Haven, though a couple of years later I would be playing on the indoor court of the Jewish Center Midgets or occasionally at the Dixwell Community House in inter-racial competition.

There was no Little League yet, and our baseball games were hardly that at all, sometimes no more than four or five kids, with one pitching and one batting while the others had to make a set number of plays in the field to get up to hit while the previous batter took the mound. No mound, really, just a roughly approximated sixty feet six inches from the makeshift plate. There was a backstop, which helped, though you wanted to hit every pitch instead of chasing the ball down--we rarely had more than one ball.

The truth is that we did more horsing around than playing ball, and that's where my father would get angry with me. He'd come by the park and pick me up on his way home from the office, and he'd find me picking on Burt, a bantam rooster sparring with a premature heavyweight. My brother had dubbed him "Man-Mountain Dietch." Heavy-set but not fat, he didn't bother to defend himself; my blows were harmless; I doubt I ever raised so much as a faint bruise. But Dad would see me striking my friend, who never ever hit back. It didn't matter that it was all in good fun, that we'd both be laughing, or that despite my size I was kind of a ringleader of the group, the kid with the ideas for what to do and where to go. Dad would yell at me when I got in the car, "How can you treat your friend that way? You don't deserve to have such a good-natured boy as a friend."

To me he was the proverbial gentle giant, though he wasn't all that big, just precociously mature. He remained my father's favorite of all my friends right through high school, though by the time we were juniors at Hillhouse we had gone separate ways, still friends but running with different crowds. The high school fraternity system had something to do with that. Burt and Joel were in Mu Sig with Jerry Sachs, and I was in Delta Rho with Marty Danzig and Jerry Weiner. Still, we'd see each other in school, played against each other in the fraternity basketball league, and went to some of the same parties and dances. Burt wrote a sports column for the Mu Sig newsletter, and when he picked me for the all-star hoops team I knew it was more a token of friendship than a rigorous assessment of ability.

Burt played some football for Hillhouse, and I didn't see much of him senior year. Both of us headed north to college, he to UConn at Storrs and I straight up the Connecticut River to Hanover, New Hampshire. As I learned much later, neither of us had been particularly happy with our choice. But in the summer after our sophomore year we came together in an odd venue.

Both of us were at loose ends, doing dreary work during the day and aimlessly hanging out at night. He had transferred and would be off to Cincinnati in the fall, and aside from the few days I spent on the Vineyard pursuing my infatuated courtship of the elusive Esther I had little to interest me of an evening--except for the poker games that seemed to materialize a couple of times a week. I hadn't realized that

Burt was a player, and perhaps he hadn't been before that summer, so I was surprised when he turned up at the table one night.

Most of the guys I played with had been in the same circle of action for years, and they included as many from my brother's generation as from mine. Phil was in the middle of his MFA program at Yale Drama School but not living at home. He was renting a mobile home in Branford, and there, on a memorably hot occasion, Burt, Phil, and I played three-handed poker through the night. Desperate for action and collectively down on our luck in several ways, we had exhausted all potential alternatives and ended up in those cramped quarters, playing for quarters.

It had never been comfortable for me to play in the same games as my brother--I was always silently critiquing his play and worrying about his losing ways--but somehow it seemed all right to be teaming up to take a little of Burt's money. Not only gentle but generous to a fault, Burt was the kind of player who never folded a hand if there was even the remotest possibility he could draw a winner at the end. And that night he did just that, hand after hand, catching the perfect card, beating the brothers Isaacs like a pair of snare drums, the only rim shots being the loud expressions of Phil's anger.

That was 1951. Fast forward a quarter century, and we were both, unknown to each other, living in Silver Spring MD. One of the annoying things about relocating is having to establish a whole new set of healthcare personnel. Fortunately, friends had recommended their dentist, Arthur Dubit, and when I went for a first visit and he discovered I had grown up in New Haven, he asked if I knew his very dear friend Burt Dietch.

Our reunion was especially pleasant because the old warm feelings were still there. He was the same gentle, engaging guy I remembered. And he still liked to play poker. He had had several entrepreneurial ventures, including some success as an inventor of small household items, and now operated a successful wholesale carpet business. It did not take long for him to get a seat at the Tuesday night game, where he was a welcome, affable addition, and not the foolishly loose player I remembered. Such good company he was that the whole climate of the game was improved. And now he was setting me up for another flirtation with fame

So, batboys. Knowing Burt's history of good and marketable original ideas, I gave it some thought and did some preliminary research. There was so little on record from this potential source of baseball history and clubhouse lore that I thought the only obstacle would be finding the sources to start with.

And just a few phone calls told me that there was no problem. Equipment and clubhouse managers, who are in charge of the batboys, ball-boys, and clubbies (as the lowest ranks of the staff are called) are generally proud of the kids they've hired, especially the ones who stayed around for multiple seasons, and liked the idea of getting them some ink. Each call gave me several other numbers to call and I was off and running.

It was an exciting and rewarding process of education. I won't go into detail here, since it's all in print in two books (*Innocence and Wonder: Baseball through the Eyes of Batboys* and *Batboys and the World of Baseball*). The latter is a serious work of cultural history in a series of "Culture Studies" from the University Press of Mississippi, treating the baseball clubhouse as a subculture of its own, with firm traditions, initiation rituals, language, values, and a code, much of it mirroring the subculture of law enforcement, including a code of silence, an *omertà*. No wonder the most common career of former batboys, next to those who wangle their way into long-term service with the game itself, is law enforcement. The former is an oral history, the product of more than two hundred interviews, with men and boys who worked for thirty- six professional teams in a period spanning more than sixty years.

The second book, I thought or hoped, would piggyback on the first and get more attention than most scholarly tomes. Indeed it gave me a brief moment of contact with fame, in the person of Senator Paul Simon of Illinois. The Press had arranged for two appearances for me at the mammoth booksellers' convention in Chicago in 1995. The first was an hour time-slot in the great hall where booksellers lined up to have their complimentary copies signed by the authors, themselves lined up at the head of a dozen or so queues. It was my good fortune to be placed next to the Senator, whom I much admired, and whom I had the pleasure of chatting and exchanging copies with. As it happened, my queue was twice the length of his, an embarrassment to me, but I laughed it off as being an indication of the booksellers wanting a free Christmas present for their sons back home.

The second event was a signing the next day at the grand old Blackstone's on Michigan Avenue, which I was to share with a local sportswriter with his new book on Chicago inner-city basketball. This event lasted two hours, and no one showed up--for either author. Okay, I thought, people might want to have this book of mine, but they won't want to buy it, signed or not. At least I had an excerpt published in the journal *Witness* and then reprinted in a book called *Sports in America*.

Innocence and Wonder, however, had a fairly successful run as a novel approach to the national pastime. It was listed with favor in several omnibus reviews of baseball books and even got a notice in *Harper's Magazine*. Sales? Not so much, though it might have had a longer shelf life had the publisher not sold its whole line to a company with no interest in sports.

I had traveled as far west as St. Louis and Kansas City for live interviews, though I also solicited audiotapes and written responses from a wider field. I was fortunate enough to track down, while they were still alive and lucid, old men who respectively had been batboys for the 1916 pennant-winning Brooklyn Dodgers (aka Robins), for Ty Cobb's Detroit Tigers, for the Pittsburgh Pirates of Paul Waner and Pie Traynor, and for the St. Louis Cardinals of the Gashouse Gang era. The last, Butch Yatkeman, had served for many years as clubhouse manager for the Cards, and the home clubhouse in Busch Stadium is named for him.

I was entertained and edified by the recurrent themes of the tales told in up- close and personal glimpses of the game and its heroes. Some of the Hall of Famers were universally extolled in these versions, such as Hank Greenberg, George Brett, Ted Williams, Willie Mays, Sparky Anderson, and Cal Ripken, while other stars got consistently bad reviews, including Joe DiMaggio, Mike Schmidt, Ozzie Guillen, and (surprise!) Barry Bonds.

One player, once a batboy, who is unanimously praised and respected by inside baseball folks, is Brooks Robinson. I was told over and over, not only by Orioles personnel but by those who'd known him in visiting clubhouses, that his public image is exactly what he is in private. As advertised, he returned my call promptly and cordially invited me to come see him in his office, then wouldn't make me wait a minute when I arrived a little early.

He reminisced about several of the batboys he knew well and how they'd succeeded after their clubhouse days. He went into some detail describing all the things the kids did for the team and individual players, then said that you wouldn't see it on the back of any baseball card but long before he played on any team in York or San Antonio he had carried the bats for teams his daddy played on in Little Rock. His "first teams," he said, "were the Fire Department and the Riverside Nursery teams."

I asked him if he would write a foreword for the book, and he said that he wasn't a very good writer. Just tell me what you'd like to say, I said, and I'll write it up for you--like I'm doing with all my other interviews. And then I'll run it by you to see if you approve before we go to press. Trusting soul that he is, he accepted my word on this (a trait that has put him into financial difficulties for relying on handshake deals), and I didn't let him down. The Foreword is almost entirely in his own words, anyway, and he was happy to sign off on it.

When Ellen and I delivered his complimentary copies to him, we brought along a 22" x 17" print of the famous Norman Rockwell cover for the *Saturday Evening Post* that shows him signing a baseball for a youngster in the first row of the stands. "Gee, thanks Brooks" is the title. He signed it, "Neil and Ellen, My Best Always. Nice to see you. Thanks for everything, Brooks Robinson," with a bold underline. Framed, it holds pride of place in our modest collection of baseball memorabilia. The writing has the backward slant of a lefthander. Few people know that Brooks, who batted and threw right-handed throughout his career, was a natural-born southpaw. Rockwell got it right, showing him signing the ball with his left hand.

My dear old friend Burt Dietch died prematurely a few years ago. I treasure the memory of how he beamed with pride at having been, as he said, the godfather of this enterprise. It was one of many gifts in his generous legacy to his friends. He steered me to two books and enabled me to inherit a new friend, Brooks Robinson.

* * * * *

One thing led to another, to summon up the appropriate cliché. It was back to basketball after the baseball rounds, with a new godfather but a repeat publisher. Masters Press, before it abandoned SportsWorld, gave me another shot. They had liked the way I worked--meeting deadlines, carefully proofreading, supplying every required signed release from my sources, furnishing exemplary photos to illuminate the text--so when I came to Tom Bast with a suggestion for another "mostly oral" sports history, he shook my hand and said we had a deal.

The subject was to be what is known as the "pioneer era" of the NBA, its first ten years of struggling to exist, 1946 to 1956. The godfather was the remarkable Bill Tosheff, co-rookie of the year in 1952, but more important the leader of a group of veterans called the Pre-1965 NBA Players Association. Not to be confused with other groups, these eighty-five men were the ones who had never received recognition from the league in the form of even the most modest inclusion in pension plans. They also happened to include those who needed financial help the most, but had never reaped the benefits of the extraordinarily successful commercial operation which would have died in its infancy without their sacrifices to keep it barely viable.

Tosh had a full roster of his members and urged them all to cooperate with my efforts, hoping that any publicity generated by the book would assist his ongoing campaign for a small share of the fortune being amassed for pro basketball players and especially the greedy proprietors of the business. Almost three quarters of the forty interviews included in the book are the direct result of Tosh's efforts.

I was not completely without other resources. My friend and colleague Jack Russell, son of the first Boston Celtics coach, the legendary Honey Russell, gave me several leads along with his own memories of those trying times. I was lucky to find that Zelda Spoelstra, who worked for Maurice Podoloff when the league was formed, was still employed in its offices. Her steadfast loyalty to her boss earned me her favor since I had interviewed Mr. Podoloff several times, published a favorable profile of him, and painted a flattering portrait of him in my novel, *The Great Molinas*. (Those interviews and the profile, with Zelda's cooperation, became the text which forms his presence as the final contributor to *Vintage NBA*.) My friendship with Arnold Heft gave me access to other former officials, and I was also able to track down two writers who splendidly covered the NBA beat back in the day, Harold Rosenthal and Leonard Lewin, as well as the historic "voice" of the game, Marty Glickman.

As with the baseball books, I took great pleasure in the process of meetings and compilations. It was a treat to hear the inside basketball talk from the great Red Holzman, the inimitable Al McGuire, the canny Zeke Sinicola, the incomparable Dolph Schayes, and the masterful Dutch Garfinkel who first showed me--in a summer game in the mountains when I was a camper--what pro basketball could be. But throughout the process and far beyond, my growing friendship with Tosh more than made the whole enterprise worthwhile by itself.

In the decade and a half after I met him I never gave up pressuring him to write his own book, with or without my collaboration, to tell the story of his incredible life. He was a natural-born storyteller anyway, but there is almost too much to tell. From Gary, Indiana, the heart of "Da Region," which he called a "beautiful resort area," he enlisted in the Army Air Corps in 1943 and did a lot of flying in the war and a lot of growing up, too. So when he got out, he chose to go to college instead of accepting an offer from the Chicago Cubs for his promise as a pitcher. At Indiana University, as a walk-on, in his first year he became a starting quarterback in football, a starting guard in basketball, and a varsity baseball pitcher.

I won't list his achievements as an undergraduate, but they were many. Drafted by the Indianapolis Olympians, he was on hand when Alex Groza, Ralph Beard, and three others were arrested for being implicated in the college basketball point-shaving scandals and subsequently banned from the NBA. Tosh struggled on with the team, contributing to their relative success despite the loss of their two brilliant all-stars, and during his tenure in the league also pitching for the Indianapolis Indians of the AAA International League (and rooming with Herb Score).

Tosh may have been an extremely gifted and able athlete, but at the time financial success was beyond the reach of someone with those qualities. So his appetite for adventure and his entrepreneurial spirit took over, and his experiences on three continents in the succeeding years would make for fascinating reading. It was his wish, however, to focus on his long-suffering, frustrating, and ultimately rewarding struggle to get the NBA to answer to what a few writers have called the league's "dirty little secret" and acknowledge the contributions of his cohort of fellow players and reward them financially. There had been some successes, both collectively and individually, and he called them his proudest moments, but he lamented that more than half his original members had died before they could be included in the arrangements he had achieved.

In his quest to expose the league's abuses of its oldest veterans, including denying some of them credit for time served in the armed forces which is supposed to be included in calculating their years of service to the league, Tosh pursued not only mass media exposure but also political and even legislative action in Congress. When I joined him in the latter effort, I was, frankly, not only obeying the voice of my conscience but also grasping at the straws of possibility for another attempt at appearing in the limelight of media exposure and the long-sought-for moments of fame.

Tosh had persuaded Congressman William Lipinski of Illinois that it was right and fair for the people's representatives to take action in support of his crusade. Lipinski, appropriately enough, put the case before his colleague from Illinois, Harris Fawell. Of the seventy-four members of the Committee on Education and the Workforce, chaired by Bill Goodling of Pennsylvania, the Subcommittee on Employer-Employee Relations was chaired by Fawell.

A public hearing was what we wanted, and with the approval of Congressmen Goodling and Fawell that is what we got. An enthusiastic committee aide, David Frank, worked hard at getting the word out so that there would be a significant media presence, and he promised us that it would happen. July 16, 1998 would be our moment in the sun, and we eagerly anticipated real-time television via C-Span as well as videotaping by the major networks, CNN, and ESPN, and reports by at least a half dozen representatives of print media.

I took great care in preparing my testimony. I knew that I was going to be the cleanup hitter in our batting order of witnesses, the anchor leg in our tag-team relay. Leading off, Tosh would present the nuts and bolts of the case, after which John Ezersky and Walt Budko would tell their personal and moving tales of woe and disrespect and discrimination. It would be up to me to provide a convincing argument that would be appealing and persuasive to the conscience of the committee.

I thought I would go for a quick laugh at the start, and so I said, "Mr. Chairman, and Members of the Committee, ever since as a student I saw my first televised committee meeting, I've always wanted to say those words." I got my laugh, but just a smattering. There was nothing near the promised and hoped-for audience, no video cameras, no radio mikes, and as far as I could tell, no sportswriters. I had even greeted those committee members I mentioned largely in absentia. Of the dozen members of the subcommittee itself, there were never more than two in attendance at any one time during our testimony.

Disappointed but not terribly surprised, I went on with my allusion to those dramatic Army-McCarthy hearings and their star performer, Joseph Welch, the Army counsel. "Now," I said, "I think it's appropriate to quote from that memorable event and borrow some words from that historic occasion and address them in absentia to Mr. David Stern. Have you no shame? Have you no sense of decency?"

If anyone got it, it must not have seemed funny because I heard nary a chuckle, and in my cynical mind I dismissed the whole discourse as pointless to an audience that was tone-deaf to history.

Nevertheless, I offered a carefully designed testimony that spent at least half my time on providing a historical perspective, charting the origins and early struggles of the NBA in counterpoint to the enormous financial success of the present-day enterprise.

Strategically, I gave credit to the league for recognizing and honoring service in the armed forces of this nation. I took issue, however, with the notion that only service that interrupted a professional career should count. "I find it no less patriotic or honorable when careers are shortened by military service that took place prior to rookie seasons," I said, adding that returning to college after service and then entering the pros should not exclude the time in service since intercollegiate basketball is clearly the main minor league supplying the pros with players.

Historical context also meant, I said, that in the decade when the league began, "virtually all able-bodied, that is, sports-capable, men were liable to have served in World War II or the Korean War, or both." And then I took the league to task for its sliding scale of years served as a criterion for eligibility in its pension plan: "Only in a state of amnesia or sublime arrogance can it be argued that five years of service from these men must be required for participation in a pension plan that includes players from the post-1965 period with three or four years of active play."

I dealt next with David Stern's oft-repeated argument that it would be "highly unusual for any business to provide new pension benefits to employees who worked in the business years ago." All that needed to be said was a listing of the many ways in which the NBA is indeed a "highly unusual" operation. I likened the league's position to defendants in infringement of copyright suits "who argue that their engineers and scientists would have come up with the same discoveries eventually, anyway, so why should we pay royalties?" The veteran players, on the other hand, are like discarded ex-spouses who worked to put their mates through professional schools only to be denied the fruits of their labor when their exes reach the highest levels of income.

Only one question was addressed to me by the committee. Chairman Fawell, who also wondered about how MLB and the NFL dealt with these matters, asked about Stern's argument that there is a "slippery slope" to the time served issue, that if we grant three years, why not two, and that collective bargaining should deal with it. My response was twofold, that all eras should in all fairness use the same measuring stick, and that a slope moves in two directions, that management could say five years wasn't enough and raise the bar to six, seven, and so on.

Was this all an exercise in futility? Perhaps so, despite the committee's publication of a 64-page pamphlet that recorded the proceedings, available from the U.S. Government Printing Office (and never mind that my name is misspelled in the appendix). The lack of media coverage clearly burst our balloons of hope. The fact that both houses of Congress passed supportive resolutions was nice, but since there was no muscle attached to these conscientious declarations the league was free to ignore it--which of course it did year after year, as the surviving cohort dwindled.

As part of my vain wish that this appearance would earn me a modicum of notice in the public awareness, I had quoted extensively from the foreword to *Vintage NBA*, written by none other than Senator Bill Bradley. Just as I had identified Brooks Robinson as my prime target for a possible foreword to the batboys book, I had focused on a genuine hero of our times, in my view, the junior United States Senator from New Jersey. Bradley's basketball credentials were impeccable. At Princeton he had been, arguably, among the best college players in history and as a New York Knickerbocker he had been the consummate team player, whose acumen in addition to his skills provided the glue for individual stars such as Earl Monroe, Walt Frazer, Willis Reed, and Dave DeBusschere, bringing Red Holzman's coaching strategies into tactical accomplishment on the floor en route to the NBA Championship.

I was awed by his intellectual brilliance as well. I admired his book, *Time Present, Time Past*, which despite my disagreement with some of his emphases, was the best political/philosophical autobiography I had ever read (until *The Audacity of Hope*). Basically progressive in his views, he would be likely, I thought, to support Tosheff's campaign for equity for those in greatest need versus the oligarchically imposed stratification of rewards prevalent in the league's policies. And so he was. Working through his young aide, Elizabeth Badavas, I was able to get my request to him and an exchange of correspondence resulted in his agreement to provide some wise and caring introductory words. I think what finally sold him on the project was my pledge to donate a third of any of my royalties from the book to the cause of the pioneer players' drive for inclusion in the league's pension plan.

With excitement and a healthy dose of pride, I made an appointment to deliver in person a copy of the book to the Senator's office in the Dirkson Building. And so I did, with what was for me a surprising result. He graciously shook hands and asked me to sit down for a while. The conversation, almost from the very beginning, became awkward, stilted, forced, and finally non-existent. I was, I'm afraid, tongue-tied and dumstruck with awe in the presence of what I believed was a great man and had hoped until the 2000 primaries would one day be POTUS. It was a veritable Henry Fonda moment, and I cannot explain it. It was not that he was larger than life. In fact he seemed to me smaller than his listed 6'5" height. (It was the opposite of my impression of Wes Unseld, who every time I encountered him, whether in a small room or a large auditorium, seemed to me to fill the space with a mammoth presence, though he was by actual measurement a bit shorter than Bradley). I was probably in the senator's office less than fifteen minutes, but it seemed an awfully long time before I found a way to make a rather sheepish exit. It was an instance when instead of glorying in the immediate presence of a prominent public figure, I felt dwarfed and out of place.

I had joked with his senior colleague from Illinois. I had been respectfully embraced by a Hall-of-Famer from Baltimore. Why couldn't I take advantage of this great opportunity, this greatly anticipated chance to connect with this man? No doubt I was humbled by his presence--or humble in his presence, but I think the real issue was the failure of the book and the hearing to achieve their goals. I had not earned the prominence I craved, so no wonder I couldn't joke familiarly with Senator Bradley. Instead, in what may be the theme of this entire enterprise of memory, the joke was on me.

XVII

BRIEF ENCOUNTERS (A.K.A. ZELIG PHOTO-OPS)

If it was not in the cards for me to become a star, there was nothing to prevent my rubbing shoulders with the luminaria and hoping to pick up some reflected glory--the "pale fire" phenomenon that inspired Shakespeare and Nabokov. Isn't that what the Boswell complex is all about? The drive to make contact with the famous in the belief that one's own fame might be promoted, as if by some societal homeopathic treatment.

So this whole enterprise may be seen as an exercise in name-dropping, which sometimes seems like self-aggrandizement to the extreme of grandiosity. Another risk is that celebrity-watching, the crowds at red-carpet events, may escalate to stalking, to groupie contact that is far more intimate than a handshake and autograph. Clearly, what may be viewed as a common garden- variety trait in this media-mad society may be carried to a pathological extreme. Think of what fixations on John Lennon, Jodie Foster, Dick Waitkus, and David Letterman have led to (to take a few random examples). On the other hand, think of all the framed photos on the walls of offices depicting the office-holder sharing a handshake, a drink, the spotlight/limelight with the rich and powerful and famous. What could be more ordinary or normal or natural, for example, than to walk into his clothing store in Providence and see displayed on the wall a picture of my friend Harvey Lapides shaking hands with George H.W. Bush, both wearing the baseball uniforms of their respective Ivy League alma maters?

And so I wonder, is this the story of my life? Is it a colossal joke to conceive of a memoir in the form of wannabe episodes of celebrity contacts? Well, I'll be a stand-up guy and say, maybe so, and maybe it is an anything-for-a-laugh attitude that inspires the project just as it may have motivated some of what is reported herein. In any case it seems fitting and proper (though what follows is often the embarrassment of the improper) to include in this memoir a selection of snapshots, a scrapbook/memorybook of occasions when the star-struck narrator got a piece of the action. Sometimes it could be something passing for speaking truth to power, sometimes the pretext is an interview as part of what is labeled "research" for tax-return purposes, but usually it is just the sound of fanfare trumpets blowing. In rough chronological order, then, here is a procession of a kind of "This Is Your Life" program for your truly.

Heisman

Our first move in New Raven was from a two-family house on Willard Street to ditto on Edgewood Avenue. In many ways it was a lateral move, from a quieter neighborhood in Westville to a somewhat nicer place closer to town. But for me there were two fringe benefits. The first, as I've described earlier, was that it was a short walk to the elementary school I'd be attending, Edgewood School, just a bit over two blocks down the avenue. The other (and also testimony to my youthful independence) was that it was just a healthy walk of maybe eight blocks to the Yale Bowl, and even in the first grade I was allowed to spend a Saturday afternoon at a football game.

Yale had a rule. Children were welcome into the Bowl but had to be escorted through the gates by an adult. No problem. You'd just camp out at the Walter Camp entrance and ask a likely-looking prospect to let you walk with him. I hit the jackpot the very first time. Picture me approaching a dashing-looking young man in a blue (of course) blazer, with a lovely young woman in a fur stole on his arm (the woman, not the stole). He seemed to be the object of much admiring attention, and finally I caught on when his name was called out repeatedly. It was Larry Kelley, just a year after graduating as the Yale captain and all-American end, and incidentally the reigning Heisman Trophy winner. He was back to cheer on his quarterback teammate, Clint Frank, who was to win the Heisman that year.

Only in retrospect do I see how much I should have been impressed by my lucky encounter. I more or less took that day in stride and indeed the whole experience of a little boy seeing some of the greatest college football of the time. Yale won back-to-back Heismans in 1936 and 1937, in just the second and third year the award was given, actually the first two with the name Heisman attached. The only other time a school repeated was when Mr. Inside and Mr. Outside, Doc Blanchard and Glenn Davis, won it in the mid-40s. I'm happy to say that I saw their Army team in the Bowl, though it was a longer walk out there from our next home, an apartment house on Boulevard.

I also saw another Heisman winner play in the Bowl, when I was still setting out from Edgewood Avenue. That was Michigan's incomparable Tommy Harmon, and I watched him make amazing runs through the whole Eli eleven, Still, none of those game-time memories impresses me now as much as being escorted into the Bowl in the handsome company of a former player, who seemed amused about it for the moment and surely forgot about it once we were inside and going our separate ways.

Dominic Frontieri

On the afternoon of June 3rd, 1949, Dom Frontieri and I were among the first seated, in adjoining chairs, at our high school senior class prize assembly. Graduation was still six days off, but this traditional gathering was the occasion for the awarding of many prizes to our graduates; we received our diplomas in the New Haven Arena, but that ceremony for nearly a thousand graduates allowed no time for prize-giving.

It's no surprise that in a class of this size Dom and I hardly knew each other. I knew him as one of the many talented musicians among us, arguably the most talented on a variety of instruments; he knew me as one of the leading brains. We sat there, exchanging joking remarks that indicated a mutual respect, and seeing his accordion case in the seat next to him I asked him what he was going to entertain the assembly with. He said, "Oh, just a couple of songs," and asked me which prizes I was getting. I couldn't tell him because each of those announcements would come as a surprise.

Then Mr. Countryman, our principal, came by to congratulate each of the prize-winners who had been instructed to come early and sit up front. Taking in Dom's accordion case, he said, "All ready to leave town, eh Dominic?" The clueless old guy couldn't tell an accordion case from a suitcase, and Dom and I had a good laugh at the administrator's expense. My classmate had played that instrument in a solo concert at Carnegie Hall when he was twelve years old, and even a clueless Countryman should have recognized what he was looking at.

In fact, Dom *was* ready to leave town, to embark on a career that would see a meteoric rise in Hollywood, where he went from accompanist, soloist, arranger, and composer to be musical director at Twentieth-Century Fox and then Paramount. TV shows also courted his services. His scores for "Outer Limits" and *The Man with No Name* were probably his biggest hits, and New Havenites took pride in his credits on both the small and big screens.

Not so much when he married Georgia Rosenbloom, widow of the Los Angeles Rams' owner. His position as Georgia's seventh husband allowed him to scalp thousands of tickets for the 1980 Super Bowl, earning him a half million dollars and a jail term for it. She waited until his short sentence was served and then divorced him, eventually moving the club back to her hometown in St. Louis, while Dominic continued his career in Tinseltown. I never saw him live after that prize assembly, but whenever his name came up I'd gleefully tell the tale of the Countryman contretemps.

The Champ's Corner

Picture me in Caesars Palace during a short stop in Las Vegas as Happy Harris and I are driving back across the country to New Hampshire for the start of the academic year of 1951-52. I had picked Hap up in Redlands, after spending a couple of weeks in L.A. with Aunt Ruth and family, including my mother who was having a short visit of her own. It was also the first and only time that I had had a date with Susie Marley, the sweet, bright Wellesley girl from Syracuse whom I was so anxious to impress that we had dinner at Lowry's Prime Rib on La Cienega, and hit the Mocambo and Ciro's on an evening that was ridiculously out of my pay range. Susie and I had become friends but never dated, though I had been the first to see her the day the bandages from her nose job came off and she was given her first mink. That was in the old Gotham Hotel at Fifth and Fifty-fifth between the Fifth Avenue Presbyterian Church and the Saint Regis. Her parents kept a suite there and instead of room service there was always a spread of haute cuisine ordered up from Le Pavillon across the street. Eventually she married into the Newhouse family, an appropriate merger of timber and paper industries with the publishing empire. I felt good enough about that friendship that years later I asked Susie to write a recommendation for my daughter for admission to the Newhouse School at Syracuse. Annie got in anyway, but that's another story for another time. (Alas, just last week I found obituaries of both Susie and Happy.)

Anyway, I'm shooting some craps at Caesars when I see a famous face passing by the table. I'd have recognized Al Weiss anywhere, with or without the cigar, the crafty manager of Rocky Marciano, the undefeated heavyweight champion of the world. He's headed for the men's room and I follow. I deliberately hitch up at the urinal next to him, and then as we're washing our hands, I say, "I've got a boy might beat your boy."

"Uh-huh," he grunts.

And I say, "He's the biggest, strongest, quickest African you'll ever see."

Without cracking a smile or even turning to look at me, he says, "That won't help him."

Lena Horne

Here I am on a Saturday night in April of 1953. It has been an eventful week, taking me from Hanover to Boston where I failed to pass one of a battery of tests that would have qualified me for the Naval Air Cadet program. A date with the charming Margie Vogel, then a drama student at Emerson, with me trying to drown my disappointment at the same time as laughing it off, ends with her telling me that I'll always be her intellectual friend--but never a sexual one. Home then to New Haven, where

I borrow my father's new powder-blue Olds 98 to pick up my Sarah Lawrence date for a night on the town.

For two years my roommate George Graboys has been touting this girl from his hometown, Fall River, as a good match for me, and after many rejections this was a first, not quite blind, date, and my intention is to make a big impression. The high point of the evening is supposed to be our reservation at the Byline Room where Mabel Mercer's performance would be the mark of an elevated and sophisticated taste, which I have acquired from my brother, a long-time Mercer fan.

Somewhat aloof but none the less very appealing, this bright, attractive blond is not proving very responsive to my insistent attempts at wit and flattery.

The harder I try, the more martinis I drink, until I am drunk enough to continue my spiel during Mabel's first set. And then I see, across a crowded room, that Lena Horne is there. She is, in my view, or at least at that moment, the most beautiful woman I have ever seen. As soon as Mercer takes a break I stagger over to Horne's table and say, respectfully if slurringly, "Miss Horne, it would be wonderful if you'd do a song for us tonight."

She is the perfect lady. "Thank you," she says, "but we're all here to listen to Mabel."

And that is the entire story of the encounter. What follows is a sequence of anticlimactic events, starting with my date's casually indicated distaste for my impertinent behavior. Then there is the vomiting in the Byline men's room, which leaves me sober but mortified, and the drive back toward Scarsdale when a freak April snowstorm has left an icy glaze on the West Side Drive.

The recovered sobriety allows me to avoid a collision when we round a curve and barely slide to a stop with six other cars piled up across the road. A slight ding in the fender is the only damage to the Olds, thanks to a genuinely brilliant piece of maneuvering--which leaves Dad furious when he sees it in the morning. No matter: I would never see the belle of Sarah Lawrence again, nor Lena Horne up close and personal.

Globetrotters

Mal Brochin, George Graboys, and I on our grand tour of Europe in the summer of '53, took a nostalgic break from our rounds of tourist-destinations to see an American movie in Rome (George, he of the steel-trap memory, has reminded me that it was the Rudolph Mates classic "The Green Glove" with Glenn Ford and Geraldine Brooks). We had climaxed our touring the night before with a visit to the Baths of Caracalla for a performance of *Aida* on the outdoor stage. It is hard to decide what made the greater impression, the live elephants in the "Triumphal March" or the holes in the middle of the concrete floors that passed for toilets in the latrine.

We had no sooner taken our seats in the movie theater when in trooped a posse of enormous African-American men. It was the Harlem Globetrotters on their annual summer tour of European capitals, and they filed into the row directly in front of us. I thought I recognized Goose Tatum, Marques Haynes, and Pop Gates among them, but one I knew best was Walter Dukes, recently departed from Seton Hall and beginning his Trotters tour before joining the Knicks. He lowered his massive black marble frame into the seat right in front of me. He turned around and kindly said to me, "I'm sorry if I block your view, but I'll scrinch down as far as I can."

He was as good as his word, resting his head on the back of his seat. The trouble was that his knees blocked my view. No wonder I have no clear memory of the movie.

Next day we headed south, where we encountered the recently crowned "Missa Sorrento Mille Novacento Cinquenta Tre" at a club on Capri. It was a very rare occasion when Mal failed to get a date with a beautiful young woman. And we were soon off on the long drive up the boot to Venice.

Why does this minuscule encounter with Walter Dukes, not even brushing shoulders with him but only overwhelmed by his presence a row ahead, rate inclusion here? Only because of the prominence of the memory in a catalog of the high points of that summer odyssey. I can still hear his voice as he apologized for the size of his frame, and the image of him sitting there right in front of me is as prominent in my tourist's-eye memory album as my photos of the Grand Canal and the Leaning Tower.

Ted Straeter

So there I am in Venice in late August, 1953, sitting around the piano bar with Mal and George where Earl "Pappy" Howard is taking requests. He's a favorite of the American tourist crowd in this popular place just over the bridge from the Bauer Grunwald Hotel. Lucky for us we stumbled on the place. We had arrived in Venice in our little rented tin can of a Citroen just as our money ran out. The bad news was that we got there during the long bank holiday and we can neither cash a check nor get a rescue wire from home.

The good news is that we were booked into the Pensione Rosa, just across from Pappy's gig, and we've been given the privilege of running up a tab for meals at the bar (some sort of mutual arrangement *a la famiglia*). Even better, we can drink free there if we can bring in some of the student tours, either from the big hotels in the neighborhood or by spotting newcomers at the American Express office.

And this we have done, with such success that we've still had time to visit the art-lovers' sites and have become Pappy's fair- haired boys.

Pappy is in the middle of his next-to-last set when Ted Straeter pops in, and a buzz seems to build up, at least to my high-toned ear. Pappy recognizes him immediately, sends over drinks on the house for him and his friend, and then is energized at the keyboard to a degree I've never seen or heard--and Straeter is cheering him on. Most of the young crowd doesn't know who Ted Straeter is, but Pappy and I both start reeling off his credits: New York society bandleader, house entertainer at some of the swankier hotels, and, most important, the guy who played rehearsal piano for most of the Rodgers and Hart musicals. Pappy calls him a latter-day Eddie Duchin.

It is a grand night at the piano bar, and then the next night is the topper. It's close to midnight when Straeter and his friend show up again. Pappy can hardly contain himself and graciously invites him to take over the keyboard. Straeter is happily in his cups and glad to oblige. Sitting right across from him, I keep calling out titles from the Rodgers and Hart songbook, and he grandly performs, playing and singing with his characteristic bravura. His young friend has written a song, and the maestro plays that as well.

Unlike Pappy's jazzy style on the standards, Straeter is the master of Broadway cabaret camp. Every time I come up with one of the more obscure titles in the canon, he gives me an appreciative smile and launches right into it. It's almost like Judy Garland at Carnegie Hall telling the audience, "Let's sing all night." In fact, he goes on without missing a beat or a glissando for about two hours, and he pats me on the back when he leaves. "Thank you," he says to me, and I'm not so overwhelmed that I can't say, "No, thank *you*."

This unexpected star turn, a showbiz bonanza from out of nowhere, was probably the highlight of the whole trip for me, and I bought a couple of his LPs to celebrate it. Ted Straeter's premature death not long afterward was, I thought, insufficiently noted in the press, so I eulogized him in a letter to the editor that appeared in the *Herald Tribune*, focusing on the generosity he displayed that night in Venice. As for his friend's song that the two of them seemed pretty excited about, I doubt it was ever recorded because I kept listening for it for a long time.

On the grand tour, with Mal Brochin and George Graboys in Pisa

With George at Cap D'Antibes

George and I flank Pappy Howard in Venice. His lessons on the opposite sex included this gem about young ladies wearing veils in the evening: "When they've got that mosquito-nettin' on, they mean business."

Harvey Swados

My four years teaching the bright undergraduates at City College were trying, demoralizing, exhausting, and variously troubled. But I worked hard enough to virtually write my way out of it, to survive a toxic atmosphere where character assassination was the predominant indoor sport, and to rub shoulders on occasion with great men of letters who visited.

I also walked away with a treasured, now more than half-century friendship with Rose Zimbardo. She was married at the time to Phil Zimbardo, whom she called the greater one to her "lesser Zimbardo." Briefly he played center field and batted third on my softball team, and in time would go on to an illustrious career at Stanford as one of the most often cited (at least in the mass media) of social psychologists. But there was nothing inferior about Rose--a great teacher, a brilliant critic, and unfailingly dear to my heart.

One perk of being a relatively presentable young man, whose wife stayed close to home with our three sons while I was free of an evening after my budget-balancing extra classes were done, was to be available for my senior colleague Henry Leffler's soirées (for men only). Some of these gatherings took place in the apartment he shared with his sister, the walls of which were blanketed with a dazzling array of fine art. For years of summer vacationing in Paris he had been assembling an amazing collection, carefully shopping the galleries and buying pictures by the great and near-great before they were recognized and rose to the top of the art market. Every important impressionist and post-impressionist artist was represented, with, for example, a pair of signed Picasso drawings in the bathroom and miraculously three of the best ten Magritte's in the world.

The other Leffler evenings took place on campus where he'd host dinners for the guest speakers in the faculty dining room and surround them with "his" posse of colleagues. In general, since he was the chairman of the committee that chose the guests, they would reflect his taste for the traditional, the elegant, the eminent, and especially the famous (again, men only). On several such evenings, before I fell out of favor with dear old Henry, I was seated next to the man of the hour. Herbert Read was one of them, the distinguished English literature and art critic, whose work I knew and greatly admired. We barely spoke, however, as he discouraged conversation by focusing his attention on meticulously boning the fish he was served. Another was Saul Bellow, who also discouraged conversation. I had much to ask this great one, but every gambit was turned away with a gross remark, a complaint about the food and the people, or a sneer.

Unlike these disappointments, I was blessed one evening to meet Harvey Swados, who had come down from Sarah Lawrence to give a talk. Friendly, gregarious, and approachable, he asked me questions and listened attentively to my answers. When I told him that I was preparing a course on the short story and hoped to include some of his classics, he said, "You must take a look at Grace Paley's work." She was then a colleague of his and he raved about her short stories. This display of generosity endeared him to me, and I followed up on his suggestion. The results of this opportune encounter were true blessings for me. I taught Paley stories for many years in my courses and wrote the first book-length study of her work (for the Twayne series on short stories). More important, I could consider her a friend, visited her place in Vermont during the preparation of the book, hosted her in my home in Maryland when she had a gig for the Howard County Libraries, and have an enchanting picture of her and my daughter Emmi, cheek to cheek and arms around each and looking like family (more below on Grace and me).

Incidentally, it was Grace Paley who, recognizing my pacifistic thinking, recruited me for membership in the War Resisters League. A fringe benefit of that was another Zelig moment, when I joined a march on the Pentagon (the event was "A Day without the Pentagon") and not only met Dick Gregory there but went stride for stride with Daniel Ellsberg at the head of the parade. In later years I resigned from the WRL over their strident anti-Israel position and a nasty habit of calling Hezbollah and Hamas "freedom fighters." Sorry, Grace.

The Paley book was one thing, but probably more important and surely more satisfying was a Swados book that I produced. It was a novel, *The Unknown Constellations*, his first but repeatedly rejected attempt at book-length fiction. It was entirely serendipitous that I discovered this property. I was teaching, at Maryland, a graduate seminar on the use of place in fiction, with New Orleans as a model, at the same time that I was working on my Paley book. A recent bibliography of her work listed an introduction to an edition of Swados's collected short stories. When I found that book I also found that the introduction was not by Paley but by Harvey's son Robin. I might have wondered about that but of more immediate interest was Robin's mention of his father's unpublished first novel that was set in New Orleans.

Surprised to learn that a writer so widely admired would not have been able to place an early work once he had become established as a significant figure in the literary world, that he had simply put it away and gone on to other things in a writerly (and academic) life that had kept him continually occupied until his untimely death from an aneurysm in 1972 at age fifty-two, I made an immediate decision to go after this buried treasure. The typescript had survived, along with the correspondence concerning it among friends, agents, editors, and the author, as I discovered when I traced it to the special collections at the University of Massachusetts Library in Amherst, where he had taught for some time.

It was not a great book, certainly not on a par with his classic short stories or his major novels, and yet it had its virtues, not only as a forerunner of the later work, but in and of itself as well. Swados's New Orleans, for example, was a worthy addition to the city as re-imagined by such writers as Robert Stone, Tennessee Williams, John Kennedy Toole, and Walker Percy. My course was clear: to find a publisher for it and to get a commitment that would empower me to write a celebratory introduction that reviewed an under-appreciated career.

The Swados family was cooperative and supportive, Richard Wentworth of the University of Illinois Press was enthusiastic, and once the terms of the deal were worked out (my role in those matters was as an arbitrator, since I was eager to have it settled though I had no financial incentive) I set to work. In this effort I had the valuable and encouraging support of Alan Wald, the University of Michigan's great historian of the American left. My thirty-five- page retrospective owes a great deal to the high standards which he pushed me to meet in my revisions.

In this context it is no surprise that I found the Swados career to be grounded in his steadfast political commitment to the principles of the Socialist Labor Party. That is why I believe *Standing Fast* is his finest novel, that his collection of interconnected stories *On the Line* is a treasure of socio-cultural history, and that his role in inspiring the creation of the Peace Corps was significant. I call *The Unknown Constellations* "my Swados book," and I am proud to have unearthed it and brought it to light, pleased as well with being given the opportunity to celebrate his value as a writer and human being.

That it, like him, received little significant notice in the public eye, I regret, but accept, in the appropriately joking cliché, as "the story of my life."

Camelot

There was a time when I was cast in the role of Stage-Door Johnny. It was during my second year at City College when I was struggling to survive financially with a wife who refused to consider living in an apartment and three young sons. I had taken on all the added evening classes I could get as well as committing to summer school. Because most of the evening classes ended about nine, I found some relief by an occasional trek from Convent Avenue in Harlem down to Broadway. I saw a number of second acts, knowing how to mingle with a ticketed crowd during intermission and slip into the theater, sometimes even into a seat.

As it happened, I had been back in touch with fellow New Havenite, Wayne Weil, who had been a fraternity brother of mine at Dartmouth. He was a guy who never turned down an invitation to go somewhere or do something bizarre, anything that relieved the intolerable tedium of schoolwork. "Leaving for Northampton in ten minutes, seats open in the car," might be heard in the hallway of the dorm on a Tuesday evening, and Wayne's door would fly open. "I'll go," he called out so many times that "I'll go Wayne" became his moniker.

Wayne was beginning to have some success in advertising/public relations, lived in a commuter town in New Jersey, and was married to the lovely redheaded Shelia, who was a chorus girl, dancing and singing her showbiz heart out in whatever show would have her. She had hit the jackpot with *Camelot*, and Wayne would meet her after the final curtain and escort her home. There came a night when he had a meeting he couldn't afford to miss, and I was asked to relieve his anxiety about her traveling alone by escorting her to the station and seeing her onto the train. Shelia sweetened the invitation by telling me she could arrange for me to see the second act from the wings, and then if I waited outside for her she'd introduce me to some people.

So there I am, in the alley outside the stage door. The person I'm shaking hands with is Robert Goulet, and the picture shows that I am the taller one. We are then joined by Richard Burton--and he is even shorter than Goulet. The conversation is perfunctory and brief, the memory vivid and long.

Backstage during rehearsals for "Camelot" Burton and Goulet play gin; as the kibbitzer I am in my paparazzo-wannabe mode

You Can't Beat City Hall

At least once I didn't even know who it was that I was insulting. It was in Atlanta during the annual SAMLA convention, and I had been invited to a private celebration at Emory to honor George Garrett. Garrett had been a cordial acquaintance who had taken to calling me a friend, whereas I had been eager to seek out his company at every possible opportunity. He was one of the very few writers in the region that I held in the highest regard, full of admiration not only for his mastery of fiction (short and long, historical and contemporary), poetry, and criticism, but also the generosity with which he encouraged and coached other writers. I gave him much of the credit for making the English Department at the University of Virginia and the whole cultural scene at Charlottesville a popular magnet for academics and artists.

I must have hit a few publishers' parties on my way over to the campus, because I was surely feeling no pain when I got there. As I made my way into the crowded scene, I saw sitting on a sofa a man with slicked down black hair and clad in full evening dress complete with scarlet cummerbund. His whole presentation of himself somehow struck me as terribly funny, and I went right up to him, shook his hand, and said, "Where's the rest of the band?"

A couple of others took me by the arm and led me away before I got a response to what I had thought was a jovial greeting, and it was then I learned that I had just insulted His Honor the Mayor of

Atlanta. I never even learned his name until years later. So here it is, with belated apologies: Sam Massell, a realtor who became Atlanta's first Jewish mayor, whose term preceded twenty years of administration by Maynard Jackson and Andrew Young, and who earned the unofficial title of "Mayor of Buckhead" by his many years of service to the neighborhood and the city at large.

Mallon Faircloth

Judge Faircloth recently retired from the bench, having served for a dozen years as a federal magistrate judge for the United States District Court for the Middle District of Georgia, but he had been duly recorded in the history books in the fall of 1963. On a damp and windy day in Knoxville he had led the Vols to a 14-0 win over Vanderbilt. It was the last game that Tennessee played in the archaic formation of the single wing.

For two seasons Faircloth had been the tailback and a record-setting kick returner on a mediocre team (despite the presence in the line-up of all-stars like Steve DeLong and Frank Emanuel). The glory years of Coach Bob Neyland's system had long passed, and the dominant T-formation had left Tennessee stubbornly mired in history. Faircloth had treated nostalgic fans to a seventy-two-yard touchdown run on that muddy field, but there were no NFL scouts looking for single-wing tailbacks to draft. Faircloth, however, had business to attend to in Knoxville, three years of law school before returning home to Cordele, Georgia for his career at the bar.

He wasn't quite finished with football yet. At U-T, touch football was a very big deal, and Faircloth naturally played tailback for the powerful law school team that was expected to win the university title. The main competition was expected to come from Sigma Chi, the fraternity champions who had easily reached the semifinals of the season-ending open tournament only to be surprised 24-12 by an English Department team, proud winners in the Faculty/Staff competition. Graduate student Mike Kelly had a big day in that game, completing twenty-one passes, fifteen to his fellow grad students Bobby Jack Fry and John Gilbert (two outstanding all-around athletes) and six more to a diminutive professor named Isaacs. The protecting line featured two other grad students (both former college players) and another young prof of considerable size and strength (John Tinkler).

The title game turned on the play in which I had my brief encounter with Faircloth. Leading a late march toward what promised to be a winning touchdown, the famous tailback threw deep down the middle only to have John Gilbert leap high to bat the pass away--into the opportunistic hands of yours truly. Intercepting a Faircloth pass was a triumphal, if universally unrecorded, moment of glory.

Robert Penn Warren

His friends called him "Red." I never got that close, nor did my brother who spent a full year in his playwriting class at the Yale Drama School. (Of course when Phil and I talk with each other, we always refer to him as Red Warren.) My brief encounter with him took place on a cool, breezy day in March of 1975 in Boone, North Carolina. Appalachian State University, on a gem of a campus in the western mountains of the Tar Heel State (where my son Daniel would matriculate to study geology a couple of years later), had decided to hold a festival in Warren's honor.

And why not honor a man who was the preeminent man of letters in the nation for his many and varied contributions as novelist, poet, playwright, essayist, critic, cultural historian, editor, anthologist? I was there as a fiction- into-film maven to give a paper on the translation of *All the King's Men* to the screen. I knew I'd have to be at my best because, in Warren's presence, I'd be interpreting some of the subtleties and nuances of a finely textured novel that were either modified, omitted, or made obvious in a movie that was no less impressive for the changes and spoke eloquently for itself. And then he and I would be sharing the stage in a relatively informal discussion before a large audience of the campus community and the interested folks of the region.

The participants had gathered for a light lunch, and in consideration for his age and with appropriate southern hospitality, the guest of honor was asked if he'd like to have some privacy or take a rest before the afternoon program began. He laughed and said no, what he'd especially like is to take a walk. He asked me to join him, an opportunity I wouldn't have given up for anything, and we were joined by several devoted fans of his, a version of intellectual undergraduate groupies, I suppose. One of these students volunteered to lead the way along a trail that led out from the campus and might present some decent views of the early spring in the mountains.

We walked, briskly, and before long it was Warren who set the pace. What I found most remarkable was not the physical vigor of the man but his ability to maintain--and dominate--the conversation as we took in the surroundings. It was like a pioneering American version of an ancient Greek philosopher holding forth while guiding his charges amid the stoae. It is those fifty minutes of trying to keep up with this wise man's running commentary and his vigorous pace that I most remember of this experience, not my anticlimactic paper, not even the affable panel discussion that followed. My only regret is that he never asked me to call him "Red."

Amused and bemused at Appalachian State, March 1975

Red Smith

On a sunny Saturday in May, I was at Pimlico for the Preakness, and I had the privilege of carrying press credentials to watch the race far from the madding (drinking, betting) crowd. (The press pass had been provided by a "friend" who shall remain nameless in this chronicle, because grievous, repeated betrayal will not earn commemoration here.)

Pimlico respects the working press to the point of providing a private betting window in the press box, and that is where I left my money that day. I was sure that Ridan, a disappointing third to Decidedly in the Derby two weeks before, would be an easy winner, with Jaipur his only serious challenger. Unfortunately, most of the crowd and the professional handicappers as well thought the same way, and the big horse ridden by Manny Ycaza was the heavy favorite. I was excited to be there and the excitement was a factor in my decision to risk a sizeable bet on the favorite.

I was also excited to be rubbing shoulders with the A-list of sportswriters, for whom Triple Crown races in those days were events as big as the World Series, the Indy 500, and heavyweight championship fights. And I found myself in line at the betting window right behind the dean of them all, Red Smith, universally regarded as the best in the business. Justly so, I thought, because the man wrote compelling prose which was as witty as it was wise, with a healthily modest attitude toward what he did for a living--writing about the "toy department" that attracted a fascinated plurality of American adults.

As a reader and would-be writer, and as a sporting fan proud of his own knowledge and analytical expertise, I regarded Red Smith as a model, an icon, a god among us. I was awestruck, reluctant to intrude on the great one's presence and not emboldened to play the tout's role. I was also exulting in the good fortune to be there, right there, just behind him in the betting queue. So I paid close attention to his transaction at the window.

"Two dollars to win on Greek Money" was all he said, calmly and quietly, as if going through the minimal motions of taking part in the event with the smallest possible wager on a moderate long shot. What I heard, however, did not deter me from the foolishly large investment I was about to make.

That race went down as one of the most exciting in Triple Crown history. Ridan challenged for the lead early and put away all the other speed horses, turning for home in front as the others faded. But on the last turn he went a little wide and a late-charging Greek Money, after trailing the leaders in fifth place much of the way, forged to the front by half a length. The big favorite came back, once Ycaza realized there was work left to do, and he caught Greek Money, Ridan's great strides taking him to a slight lead. In the last twenty yards Greek Money came on again and finished a nose in front--only to have Ycaza claim foul against John Robb for coming out and bothering his horse in the stretch.

I had lost sight of Red Smith during the race, my attention focused on the action, but as the judges looked at the race films I distracted my anxiety by trying to see how he was reacting. And there he was, calmly waiting out the delay as if it were of no consequence, not stoic exactly, because it really was of no significance to him and he never needed to be right about a prediction of something so full of chance as a horse race.

The films, of course, showed Ycaza in mid-stretch, carried away by his competitive drive, brazenly reach out and drive an elbow into Robb's chest. Ycaza was the one who had committed the foul, Red Smith was the one who had made the right bet, and the degree to which I had been crushed by the result was outweighed by my feeling of having been blessed for what was, after all, the near miss of an actual encounter with a great one.

Two years earlier, it so happens, I had in fact exchanged letters with Red Smith. Based on my own brief experience as a teenage boxer and some ensuing attention to the fight game, I considered myself something of a boxing maven. In the aftermath of the Gene Fullmer/Joey Giardello middleweight championship fight, in which the champion held on to his crown because the split-decision/draw failed to acknowledge the challenger's apparent win, I wrote a detailed analysis of Fullmer's brawling style, arguing that he could have lost eight rounds in that fight on fouls that were ignored while the superior boxer lost one for a head-butt that was deliberate but retaliatory.

Addressing a letter to Red Smith, however, I knew I had to be amusing, so I ended this way: "If, for no other reason, though, Giardello deserved the decision for acting like a boxer during the fight and after. It was refreshing to hear, 'I the champeen! I win! Who ever heard a draw in a champ'nship fight?' Fullmer may feel at home teaching Sunday school or scrimmaging against Don Huff, but he doesn't belong in a boxing ring. He fights not according to the Marquess of Queensbury but according to Marquis de Sade."

The punch-line came back under the *Herald Tribune* letterhead: "Just a note on your nice letter sent so long ago: Didn't you know? De Sade had a glass jaw." In Baltimore, I had the good sense not to remind him of that exchange, knowing that Red Smith would always land the final winning blow.

Sam Jones

The truth is that I can't remember who it was, during the days when I was actively researching my books of hoops history, that told me Sam Jones was actually a neighbor of mine in Silver Spring. It could have been almost anyone in the Bullets organization or any of the visiting NBA players or coaches, or maybe it was K.C. Jones--the most likely suspect as Sam's running mate with the Celtics, who despite his reputation for reticence, when it came to memories of games he played at the University of San Francisco or for the Celtics would display an amazing play-by-play memory.

Anyway, I jumped at the opportunity to contact Sam and met him first for an interview in his suburban home. By coincidence, it turned out that his son Aubrey was a schoolmate of my son Jonny at Sherwood High School and that they ended up the number one doubles pair on the Sherwood tennis team. What made that coincidence uncanny is that Sam and I formed a doubles team ourselves, playing together in some "celebrity" tennis events around town. Sam is a foot taller and at least that much better a player than I am but we worked well together--until our last pairing when the host of the event decided to give the old boys a lesson and matched us in the first round against a couple of collegiate hotshots who blew us away. (See photo of Sam and me, with our game faces on, waiting to get on the court for a match.)

What endeared Sam to me, however, was his willingness to share, not only with me in private but openly on his visits to my classroom, his intelligent and candid opinions of basketball luminaries, especially those who tended to underestimate his ability and whom he far outshone on the court. As for his legendary coach, Red Auerbach, he never quite articulated his support for my negative opinion, though there were signs of his tacit agreement. In my case it was largely a matter of character, while for him I think it was a matter of how Auerbach favored Bob Cousy over him.

Parenthetically, piling coincidence on coincidence, though only perceived in hindsight, was the fact that my only first-hand meeting with Sam's Celtics teammate Bill Russell was occasioned by a chance meeting between our young sons on the beach at Martha's Vineyard. The boys played in the sand, his towering over mine though younger by a year or two, but I was thrilled to introduce myself to the man who changed the way the game was played and was most responsible for the Celtics' run of championships. Sam wholeheartedly agreed with that assessment.

I respected Sam Jones's intelligence and sophistication enough that I asked him to give a pre-publication reading of *The Great Molinas*. He did so, gladly and quickly, and honored me with an eminently quotable blurb: "Isaacs is not only an outstanding student of sports but a skillful and knowledgeable storyteller as well. ...you will not be able to put this down." I am forever in his debt.

Len Elmore

Though he was an English major at Maryland, Lenny never took a course with me. He knew me well enough, though, through my close relationship with the basketball team in those days, that when he and teammate Owen Brown were having trouble in a tough Chaucer course, they cornered me in the locker room after a game and said, "Where were you when we needed you?"

At the end of his junior year, Lenny had another kind of problem, the kind that my father used to call a high-class worry. He had to decide whether to come back for his last year of eligibility as a senior or to go the Spencer Haywood-hardship route and enter the professional draft. I told him I'd help him decide by asking around among my contacts with coaches and scouts about what his prospects were likely to be. I found that there was a general consensus that he would do better to play another season of ACC ball, improve certain skills, and earn the high draft spot that his physical stature and ability, his basketball pedigree (he had gone to Lou Alcindor's high school), and his intelligence might earn for him--and the salary that could go with it.

I met with Lenny and told him what I had heard. "They tell me that they want to see more of an offensive threat from you: some range on the jumper, that you can create your own shot, and that you can shoot off the dribble." These were things that he'd not been able to showcase because they didn't fit in with Lefty Driesell's narrowly focused schemes. And then I told him, "During the season, regardless of what Coach says to you, you need to demonstrate those skills. You're not going to be benched, and your future really depends on what you can show the scouts."

He paid attention and did just that, I assume, not just because I said so and he respected my basketball insights but because he was getting similar advice elsewhere. In any case, I was glad I had made the effort and proud of Lenny when he became a top draft choice both in the NBA and the ABA, choosing the latter when the Indiana franchise offered him a seven-figure contract. Maybe I was a little too proud because I used to say fairly often that I made Elmore a millionaire.

My pride in Len Elmore grew when, while still an active and moderately productive player in the pros, he pursued a law school degree at Harvard and was prepared to launch his next career as soon as he quit playing. Seeing an opportunity to combine his credentials, he subsequently opened shop as an attorney-agent for players. Again I was proud when he shut down that operation because he had been playing strictly by the rules and not indulging in unethical practices. The latter, apparently, was the kind of conduct that both earned agents a bad name and attracted me-first and money-hungry athletes into their clutches (or Klutches?). Lenny and I talked occasionally during this period, especially when my son Jonathan, himself a law school grad and recent passer of the bar, was considering the same specialization--only to abandon that ambition for similar reasons.

By the time Elmore became a regular analyst for televised college basketball games, he had more or less deleted me from his speed dial. That is, he had stopped taking my calls. I can't say I am proud of him as a broadcaster, his commentary being repetitive and cliché-ridden, but I admire his accomplishments along the several career paths he has pursued. What I don't get, frankly, is the fact that he has never so much as said thank you. And I feel like Lenny Bruce's "Masked Man," who was wont to say, "I must have a thank you."

Tony Kornheiser

Having been graced by his visit to my classroom, I had the temerity to ask Kornheiser to read *The Great Molinas* and consider providing a blurb as well. Once he started writing a regular column on the Washington *Post* sports page Tony had become recognized as one of the sharpest and wittiest writers around. I thought that a word from him would be a golden asset for the book and hoped he would find something good to say about it.

Scoring a direct hit on the heart of the matter, he obliged me with this: "Jack Molinas was brilliant, ambitious, the best basketball player in the country, and totally corrupt. This is a fascinating, cautionary tale."

I expressed my gratitude for this gesture and hoped for a relationship between us to grow. I suspect I know why, despite my efforts, that never happened. Never having forgotten the dramatic context of his appearance as a guest in "Sports Culture, USA," I used the incident as the basis for a short story in my collection, *The Miller Masks: A Novel in Stories*. In fact, it is the last item in the book, an attempt to put the finishing touch on a major theme: how writers are driven to invent themselves every time they try to shape experience into narrative or adopt a narrative voice.

Tony had visited my class on the very day that the news had broken about a Washington *Post* writer who had to surrender her Pulitzer Prize when it was discovered that she had faked chunks of her résumé and had fabricated most of her prize-winning feature. He was visibly distressed about this event, both for his newspaper being victimized by a hoax and for the way his journalism profession had been besmirched.

Yet when it came to the Q and A time that always followed the interview in my class sessions, the students tended to ignore the headline news of the day and focus on a recent column Tony had written. He had been assigned to do a profile of a local radio sports-talk host who had a large following in the area; but when he discovered that the man was guilty of inventing an athletic history for himself, of fabricating as fact many details of sporting events to support his controversial opinions, and of reporting the findings of a non- existent network of informants, Tony and his editors decided to kill the piece rather than indulge in an exposé of a relatively insignificant figure.

This radio host, after realizing that Tony had the goods on him, tried for a preemptive strike by getting a puff-piece about him published in the cross- town rival paper, the *Star*. The *Post*, then, decided it had to respond, and so the devastating Kornheiser pen struck its mighty blow, a "poison pen" as one of my students called it. I was somewhat embarrassed that my class had neglected the big picture of the fraudulent Pulitzer and rushed to defend its trivial equivalent in a radio personality whom they listened to faithfully--and probably accepted at (false-)face value. I had my own issues with the radio guy and added details of some of the howlers I had heard him utter on air.

In my short story, I have Jesse Miller, the professor, and his guest, Sandy Hyweier, engage in what I thought of as clever dialogue touching on the issues and personages involved in that day's classroom interview and discussion. I thought I made Kornheiser look good in his guise of Hyweier, though perhaps he took offense at the name I gave him. He may also have taken offense that I had "used" him as a vehicle of my fictional pretensions. If that story, unlike most of those in the book, was a textbook example of a *roman à clef*, then identifiable subjects could be entitled to some resentment, I suppose.

And yet, the name of the story is "Inventing Myself," and the objects of its probably ineffectual satire are not just the ersatz Pulitzer reporter and the absurd radio sports guru. The primary subject being held up to scorn or what I hoped was self-deprecating humor was myself, Neil D. Isaacs, in his transparent guise as Jesse Miller. If Tony Kornheiser took it amiss, I can only guess, because I never heard from him about it. In fact, I never heard from him at all. When Tony became a radio and an unlikely television personality himself, I became persona non grata to him (though his colleague Michael Wilbon maintains a courteous manner in our occasional exchanges).

One might infer from this a lesson about the effects of fame: that the non- famous are no longer acceptable associates to those who have actually achieved what has been the elusive goal of some of the rest of us. I like to think I would be above that, but I haven't had the luxury of testing that belief.

Roy Jefferson

I can't be sure of the year, but it had to be in the late 1970s because Jefferson had retired in 1976 after a dozen years as a star wide receiver in the NFL. After five years in Pittsburgh, where he had been a league leader and the Steelers' best offensive weapon, he and coach Chuck Noll had had a well- reported falling-out and Roy was "exiled" to Baltimore where he helped the Colts win the Super Bowl. And then came the trade that sent him forty miles down I95 for his six years with the Washington NFL franchise. Again he was instrumental in helping a team to the Super Bowl, but with diminishing prominence while still in good health he had called it a career.

The occasion was an evening of tribute to a charismatic personality who had stayed on in Washington, despite a brief Hollywood sojourn (he was articulate, witty, and good-looking, too), to pursue business interests and a great deal of charity work. I was honored to be asked to take part in the program by the organizer, Harold Bell, a well-known man-about-town whom I had met on several occasions and added to my guest list for Sports Culture, USA. Remembering that Jefferson and I had a slight acquaintance, Harold decided to return the favor of an invitation to appear and perform.

Harold Bell, to his credit I thought, was pushing every opportunity he could drum up to draw attention to himself. He had been a star schoolboy athlete in the District, had made physical fitness a crusade, had attracted the recognition of President Nixon who appointed him to his Athletic Commission, had a sports-talk radio show, and was trying to launch a political career. When he asked me to come to the club on upper Georgia Avenue that he had negotiated for the event, I took it as an offer I had no idea I could refuse.

When it was my turn, early in the program, for my roast/toast of Roy, I took the mike in my slightly shaking hand and decided to make a point of my presumed role as a token white face in an African-American setting with a predominantly African-American audience. "When Harold Bell asked me to appear here tonight," I began, "I said to him, 'Harold, are you sure you want me to be a part of it, because you know I'm part white,' and he said, quick trigger as always, 'That's okay, Neil, so's Roy.'"

The big laugh was encouraging, my hand steadied, and I began my shtick about the people I had been pleased to see in the club, all here to honor Roy Jefferson's contributions to the community. The climax was my assertion that I had failed to see Roy Jefferson himself among the celebrators--pause--but I had been glad to see Johnny Mathis here. That was the other big laugh I had been hoping for, because Jefferson was an uncanny look-alike for Mathis.

That was my exit line (always leave 'em laughing, as my dad and Fred Allen liked to say), but I stayed on in the club because I wanted to hear how Roy thanked and responded to the "testimonials." And I got a bit of an appreciative thrill when the first thing he did when he took the mike from Harold Bell, was immediately sing the first few lines of "Chances Are." And he sounded like Johnny Mathis, too.

Roy Jefferson and George Nock listen closely to the old professor--there might be a quiz. Nock was a fullback and also a gifted artist. A lithograph from his "Spirits" series decorates a wall in our house

Bob Fachet

I've already mentioned my admiration for the way Fachet covered the Montreal Olympics in a whirlwind of reporting as if he had sideline cameras on dozens of events happening at the same time (on his visit to my classroom he modestly dismissed that accomplishment as just normal for a reporter). Another occasion on which he earned my admiration happened in the press box at a game between the Toronto Maple Leafs and the Washington Capitals. It was a case of a journalist's integrity overcoming the familiar proscription against cheering from the press box when his voice needs to be heard loud and clear.

It was early days in the history of the Caps franchise, but the thuggish play of the Leafs on the ice was as embarrassing as the earnest but often unproductive play of the home team. Much more distasteful from virtually any point of view was the antisocial behavior and verbal abuse polluting the press box from the repugnant presence and nasty mouth of the visitors' owner, an ex-con and more of a thug than any Toronto player on the ice, one Harold Ballard. It was Bob Fachet who stood up and dressed him down. I congratulated him that night and remembered to praise him again in my obiter obit that followed his untimely death.

Dick Darcey

A welcome and illuminating guest in my classroom was the brilliant sports photographer, Dick Darcey. As I wrote to the *Post* after Dick's death, there were two things that distinguished his work. The first was that he considered himself a reporter. While other reporters would caucus after an event to define the key moment or play or shift of momentum, Dick would have anticipated the crucial and telling action, positioned himself, and caught that defining moment. Because he was trying to tell the story rather than frame an artful picture, he often got the shot that everyone else missed--like Charley Taylor breaking free to beat the Cowboys or Patrick Ewing dunking over Ralph Simpson in the classic Georgetown-Virginia showdown (a picture that told a story larger than the particular game, which was why it graced the cover of the second edition of my history of college basketball).

The second was that he recognized the emotional power in the faces of athletes and other figures in the world of sports. His close-ups rival those of the great portraitists of photography. I think of the penetrating grasp of his look at the many faces of Muhammad Ali, at NBA referee Manny Sokol (see below), at aging fighter Emile Griffith, at jockey Chris McCarron, at Rod Laver (see below), at Satchel Paige looking back after all, or at Karl Wallenda (see below) with the lines of his flying and stressful exhilaration engraved on his face.

In my first interview with Dick, I was startled to hear that there had never been a book devoted to his art, and after class I asked if he'd allow me to write a proposal I could use to query possible publishers--and then, if I could elicit an offer, write the text for the book. Yes, he said, to both questions, and he soon presented me with a selection of prints that demonstrated his remarkable production.

I called him the Cartier-Bresson of sports. He managed to capture a complex and emblematic sports personage with a close-up of the visage at the very instant of a climactic movement: a Mickey Mantle swinging in pain, a high- jumper at his peak, a referee making a tough call, and a half dozen flashes of Ali in action. He was, in my view, a genius at his game, but I couldn't interest a single editor, publisher, or agent. The provisional title was "The Faces of Sport," and my disappointment that it never got past the drawing board is somewhat relieved by the portfolio of his gems in my possession. I am privileged to present an all-too-meager sample herewith.

Georgetown-VA showdown; Darcey called this "Awe American"

Manny Sokol

Darcy called this simply, "Rocket"

Karl Wallenda

The last sample here is long-distance runner Erich Segal, author of "Love Story"

K.P. and the Gang

Hanging out at the Capitol Centre with the Washington Bullets in the late '70s gave me the freedom to indulge in a fan's fantasy of familiarity with professional athletes. Not only could I have a front-row press seat at the games themselves, but I could have a meal in the press room before games and, best of all, visit the locker room after games. I enjoyed listening to reporters discussing the games as they reached a consensus about what their leads should be.

Often the loudest voice in the room was Boston's hoops maven, Bob Ryan, whose observations came to shape most of the media perceptions about what had happened on the floor. I learned little about the game that way, but a lot about sports-writing. The reporters whom I leaned to respect, like Steve Hershey, Dave DuPree, and David Aldridge, typically ignored Ryan, and I found that my appreciation of the games (the key moments, the decisive shifts, the strategy and tactics) most nearly matched their perceptions.

Many of the players enjoyed talking about the game, not the specific one they had just played, but the one that exhibited their talents and defined their lives. Dave Bing offered concise gems. About defense, for example, he said, "If you take something away, you're always giving something up." (That reminds me of a gem I overheard tossed off by legendary coach Frank McGuire during a Big East tournament half-time at Madison Square Garden: "It used to be pass and move to the ball; now it's pass and screen away.") Clem Haskins, on the other hand, would expound at length on the game and his long experience, especially after games when he had played very few minutes. Wes Unseld and Mike Riordan wouldn't talk much, but that didn't mean they had little to say (they were the only players, to my knowledge, who read books on road trips), and Elvin Hayes was usually quickly dressed and gone, pursuing other pleasures elsewhere.

Kevin Grevey was particularly welcoming and amiable (no wonder he succeeded in running his tavern later on), and we often stayed on after games to play some table tennis in the players' lounge. He was a good player, but this little old college professor played him about even. Imagine that! Kevin and I thought we owned that table--until Truck Robinson started to join the competition. We were good, but Truck was better.

Kevin Porter ("K.P." to his teammates) and I had had a good rapport, maybe because we identified with each other as under-sized playmakers. He played a key role in the two incidents I remember most vividly from those days. The first was during a mid-season game against the Chicago Bulls, when he was matched up against his fellow St. Francis graduate, all-star guard Norman Van Lier. I had the perfect vantage point from the courtside press table, when the two collided near mid-court. Van Lier fell to the floor and the referee called a charging foul on Porter. As Van Lier was about to pass the ball inbounds, I said jokingly, "Good act, Norm." He whirled around and began to climb across the table to get at me, when K.P. grabbed him around the waist and said, "No, Norm, he's all right."

While I didn't literally have my life flash before my eyes, I did make a silent vow never to address a competitor of such intensity during actual play--or any player, for that matter. A few years later, when I mentioned the incident to Dick Motta, who had coached Van Lier during his time with the Bulls, I heard a frightening summary of incidents dramatizing how heavy a burden it was to monitor his tenacious point guard's behavior during road trips.

The second incident of my debt to K.P., life-enhancing rather than life-threatening, came that same season, on the singular occasion when I flew on the team plane back from Boston during the playoffs. He came to me at my seat and invited me to join a few of the guys playing blackjack at the rear of the cabin. This was more than an opportunity to enjoy some card-playing but an ego-boosting gesture of my being a part of the gang. I even managed to win some walking-around money, mostly because of the presence of rookie Nick Weatherspoon among the players. "Spoon" had a unique way of playing. No matter what cards he was dealt, he'd just keep saying, "Hit me, man," until he could say "Shit, man, I'm busted." He apparently thought the idea of the game was to get to exactly twenty-one, never mind getting closer than the dealer to the target.

Kevin Porter, my life-saver

Truck Robinson, table tennis terror

Spoon Weatherspoon, blackjack novice

Chet Forte

We never met in person, and our exchanges of mail, phone, and live radio interview came near the end of his life. But what a remarkable life it was. At Columbia in the mid-'50s Forte was a prodigious basketball scorer, though only 5'8", competing with West Virginia's Hot Rod Hundley and Seattle's Elgin Baylor for national scoring titles and beating out Kansas's Wilt Chamberlain for player-of-the-year honors in 1957. Released after a brief stint in the NBA, he played on Jack Molinas's team in the Eastern League, where he remembered a night when Molinas was driving his players to a game and suddenly pulled off the road when he heard on the radio that a game had tipped off at 7 o'clock instead of an announced 7:30.

Forte had not yet started betting on games, but he and the whole team knew of their coach's apparently manic gambling habit and they were roaring with laughter as they watched Molinas run for the nearest phone booth. They believed that he was calling his bookie to get down a "past-posted" bet on a game that was already underway. "You all got it wrong," I told Chet the Jet when he told me this story. "He was calling Joe Hacken, his partner in a bookmaking operation of their own, to make sure they were covered on the game."

As a television producer, Forte achieved more fame as a result of his talent and accomplishments. In twenty-five years at ABC as producer and director, he was largely responsible for making Monday Night Football the crowd- pleasing spectacle it became, with his innovative coverage and his instinct for in-the-moment decisions. "Wide World of Sports," the Olympics, Triple Crown races, the Indy 500, and championship prize fights were also on his list of credits, yielding twenty-seven Emmys. His growing gambling habit, however, overwhelmed his success, ended his TV career, and nearly cost him his family and his freedom.

Forte had given my book a rave review, saying, "Neil Isaacs has written a very scary book about the second greatest basketball player I've ever seen, Jack Molinas (the greatest being Magic Johnson). THE GREAT MOLINAS will scare you and make you sweat. Isaacs has captured all the diverse personalities of one of the greatest players and gamblers to ever play at *both* games."

After I contacted Forte, he became a textbook case in my study of pathological gambling. As a sports-savvy, highly intelligent man in possession of much inside information, he might have been expected to be a big winner. But, always concerned to avoid even the appearance of a conflict of interest by betting on events he was screening, he was not only losing more than he won but escalating his action on wild casino jaunts and long- shot parlays.

A first-hand source told me a story I never had a chance to confirm with Chet. He was producing the telecast of a Thomas Hearns-Sugar Ray Leonard fight in Las Vegas. He and his director were getting paid $15,000 each for the show, and they had bet it all on Leonard, a three-to-one underdog. Hearns had dominated the fight into the thirteenth round, when Leonard suddenly turned it around and knocked him out. The director was shouting with joy and questioned the glum look on his producer's face. "You don't understand," Forte told him, "I had three baseball losses and I'm out sixty thousand for the night."

When he took a buy-out to leave ABC, it was not to cover his loans on his lavish Saddle River NJ home (or his daughter's pony), it was to stake him on his betting efforts to get even. When they inevitably failed, he did what many addicted gamblers do out of desperation; he turned to white collar crime. Convicted of bank fraud, he had hit bottom--but, sentenced to five years on probation, his luck turned. He quit gambling cold turkey and never relapsed. Supported by Gamblers Anonymous and treated by Arnie Wexler, one of the most successful therapists in the field, he also allowed himself to become a poster-boy for the dangers of the gambling habit.

My contact with him came during his last career, as a radio talk-show host on XTRA in San Diego. We talked frequently, on and off the air, and I always found him to be engaging, intelligent, respectful, generously forthcoming, and even inspirational. He died of a heart attack in 1996, at 60, more than four years before my book in which he has a place of honor came into print.

A footnote to several of the preceding entries. Soliciting blurbs from people of consequence, household names in their fields, has been a way not only of promoting my publishing ventures but also, metaphorically, to rub shoulders with those celebrities. In addition to those mentioned above, my books have been graced with the kind words of such writers as George Garrett, Irvin Faust, Jay Neugeboren, Tom LeClair, Jerry Klinkowitz, Dave Kindred, and Susan Leonardi; of the publisher Dan Simon; and of masters of mental health Irvin Yalom, Gordon Livingston, and Paul Ephross--each one, in Pound's phrase, *il miglior fabbro* from my perspective.

E. L. Doctorow

I only met him the one time, and only very briefly. The occasion was a Pen- Faulkner meeting, and I was introduced to him and his wife, I forget by whom but it may well have been Grace Paley, in the lobby of the convention center. A moment later the three of us were together, sharing an elevator. The Henry Fonda *tête-à-téte* still fresh in my mind after five decades, I had something ready to say to this great one.

"As a faithful and appreciative reader of all your work, there's a question I've always wanted to ask you. When I read *Billy Bathgate* I was struck by the passage describing the gangland assassination, because it seemed in all its details to be familiar to me. Not just well-known legend and lore, but the entire sequence and approach. It was identical to the corollary scene in Coppola's *Cotton Club*. Is that where you got it?"

"No. I never saw the film."

His wife interrupted immediately. "Yes we did see it, Eddie. Don't you remember?"

"Thank you," I said, in the general direction of both, and got off at the next landing.

Now, I know that writers, like gamblers, addicts, and politicians, tend to lie-- to themselves as well as to others. And I also grant that writers are often not consciously aware of their sources, influences, and inspirations. But this seemed uncannily derivative if accidental.

I also know that I am capable of confusing, misremembering, conflating details of what I've seen--or think I've seen. (See Chapter XIII above for an example.) This time I went back again to the text and re-screened the movie to validate my perception. And this time I was spared the embarrassment of an impertinent error. Instead, I was somehow embarrassed for a famous writer, and I take it as an indication that at times I might want to avoid continuing a conversation with a celebrity or sacrifice even the remote possibility of developing an acquaintance with one. An example of delayed maturity, perhaps, or a spontaneous heeding of the superego's voice?

John Barth

One of the things I always liked about the world of academe was the way mutual admiration could nurture friendships. My best personal example is my friendship with Jerry Klinkowitz. I don't remember just when or why we began to correspond. It could have had something to do with our mutual appreciation of Grace Paley's stories, or to our mutual expertise in baseball fiction or to any number of shared interests. It soon evolved into a reciprocal listing of each other as readers of our book manuscripts under consideration by publishers--and that in turn led to the appearance of blurbs by each on book jackets for the other. It was my pleasure to include his book of short stories (based on his experience as a part-owner of a minor league baseball team) on my syllabus for a course on baseball fiction--and his pleasure to recommend that I join the editorial board for the "Writing Baseball" series then underway at Southern Illinois University Press.

I came to know him as one of the most prolific and versatile of writers I've ever known and for his apparently limitless capacity for generous attention to the work of others (including his invaluable advice on the present project). So it came as no surprise that when he was unable to accept the honor of delivering the annual Craig Daniels Lecture at The Johns Hopkins Writing Seminars he suggested that I be invited to do so in March, 1997, with Stephen Dixon, his friend and writer of avant-garde fiction who was on the Seminars faculty, acting as intermediary.

I was asked to offer an overview of the current status of American fiction, and I proceeded to honor the contributions of many writers, expressing some disappointment about others, and reserving my highest praise for Thomas Pynchon, David Foster Wallace, and John Barth. The last had been for many years the most prominent member of the Seminars faculty and the subject of one of Wallace's funniest stories (and the subject of one of my chapters in my recently published "The Triumph of Artifice"), and within the constrictions of the time allotted to me I believed I had adequately celebrated his work.

Soon thereafter, Barth was named to receive the annual award for contributions to American literature at the F. Scott Fitzgerald Literary Conference. My colleague Jack Bryer, a leading member of the board for the conference, asked if I would introduce Barth at the climactic session on a Saturday night in October. I was proud to do so and diligently prepared my remarks, though again I had only the fraction of the time I would have liked to do justice to one of the iconic geniuses of our literature.

I have no idea of how the large audience felt about my performance. I assumed that the loud applause was for the honoree himself. But when he approached the lectern, grinning at me, and gave me a hearty if awkward *abrazo* (he is much taller than I am) he said, "That was the best introduction I've ever had." That was the greatest sign of appreciation I could ever have wished for, and I treasure the memory. Those pictures on my wall, with Barth and with Warren, are like trophies to a presence I never earned. Still, I would go to great lengths to have shots of me with great figures in American literature, like the picture of me admiring a portrait of Flannery O'Connor in her family home in Savannah or the one of me with a sculpture of Mark Twain in Santa Fe. Even second or third hand, the proximity to fame was tonic.

The latter two photos by Ellen Isaacs, 1998 and 2011

Grace Paley

Seven years later I was back at the same place, asked to introduce Grace Paley for the same award. (It so happened that I had been called to the rostrum earlier in the evening to receive a runner-up prize in the Fitzgerald Short Story Contest, and so I was doubly happy to be there.) Barth and Paley were friends; she had for a time been part of the Hopkins Seminars; and I truly valued their work to the extent that whenever I taught a course in the short story, Barth's *Lost in the Funhouse* and Paley's *The Little Disturbances of Man* would grace my reading list.

Whereas my personal connection with Barth had been limited to that single brief encounter, my relationship with Paley was far more personal and, as I see it now, complicated. Long an admirer of her short stories, I was delighted to be given the opportunity to write the first book-length critical study of her work. It was to appear in one of the Twayne series of books published by G. K. Hall, recognized as a standard of critical texts of American literature. In this series, "Twayne's Studies in Short Fiction," under the general editorship of Gordon Weaver, my Paley would be in the distinguished company of the book on Malamud's stories by Robert Solataroff (Ted's wittier brother) and James O'Hara's book on Cheever's stories.

My initial problem was with the word "standard," an indication of policy, consistency of format, and a company formula for these books. I wanted to push the envelope or think outside the box, metaphors in this case for my unwillingness to take on my subject under restrictions that would prevent me from doing what I thought Paley deserved--given the total absence of book- length attention at the time. I therefore designed a unique format, contacted Grace to be assured of her cooperation, submitted my proposal, and held my breath while the corporate consideration took place. Gordon Weaver, who supported the plan, finally gave me the go-ahead.

It was a tripartite design. In Part 1 I would present a "reading" of all of the published stories. Part 2 would be called "The Writer," not a biographical sketch but a coherent autobiographical narrative derived from the many published interviews with this extraordinarily generous writer (her willingness to talk publicly about her work, its relationship to her life, and her beliefs about the craft of writing are perhaps unmatched in our literature).

Part 3 would be a survey of critical articles and reviews. Finally, I would compile an appendix of all her published work and all the published commentary on her I could find.

It was the second part that Grace had promised to vet, with my assurance that I would edit it according to her wishes. That led me up the road to her Vermont home one pleasantly warm day to discuss her reading of the draft.

As many others had said, she was voluble, decisive, and engaging. I promised to run my revisions by her before publication, and that was that. The book was published in 1990. I was very pleased with what I had accomplished, but I have no idea whether Grace was--or not. She never mentioned it in our several conversations thereafter, including one visit to Maryland when Ellen and I hosted her while she made some public appearances (and when she hit it off with our daughter Emmi as if they were close kin). Other books on Paley have followed, and neither they nor any appropriate reviews have acknowledged my work. That isn't surprising: the Twayne books in general are too academic for the popular media, too unsophisticated for the academy.

My debts to Grace Paley are considerable. She has given me many hours of entertaining reading, rich material for classroom study, active participation in the production of that (neglected) book of mine, and the always appreciated opportunity to meet several celebrities. But the reason that she is relegated here to "brief encounters" is that, despite a connection that was not brief at all, it was so insignificant that she could never be bothered to acknowledge my considerable efforts on her behalf. I am less troubled by that slight, however, than by her failure to honor her commitment to write the introduction to the edition of Harvey Swados's collected stories. She owed him much, and I am as bewildered by this omission as Swados's surviving family members have told me they were. Dismay is a better word for it than disappointment.

Grace Paley with my daughter Emmi,, 1996

David Ignatius

One of the original courses I introduced at College Park was called "The CIA in Fiction." Inspired by Mailer's novel, *Harlot's Ghost* (actually just half a novel because, long as it is, it promises a second act that never got written), I came to understand that the Agency had taken on a legendary life of its own as a figment of creative imagination and the vehicle of whatever bias the writer wanted to color it with. Not only Mailer, but other major mainstream writers (John Barth, Don DeLillo, and Robert Stone to name a few) had employed its mystique to an effect that took it far afield from the generic spy fiction in which it was a staple. As a plot element the Agency a.k.a. the Company had become a common trope, a veritable meme.

Through my dear friend Mary McCarthy (see the item below) I had some contacts in Langley that assisted in my research, providing me not only with long lists of publications but with a familiarity with the process by which the Agency screened such material, especially when one of their own had become an author. Ironically, this knowledge was too much of a good thing, and I realized that my original thought that I could get a critical book out of the subject (and the course) was misguided. It would require a decade's work I was unwilling to undertake--a woulda coulda shoulda item, one that remained subjunctive perhaps out of sheer laziness or maybe just a feeling of being overwhelmed.

The syllabus for the course had a reading list that included Robert Ludlum, William F. Buckley, Jr., Tom Clancy, Nicholas Proffitt, Joseph Finder, Aaron Latham, and John Horton. The last was on the list, not just as an example of the traditional genre, but because I had made contact with the author, a retired case agent living a quiet life near the Chesapeake Bay, producing potboilers, and he kindly agreed to meet with the class for an enriching discussion.

Also on the list was the recently published *Agents of Innocence*, a first novel by the distinguished journalist, editor, and columnist David Ignatius, which was an utterly convincing and harrowing story of the 1983 disaster at the Marine barracks in Lebanon. I reached him at his office at the *Post* and he cordially accepted my invitation to visit the class one day. It was the highlight of the semester. Generous with information and opinions, he not only delighted the class with his knowledgeable candor but acquired about thirty devoted readers from then on--including the professor.

How he manages to do it I cannot imagine, but in the years since that debut he has produced more than half a dozen novels of wide-ranging interest while maintaining a writing, editing, lecturing, traveling, and information-gathering schedule that can hardly leave time for sleep. We have corresponded often and he insists that the visit to my class remains an outstanding memory in a career that has made him an acknowledged authority on political, economic, and especially intelligence matters around the world, especially the Middle East.

Valerie Plame

At first, I wasn't even aware she was in the house, Tony Lake's very comfortable and tastefully decorated home near DuPont Circle, never mind the very room where a pleasantly mixed and mixing crowd was enjoying drinks, finger food, and conversation. But when Ellen nudged me and said, there's your dream girl, my eyes were drawn to her--like a moth to a Plame? She sat alone in a white easy chair, and it struck me immediately that news photos of her had not done justice to her beauty. Well, I thought, she's fair game as she sits there, and I should go talk to her. But before I made my move I learned that Joe Wilson was not there--someone had to stay home with the children--and I was glad that crazy Joe and not serene Valerie had the duty that night.

So what did we talk about when I had the temerity to approach her, introduce myself, and tell her of my admiration for what she and her husband had done? Twins--her well-publicized pair and what a challenge they were and my daughter Annie's treasured Jessica and Ilana, the sororal, anything-but- identical, twinned joys of my grandparental life. For someone who had been for months a media sensation, she seemed placid, diffident, unaffected, a little bored perhaps, and a little boring, too. We didn't talk for long.

The occasion was a retirement party for Mary McCarthy, Michael's wife, who had resigned from the CIA (like Valerie) and though under an unjustified cloud had stayed out of the public spotlight (unlike Valerie) after a couple of frenzied days of escaping paparazzi and such. The McCarthys were old and close friends, dating back to the days when he was a colleague in the American Studies Department at Maryland and she was a consultant before becoming a full-time public servant with the Agency and as Sandy Berger's right hand in Bill Clinton's White House. Ellen and I knew few of the other guests, who included familiar names from Democratic politics and diplomatic think tanks like our host Tony Lake, Richard Clarke who was co-hosting, John Podesta, and Susan Rice.

If Valerie had been the victim of an unauthorized leak, revealed publicly as a clandestine agent, Mary had herself been falsely accused as a senior executive who had been an anonymous leaker of operations like the "extraordinary rendition" of prisoners to foreign locations where they would be tortured for enemy secrets. Among Mary's many friends were distinguished journalists like Jane Mayer of *The New Yorker* and Dana Priest of the Washington *Post* (neither one present at this party), but only guilt by association could ever be attached to her. She was close-mouthed and loyal to a fault, and we, like her other friends, were astonished and appalled that she had been fingered as a leaker. Some of her friends thought that the threat of a lawsuit against the Agency for improper and perhaps illegal termination had been settled at considerable expense, but such speculation could not be confirmed. To this day it remains an unverified and unverifiable assumption, because Mary McCarthy would never leak such sensitive information.

When the time came for toasts to the evening's honoree, there was a series of warm tributes to a woman who had clearly earned the admiration and affection of her colleagues. And, near the end of the laudatory sequence, Ellen and I rose to make our own contribution. It had become our habit to perform a little original song at celebratory occasions. At Mercy Coogan's sixtieth birthday party, for example, to the tune of "Frere Jacques," we had sung, "Mercy Coogan, Mercy Coogan, you got old, you got old-- not as old as Bobby, not as old as Bobby" (her husband, my colleague), "what a pair, what a pair" with several verses intended to be comic between the repetitions of that refrain.

This time, Ellen came up with the idea to use "Maryland, My Maryland" as a model for a comic tribute to Mary, with the refrain of "0h Mary-0, my Mary-0, CIA said time to go." I won't reprise all the verses here, but one will suggest the flavor of the whole:

> Your private-sector hat you'll toss, A grievous governmental loss-- Which can't be said
> for Porter Goss, Mary-0, my Mary-0.

That was the line that got the most vigorous laugh from this highly partisan crowd, though we were roundly applauded and for the rest of the evening many times complimented. (Mike McCarthy says it's the best thing I ever wrote--and I needed Ellen as co-writer to do it.)

The one person who seemed to ignore the performance was the iconic Valerie Plame, so aloof as to distinguish herself from the crowd. And she was so skilled at not being noticed, an attribute better suited to a spy than to a media cynosure, that she slipped away from the event without anyone apparently taking notice. Except for me, a smitten fan if there ever was one, perhaps alone in my belief that the beauty of Naomi Watts hardly did justice to her real-life original's historic attractiveness.

Barack Obama

Pride of place in this photo album of memories belongs to the POTUS. May 23, 2007 in Washington, D.C., was clear and warm, with low humidity, a perfect day, not for banana-fish, but to meet the next President of the United States. The event was held in the lovely side yard of George Stevens's home in Georgetown. Ellen and I were excited about seeing and hearing Barack Obama at this campaign event. Seventy or eighty people had been gathered, at a thousand bucks a pop, so it was one of many successful small fundraisers.

The tickets were arranged by my good tennis friend, Bob Bates, another early supporter of the Obama candidacy, who was working as part of a team for a major bundler.

We arrived early because we were also pleased to be meeting George Haywood there. We'd been hearing about Haywood for a long time, from my son Ian who had been doing business with this major investor for years. George is a scion of Black D.C. nobility as it were, Harvard-educated, a world-class track athlete (three years later, at fifty-eight, he would compete in the most grueling event, the 400-meter hurdles, and finish second in the world, first among all Americans, in his age group), and a long-time intimate of Obama, who would talk with him several times a week. George ordinarily would avoid this kind of event but promised to be there because it was just a short walk from his own home. Haywood turned out to be even more than Ian promised, not only cordial and warm but movie-star good-looking, dressed in a dark summer suit over a pastel tee-shirt.

I had brought along my copy of *The Audacity of Hope*, hoping to get it signed by the author. Obama's spiel from the steps of the back porch was disappointingly formal, standard stump-speech stuff, though pleasing in substance to the supporters present. But when he took questions from the crowd the whole atmosphere changed with his informal, expansive, engaging remarks. His manner declared that he was one of us, listening to what his friends had to say, and generating a cheering wave of welcome.

When he was done and the applause died down, I hustled up to the porch with my book held high. A security guard stopped me and said there would be no private interviews because the Senator was running late for his next event. I was disappointed that there would be no pressing of the flesh at this event, but I tried to make my case. My son and daughter-in-law (Ian and Rita), I said with parental pride, wanted me to convey personal greetings. Well, go see his aide there, he said, and I got to the inner level of gate- keepers, only to be turned back once more, with regrets, as Obama began to make his getaway around the opposite side of the house.

Undaunted, I moved quickly in the opposite direction, hoping to catch him at the front of the house. By the time I got there through the thinning, exiting crowd, I was delighted to see that Obama was sitting at a little table in front, in private conversation with my new friend, George Haywood. This time I walked right past the guard and the aide as if I belonged there, walked right up to George and said, "Can a father of a friend get a friend's introduction?"

Indeed I could, and when the next president smiled at me in recognition of Ian's name, he said what I'll never forget, "I love that guy."

Handshakes and book-signing followed. The inscription reads, "To Neil-- thanks for the support." The snapshot in my mind shows me walking on air back to the car.

Michelle with my son Ian

Barack with Ian, Rita, and Mickey

XVIII

ENVOY

So it goes. Sometimes I feel like a small child in the playground, calling out to parents or care-takers, "Look at *me*! Look at *me*!" only to understand that the collective response of all within hearing range simply adds a letter to say "Meh!" Probably most small children undergo that stage of reality-testing, but what about taking a lifetime to experience it over and over again, living more than eighty years (now ninety) with a universal "Meh"?

Perhaps the only times when I had a genuine impact, with the kind of performance that becomes firmly etched in an audience's memory, was when I was not seeking attention at all. I can think of two such memorable events, and they both occurred when I was a self-medicating undergraduate, that is, during my drinking days. And neither one lasted more than thirty or forty seconds.

I have given both these occasions to my fictional alter ego, Jesse Miller, and I don't think I can do any better than to describe them in his words from *The Miller Masks: A Novel in Stories* (2000). The first occurred in Saratoga Springs, where three of my classmates and our four comely Skidmore dates had piled into Shy Salitsky's Plymouth to race back to campus, hoping to beat the ticking curfew clock so the girls would not suffer the consequences of violation (standard practice in the early '50s single-sex colleges).

Skidmore at that time had made a virtue of necessity and converted several private homes near the campus into dorms, saving a fortune in capital outlay and presumably supplying a healthy environment.

The problem was that I was so tanked up on beer that I didn't think I could hold my water for the wild ten-minute ride. Jesse phrases the scene in the present tense:

> My three friends and the girls pour out of the car and join the crowd at the door [with a minute to spare]. I am immobile, curled up, knees tight, whole body aching for release. I know I can't move. And then I know that I can't *not* move. I unwind out

the door, stumble onto the front lawn, assume the wide stance, unzip, fish out, and cast my water in a delicious, steaming, interminable high arc. The pleasure is extreme. I look up in my ecstasy and girls are crowded into all the front windows watching the spectacle. Not, some girls are applauding, others holding hands over faces. But whether in horror or mirth I'll never know.

What I do know is that the whole scene will be instantly fixed in my memory-book, like an emblem of that whole time. The light from the front door gives almost a spotlight effect on my face. The girls' heads are lovely, backlit by the lights in their rooms, their shining hair framing soft-focused faces. The other boys are an unseen or unidentifiable presence, grouped in the walkway in front of the door or dispersing to their cars. All the light is picked up in sparkling points along that gleaming arc as, gloriously, eternally, I piss my youth away on the Skidmore lawn, and the only sound is an a cappella "ah."

The point here is that I'm sure my clear memory is etched just as unforgettably in the impressionable minds of eighteen or twenty young women I'll never know.

With two exceptions, the much larger audience of the other scene was also made up of anonymous witnesses to a totally unpremeditated exploit. The setting was the Cornell football field in Ithaca on a late-October Saturday. I had traveled a long way to see John Clayton, Dartmouth's stylish T-formation quarterback, fail to pull off an upset over the Big Red, while I blunted my disappointment by sipping a potent martini mix from a pint flask (initialed leather from Mark Cross, a go-to-college gift from my mother). Jesse Miller, again:

As the undersized Big Green moves for a final, meaningless score, I am moving with equal determination toward the field. As my team goes for the goal line I make my decision to go for a piece of the goal post.

Dartmouth scores. I edge toward the sideline. Maybe a hundred others have the same idea. Cornell runs out the clock. At the gun the small mob sprints in a massed post pattern. Dozens of hands grab each upright and start rocking. I have a stratagem to dupe the enemy hosts. "For Russell Sage," I cry disingenuously, invoking the name of my dorm in Hanover, which also happens to be the name of a girls' school in Troy, familiar to most Cornellians.

The goal resists stubbornly. A couple of leapers go for the crossbar and miss, but I can see that that's the way to bring the quarry to earth. A loutish face full of Big Red acne leers toward me and shouts, "Let's lift this little guy up." Up I go, locking arms around the bar, while the crowd tugs at my legs to topple the trophy. It's a wonderful feeling. I'm at what they call the point of attack. I am the focus, the fulcrum, the cynosure.

And I am not the weakest link: the goal posts begin to give. But before anything else comes down, my pants do. And it is at that instant that I realize that this game is on regional television, that if the director is no nitwit he'll have a camera on this scene, and just as the whole thing falls I catch sight of the sideline camera with its acknowledging red light beaconing toward me, and as I fall into the crowd, still clutching the crossbar, I am grinning directly in close-up into the astonished faces of my parents back home in the den of their New Haven apartment. It is the first recorded occasion of the "Hi Mom" greeting on TV. 1950. You could look it up.

Somewhere in a junk pile of hoarded souvenirs I still have a four-inch piece of that white-painted wooden trophy. If I could find it, I'd throw it away now. It is after all just a painful reminder that at the time when, reaching my largest audience if only for less than a minute and only "regionally" located, only my mother and father would know who it was up there--and probably wished they didn't.

As a medievalist, I often admired the convention of the "envoy" (or, after the French, *"l'envoi"*) with which a manuscript or poem would end. No epilogue, no coda, no afterword, but a postscript addressed to the piece of composition now completed and being sent on its way with humble apologies, perhaps a moral to be derived from the piece, often a prayer for forgiveness and blessings on what hath been wrought.

The best-known envoy, perhaps, is the final section of Chaucer's "Troilus and Criseyde," a dozen stanzas in the seven-line "rhyme royal" form of the entire poem. It begins with the simplest of invocations: "Go, litel bok, go...." It seems to me oddly ironic that this work of more than seven thousand two hundred lines is sent on its way with a characterization of its smallness.

Never mind its length, its artistic accomplishment places it within the best half dozen works of the whole period, with only "Sir Gawain and the Green Knight" surviving in Middle English as its extant rival.

Studying "The House of Fame," I learned that what Chaucer was talking about in his dream-allegory was something far different from my concept of fame. The word itself could mean rumor, reputation, or renown--celebrity had nothing to do with it, nor did associating with the famous or the in-crowd. There was no accommodation for a Zelig or a Boswell in that medieval house.

A writer's words would outlive him, Chaucer's dreamer learns, but eventually they would turn to dust, too, like the statue of Shelley's Ozymandias. The goddess of fame bestowed repute--good and ill--whimsically and randomly, without regard to the virtues and vices of the nine different groups of suppliants who asked her blessing, some of them in fact seeking anonymity (here late in the fifteenth century is the first argument in English for privacy rights).

Among other things, Chaucer was a master both of understatement and of irony in its many forms. His use of the conventional envoy in the "Troilus" puts both to work in its expressions of characteristic modesty. Here, then, in part in tribute to one of the great masters, is my own envoy to this "litel bok." And wouldn't it be ironic if this whole lament for my failure to achieve personal celebrity or any lasting fame for my lifelong efforts of putting words on paper--either in the world of Grub Street or in the groves of academe--is what allows me to reach the long-strived-for goal and emerge from the retreat into the resignation of accepted anonymity.

I take it as a final irony that Geoffrey Chaucer himself wrote a long dream-allegory called "The House of Fame," but neither finished the work nor composed an envoy for it. Among the many things I learned from him, I should probably add this: that a quest for ephemera is a vain and never-ending pursuit, that celebrity is a fleeting fancy, and that those who pursue either or both of them had better know how to make fun of themselves.

"Troilus and Criseyde" is a poignant and prodigious tragedy; "Flirtations with Fame: Memoirs of a Celebrity Manqué" is a long-running joke. So, go little book and let's have a good laugh.

ACKNOWLEDGMENTS

Among those who read drafts or fragments of this work in progress, I am grateful to Jerry Klinkowitz, Tom LeClair, Jack Higgs, Larry Harrison, Mike Olmert, Jon Reiner, and as always my brother Phil, for constructive criticism and encouragement. In a more meaningful way I am also grateful to the many people (including most of the above) who appear in these pages: just knowing them, even in the slightest way, has enriched my life. To try to name them all, however, would be to make a virtual index to the book--and it's not that kind of book.

Special thanks to Amy Richards, my assistant and technological guide. For this ebook in particular, her work on the photo-shopping spree (starting with the cover) has exemplified and enhanced the whole effort. For this revised text, my wife Ellen has been most helpful in any ways. From Westpoint Press, thanks to Melissa Gilbert who recruited me and Allen Mathews whose editing skills thoroughly guided the process.

The original version had a long chapter called "The Four Families," a detailed account of my origins traced back to eight great-grandparents. My cousins June Isaacs and Nancy Myers, my aunt Juliet (Uncle Mel's widow), and of course my brother were important contributors (I had yet to subscribe to Ancestry.com). But I was persuaded to drop the whole thing because it was too complicated, recited too many names, and contributed virtually nothing to the whole focus of the enterprise. The chapter, however, will be duly dispatched to all surviving members of the immediate family. And the "family-photo album" that follows and closes the book will do a better job of commemorating the heritage.

Conspicuous by its absence--and unlike every other book I've written--there is no dedication in its customary place up front. That is because, as intended all along, I mean to dedicate this (an effort that has given me a great deal of pleasure and I hope will amuse its readers) to my entire family, going back three generations and forward another two. It is fitting that I echo here the last words my grandmother, Annie Braun, said to me from her deathbed: "Neil, you know how much I loved you all."

Colesville MD, February 2014.

FAMILY ALBUM

Great-grandparents, Benjamin and Frances Levy

Great-grandparents Mark and Sara Isaacs

Great-grandfather William Greenbaum, whom I called "Grandpa Great"

Grandma and Grandpa Braun

Great-Uncle Morris Green (here as a young man probably in costume) was a Broadway talent scout and producer of Blackbird Revues and Eugene O'Neill's "Desire under the Elms" and later in Hollywood a drinking buddy of Douglas Fairbanks and Dave Chasen

Grandpa Isaacs with Dad and Uncle Bert

Dad with his Aunt Kitty and Aunt Eva

Uncle Irving and Aunt Flo. Irving was the oldest of the Braun siblings; before being gassed and disabled at the front in World War I, he had introduced his school-chum Mory Isaacs to his sister Florence (Mother and Dad)

Uncle Sid, Aunt Mabel, Uncle Walter (Lowenbein) and Aunt Betty in the foreground, at my great-grandparents' fiftieth wedding celebration in 1926. When my brother cited Voltaire during a toast at a family gathering, Uncle Walter famously jumped up and said, "That's me, Uncle Voltaire"; Aunt Betty laughed more than anyone in the family; I never knew my Aunt Mabel (Angrist), who did not survive the birth of my cousin Nancy. Uncle Charlie remarried, providing a loving step-mother and subsequent half-brother.

Uncle Sid and Aunt Marie

Uncle Mel and Aunt Juliet

Aunt Ruth and Uncle Lou (Lasarow)

Honeymooners: Mother and Dad in Lakeview NJ, 1922

Ellen and I in Negril, 1984

Ian and Rita (Karpin), 1991

Daniel and Tammy (Sterman), 2000

Emmi and Los (Suarez), 2008

My brother and I both got very lucky in our second marriages, Marilyn Swist and Ellen Lichtman

Neil the aisle-walker, with Annie

Neil the aisle-walker, with Emmi

My brother goes off to war, 1943

My cousins on the Braun side: Patricia (Sid's) visiting Nancy (Mabel's) at Mt. Holyoke. Nancy (Myers), a year my junior, graduated, earned her doctorate and earned her professorship before I could ever catch up. Patricia a "blue baby" at birth, had health issues throughout a sadly short life.

Michael (Betty's), of whom more below

Peter (Sid's) with his big sister

(Ruth's) Marilyn and Eddie (who tragically succumbed to leukemia as a teen) with their oldest cousin, Phil

Gil, Ed, and Doug (Mel's)

Ellen's parents: Joe and Sylvia Lichtman

My dear mother-in-law Syl with her sisters, Eddy Taylor and Cecille (Aunt Cissy) Abramowitz

Ellen's sister Ronnie Blumberger, with David and their sons Jeffrey and John

Peter Gordon Isaacs, my brother's only child; with his loving grandmother

Pairs of sibs: Phil and I

Sons Ian and Jonny

step-kids Josh and Emmi (with Gwen for Guinivere, the Airedale, and Violet, the Irish Terrier, our last two dogs)

Samson and Delilah (our last two cats--1 had wanted to call them Pelleas and Melisande, Pell and Mell for short but was unanimously outvoted)

Sara and Anna

Jessica and Ilana

Jacob and Makaela

Xavier and Damian, the Suarez sons of Emmi and Los

Group shots: Ian, Rita, and kids

Jonny, Liz (Kraus), and kids at the Outer Banks

Daniel and Tammy and kids

Annie and Paul (Moyer) and kids

Emmi and Los and kids

Stairway shots of me and ten grandkids (tradition of gatherings where my original ten grandchildren pose with me)

This one includes David's wife Laura and Anna's boyfriend Steven

Grins all around at Annie's second wedding

Equestrienne Marjorie

First of ten to be called to Torah

Twin bat mitzvah celebration

First of ten to marry (Laura Fornier)

GrandE, the hike-leader, on top of Sugar Loaf with Adam, Jessie, and Ilana

Ellen and I on tour; in Florence,

in Tuscany,

in Rome,

in Venice (the Hotel Flora is the gentrified version of the Pensione Flora where George, Mal, and I stayed in 1953),

and at Giza

Ellen and I in mixed doubles competition

Sir Rufus Isaacs, 1st Marquess of Reading, Lord Chief Justice, Viceroy and Governor-General of India, etc.: not a close relation despite my hopeful research.

Finally, in memory of my cousin Michael Lowenbein, here are four samples of his work as a rising art-star. One of his creative modes was to take old snapshots, many of them of family members, and re-create them as paintings. These, then, are pictures of paintings of pictures:

Grandma Braun at Yosemite in 1931 with Uncle Mel and Aunt Betty, the artist's mother (this painting hangs over the fireplace in Ian's home in Ketonah NY)

EDDIE and BOOTS   Michael Lowenbein 2002   Oil on Canvas 24x36

Grandpa Braun with Boots (my first dog) at Momauguin CT in the summer of 1938)

SELF PORTRAIT Michael Lowenbein 2000   Oil on Canvas 24x36

A self-portrait at work with live model

Me on horseback in 1936--the only time I have ever been on a horse, except in a pari-mutuel way

My great-granddaughter Emily was born on December 20, 2018. She is the first member of the seventh generation of the Isaacs family seen here.

*****

PRAISE FOR THE GREAT MOLINAS

Jack Molinas was the quintessential amoral hero of our time, and his story has been begging to be told. Well, it finally has been told, and superbly, by Neil Isaacs. He has done it the best and most meaningful way by turning it into a novel in which he and his dark angel intersect on a series of pivotal levels. No writer could possibly have invented Jack Molinas, but Isaacs has re-invented him with skill, courage, and an artfully sustained intensity.

-Irvin Faust, author of The Steagle

I couldn't turn the pages fast enough. Neil Isaacs has produced a powerful profile of a sport original, a fascinating study of a complicated man with enormous talent and strange personality

-Mort Olshan, editor/publisher of The Gold Sheet

…a very scary book that will make you sweat. Neil Isaacs has captured all the divertse personalities of one of the greatest basketball players and gamblers to ever play at both games. It reads like fiction. The scary part being that it's true.

-Chet Forte. late producer of ABC's Monday Night Football

The spellbinding story of the legendary Jack Molinas is more than a court-long shot at the buzzer, and Neil Isaacs tells it with the depth and feeling it deserves. Unlike the many ways this novel could have been handled, Isaacs does it as a narrative that investigates itself—and its teller—even as Molinas's fascinating tale is told. To some extent every good writer becomes his subject, and that happens here. The Great Molinas is a novel about basketball and everything else, too.

-Jerry Klinkowitz, author of The Short Season

PRAISE FOR THE DOAKER'S STORY

This book says all the right things about sports in America and says them memorably.

-Dave Kindred, author of The Morning Miracle

This terrific novel is a compelling tale that reveals the dark underside of contemporary sports. Isaacs js a splendid story-teller and has written a novel memorable not only because of its eye-opening revelations, but, more, because of its unerring rendering of the mysteries of heroism and friendship.

-Jay Neugeboren, author of Imagining Robert

This truly charming book is very original in its portrayal of sport and sports journalism in America. It also engages with the current media situation in a most fascinating way—the great focus on tabloids and such. The friendship displayed in the story is very intriguing;

-Dan Simon, Seven Stories Books

Billy Doakes comes across as too good to be true, but thanks to Isaacs' artistry, he enchants us and we root for him even as we know he is too good for this world. Have no fears when a savvy craftsman is at work. Isaacs does it and in the doing he grabs you and pulls you in and never lets go.

-Irvin Faust, author of Willie Remembers and Jim Dandy

Praise for The Great Molinas

Jack Molinas was the quintessential amoral hero of our time, and his story has been begging to be told. Well, it finally has been told, and superbly, by Neil Isaacs. He has done it the best and most meaningful way by turning it into a novel in which he and his dark angel intersect on a series of pivotal levels. No writer could possibly have invented Jack Molinas, but Isaacs has re-invented him with skill, courage, and an artfully sustained intensity.

Irvin Faust, author of The Steagle

I couldn't turn the pages fast enough. Neil Isaacs has produced a powerful profile of a sport original, a fascinating study of a complicated man with enormous talent and strange personality

Mort Olshan, editor/publisher of The Gold Sheet

...a very scary book that will make you sweat. Neil Isaacs has captured all the divertse personalities of one of the greatest basketball players and gamblers to ever play at both games. It reads like fiction. The scary part being that it's true.

Chet Forte. late producer of ABC's Monday Night Football

The spellbinding story of the legendary Jack Molinas is more than a court-long shot at the buzzer, and Neil Isaacs tells it with the depth and feeling it deserves. Unlike the many ways this novel could have been handled, Isaacs does it as a narrative that investigates itself—and its teller—even as Molinas's fascinating tale is told. To some extent every good writer becomes his subject, and that happens here. The Great Molinas is a no vel about basketball and everything else, too.

Jerry Klinkowitz, author of The Short Season

Praise for The Doaker's Story

This book says all the right things about sports in America and says them memorably.

Dave Kindred, author of The Morning Miracle

FLIRTATIONS WITH FAME

This terrific novel is a compelling tale that reveals the dark underside of contemporary sports. Isaacs js a splendid story-teller and has written a novel memorable not only because of its eye-opening revelations, but, more, because of its unerring rendering of the mysteries of heroism and friendship.

Jay Neugeboren, author of Imagining Robert

This truly charming book is very original in its portrayal of sport and sports journalism in America. It also engages with the current media situation in a most fascinating way—the great focus on tabloids and such. The friendship displayed in the story is very intriguing;

Dan Simon, Seven Stories Books

Billy Doakes comes across as too good to be true, but thanks to Isaacs' artistry, he enchants us and we root for him even as we know he is too good for this world. Have no fears when a savvy craftsman is at work. Isaacs does it and in the doing he grabs you and pulls you in and never lets go.

Irvin Faust, author of Willie Remembers and Jim Dandy

Praise for Bay Area Trio

Neil Isaacs is a master of short tales with long tails. A former literary historian and psychotherapist, he gives you three interlinked stories about a wedding planner. A sleeper agent, and a self-analyzing clinical social worker. All three have surprising complexity with deep pasts, up-to-date psychology, and reappearances across Bay Area Trio. Unlike fiction writers who flaunt their learning, Isaacs is a storyteller who immerses you in settings, creates and resolves plots, and gives characters familiar ways of talking to provide out-of-fashion but appealing intimacy. Why wait for "realists" working on huge multi-volumes when you have here Neil Isaacs's compact triptych of linked American families?

Tom LeClair, author of The Art of Excess and a quintet of intriguing novels with titles of
"Passing" and phrase-endings "Off," "On," "Through, "Away," and "Away Again."